OLD-TIME SCHOOLS

Metildah Upham
her Book 1791
if I this Book do lend
and you it borrow
Pray read it through to day
and send it home tomorrow

AND SCHOOL-BOOKS

A Schoolmaster of Long Ago.

OLD-TIME SCHOOLS
AND SCHOOL-BOOKS

BY CLIFTON JOHNSON

WITH MANY ILLUSTRATIONS COLLECTED

BY THE AUTHOR

WITH A NEW INTRODUCTION BY

CARL WITHERS

DOVER PUBLICATIONS, INC., NEW YORK

Published simultaneously in Canada by McClelland and Stewart, Ltd.
Published in the United Kingdom by Constable and Company Limited, 10 Orange Street, London W.C.2.

This new Dover edition, first published in 1963, is an unabridged and unaltered republication of the work first published by The Macmillan Company in 1904, to which has been added a new Introduction especially prepared for this edition by Carl Withers.

Library of Congress Catalog Card Number: 63-17906

Manufactured in the United States of America

Dover Publications, Inc.
180 Varick Street
New York 14, N.Y.

Introduction to Dover Edition

Good children must

Fear God all day,
Parents obey,
No false things say,
By no sin stray,

Love Christ alway,
In secret pray,
Mind little play,
Make no delay

In loving good

Clifton Johnson's *Old-time Schools and School-books* has long been out of print and much sought on the rare book market by librarians, Americana collectors and scholars. That Dover Publications has reprinted it attractively at low price is a happy fact not only for antiquarians but for professionals in many fields. Historian, educator, psychologist, anthropologist, folklorist, student of the graphic arts and early photography—all will find in it much to delight and inform them.

In a style notable for natural grace, clarity and kindly humor, the author traces out the early history of education in our country, from the first colonial efforts in Puritan Massachusetts to establish private and public ways to instruct children in their abc's, religion and other knowledge that was considered useful. He tells us most about schools and schooling in New England, but amplifies the picture with much additional information about similar developments farther south, from New York and Philadelphia to the Virginia and Carolina plantations, and on the faraway midwestern frontier. The book ends at about 1850, when elementary schooling had become relatively universal and secularized throughout the still expanding young Republic.

Through copious extracts and quaint illustrations, taken from the early primers, and from the later spellers, readers, geographies, histories and other textbooks which were gradually added to the school curricula, Johnson gives us a vivid impression of the scope and flavor of the offerings to young learners during two centuries. He adds many photographs taken by himself of old schoolhouses, schoolbooks and the meager schoolroom equipment that had survived until his day. His delightful text describes the early schoolrooms in which boys (and sometimes girls) received their first instruction, the men and women who were available and willing to teach them, and the methods of instruction. He tells us much of the families, and of the communities and their folkways, in which the children grew up. We also learn much about the children themselves, from the author's anecdote and commentary, and from the rhymes and remarks, sometimes satirical, which they scribbled into the flyleaves and margins of their books. Most of the book is about elementary education, but it includes accounts of the early grammar schools and academies. There are also fascinating glimpses of the colleges, especially Harvard, when its role was to train preachers, missionaries to save the souls of the American Indians, and schoolmasters.

We can see clearly throughout the book the pedagogic assumptions, and the assumptions regarding the nature of childhood and of man, which governed the selection of textbook materials and their mode of presentation. What "good children" were long supposed to *do* and *be* is succinctly summarized in the two stanzas of ingenious doggerel that head this introduction. They come from a late (1797)

Philadelphia version of *The New England Primer*. Similar
moral aims are reiterated in many rhymes, fables and
stories which the author reprints from early textbooks.
The purpose of Puritan education, he reminds us, was to
thwart Satan by teaching children the principles of religion
and the laws of their country, and to train them for useful
labor and commerce.*

Teaching was by rote and drill. Encouragement was
by the rod. Obedience (to God, parent and teacher) was
the foundation rock for the mansion of learning. Most of
us have so completely forgotten our traditional religion
and our history that the educational aims and methods
described in the present book will seem incredibly harsh
and alien. There were dissenters from them even in
colonial times—as there were dancers around Maypoles—
but they were a minority. The textbooks reflected, and
helped gradually to reform, majority opinion. They
changed in content as the nation grew and changed. The
opening wedge for the changes that were to come was the
effort to make textbooks "attractive" to children. Before
1850 enough softening of viewpoint and method had taken
place—and is revealed in these pages—to forecast the
prevailing secular and progressive (or quasi-progressive)
educational aims that we know today.

In 1904, when *Old-time Schools and School-books* appeared,
the teaching and learning system it describes was already
so remote from American cultural values that the particular

*In regard to Puritan theological assumptions about the nature of
childhood, Johnson somewhat distorts (on page 99) Jonathan Edwards's
meaning in calling children "young vipers." What this sweet-natured
and fiery divine actually wrote was (italics mine): "As innocent as
young children seem to be to us, yet *if they are out of Christ* they are in
God's sight young vipers and infinitely more hateful than young vipers."

point chosen for comment by a reviewer was the book's humor. "Mr. Johnson has made a most entertaining volume," he said. "Few professionally humorous books contain so much that is genuinely funny." With more sense of history, another reviewer called it "a storehouse of delightfully quaint reprints of texts and cuts, and a mine of information concerning educational beginnings in this country."

During his long lifetime Clifton Johnson (1865–1940) wrote, edited or illustrated over a hundred books. Their range in subject matter, at first glance, seems extremely wide. But most of them were concerned, directly or indirectly, with folk history, folkways, folklore or nature. He was steeped from earliest childhood in the history, traditions and landscape of New England; later he traveled widely in the rest of the country and elsewhere. A self-educated man with only a few years of formal education, he became a skillful and facile writer, who had an unusual eye for subject matter and an audacious, original approach to it. He became also one of the most original and poetical photographers of his day. He had set out in life to be neither writer nor photographer, but to be an artist.

He was born near Hadley, Massachusetts, the son of a New England small farmer. According to an article based on an interview with him in *The New England Magazine* (1901: **24**, 661–671), he had as a boy little experience beyond his native village, sometimes traveling as far as Northampton or Holyoke "to peddle berries," and going annually to town to see a circus *parade*. His family disapproved of "shows," he told the interviewer. He went

first to a rural school, and later to a nearby academy. As
a schoolboy, "he disliked classics and mathematics, but
liked history and natural science"; and "botany was a
passion." He left school at age fifteen to work in a
bookstore in Northampton. Here he developed a great
liking for books and pictures and decided to be an artist.
He spent several winters studying at the Art Students'
League in New York, supporting himself by drawing and
"hack writing."   At about age twenty, having developed a
small market for his illustrations, he returned to the family
farm at Hadley, which was his home for the rest of his life.
About 1890 he bought a small camera and began to take
photographs as an aid to his drawing. He showed some
to a publisher to suggest the subject matter of intended
drawings, but the publisher, instead of commissioning the
drawings from the young artist, bought the photographs
instead. Soon Johnson began writing books as a way to
sell his photographs, though he continued for a time to
illustrate books—his own and those of other writers—with
his original drawings.

Clifton Johnson's earliest interest, in photography and
writing, was in New England. To gather pictures for a
series of lavishly illustrated volumes (with many contribu-
tors) about his own and neighboring counties, Johnson
traveled into every nook and corner of the region, visiting
the remotest farmhouses, photographing, sketching, and
writing down the stories people told him of their own lives
and of earlier days. He developed these and other materials that came almost wholly from intimate personal experience and observation into a remarkable series of books:
The New England Country (1892), "a study of old times and
of . . . nature"; *The Farmer's Boy* (1894), a kind of "natural

history" of New England boyhood which covers outdoor nature, family life, work and amusements; *The Country School in New England* (1895); *What They Say in New England* (1896), a collection of folk sayings, tales and legends—which will be discussed separately later; and *A Book of Country Clouds and Sunshine* (1897), a study of contemporary life on farms and in rural villages. All these volumes supplement each other in giving a full and flavorful picture of New England social history. All are lavishly illustrated with photographs, sometimes interspersed with Johnson's own drawings, except *What They Say in New England*, decorated with the author's charming line drawings, but without photographs. From his studies of New England history, Johnson also wrote and illustrated during this period a small book, *An Unredeemed Captive* (1897), about a colonial girl kidnapped by Indians in the famous Deerfield Massacre, and *Old-time Schools and School-books* (1904). Later (1917) he published *New England: A Human Interest Geographical Reader*, for school use, and in old age he wrote two county histories, one of his home county, *Historic Hampshire* (1932) and, for publication by the American Historical Society, a three-volume history of neighboring *Camden County* (1936).

But before the turn of the century he began to publish his long series of very unusual travel books. His photographs had become famous. Between 1895 and 1900, several publishers sent him on trips abroad to take pictures for reissues of a number of popular books; they included White's *Natural History of Selborne*, Maclaran's *Beside the Bonnie Briar Bush*, Barrie's *A Window in Thrums*, Jane Barlow's *Irish Idylls* and Dickens' *A Child's History of England*. Johnson visited not only England, Scotland and Ireland, but also France. He returned from his trips

with portfolios filled with photographs and drawings and
his notebooks full of the impressions from which he wrote,
illustrated and published a book about each country:
Among English Hedgerows (1899), *Along French Byways* (1900),
The Isle of the Shamrock (1901) and *The Land of Heather* (1903).
In picture and easy narrative he captures the special folk
flavor of each country. He visited mainly the farms and
rural villages, rambling down byways and country lanes
to look at nature, and listened attentively to the talk of
villagers, farmers and farm laborers. He devotes a chapter
of his book about England to a long walk with a small boy
who, after initial shyness, tells him a large childhood lore
of sayings and rhymes about flowers, birds and their ways,
and snails. (He was as skillful in eliciting the confidence
and talk of children as he was with adults.) He avoided
the largest cities as too cosmopolitan to be typical. One
noonday he arrived in London, intending to spend several
days. "But the big town," he wrote, "seemed so dingy
and commonplace, and there was so much of crowds and
noise, that I changed my mind and toward evening took a
train that carried me northward." Over a third of the
illustrations in *The Isle of the Shamrock*, *The Land of Heather*
and *Along French Byways* are drawings, so pleasing that one
wishes Johnson had not later given up this mode of illustration, even for his excellent photographs.

His first American travel book, *New England and Its
Neighbors* (1902), was followed, during the next decade or
so, by many others. He seems to have been indefatigable
as a traveler and a writer. He wrote (and illustrated with
his photographs) a ten-volume American Highways and
Byways Series. The first was called *Highways and Byways of
the South*. Others in the series covered the Mississippi

Valley region, the Rocky Mountains, the Great Lakes, the Pacific Coast area, the great stretch from the Saint Lawrence River to Virginia, the New England states, and Florida. To get text and pictures for these, and for two additional books about rivers—*The Picturesque Hudson* and *The Picturesque St. Lawrence*—the author took long journeys throughout the United States and Canada, traveling by train, stagecoach, river boat, canal barge, hired buggy or horse, and (often) by foot. Wherever he went, his interests lay more in the byways than the highways, more in unspoiled nature and the lives of typically simple and average people than in cities, factories, or tourist "attractions." He preferred sleeping in farmhouses where he could observe habitual behavior and hear the talk of daily life, to staying in hotels. He was interested in typical ways of life, modes of livelihood, extant and vanishing crafts; how people came to be where he found them, how they viewed their environment, what they remembered of the past. With keen ear and nimble pencil he took down, as nearly verbatim as possible, their picturesque speech patterns and the tales, legends and superstitions that came out naturally in conversations, as well as realistic pictures of daily life.

Johnson recognized the value of the "life history" technique before it was invented by modern social scientists, and was without peer in knowing how to gain "rapport" with people everywhere. Long passages in his travel books read like the field records of an anthropologist, trained to ask "non-leading" questions and to take down the answering flow of thought. By the same methods he collected, over years, the experiences of people who remembered the Civil War—old soldiers from both sides, ex-slaves, and non-participants who were in the war's pathway. From these memories he compiled a valuable book called *Battleground Adventures in the Civil War* (1915).

What remains to discuss is Johnson's specific contribution to folklore and his literary involvement in the field. Scattered through all his travel books is a large quantity of folktales and legends, anecdotes, rhymes, superstitions, proverbs and other folklore, taken down directly from people with whom Johnson talked during his travels, and reported as direct quotations. (Two examples only: in one book he prints, in presumably the narrator's dialect, three Brer Rabbit stories he heard from a Negro tar-burner on a North Carolina mountainside; in another he rather gingerly reports an elaborate tall tale heard from the famous John Hance at the rim of the Grand Canyon.) The little chapter on "Fly-leaf Scribblings" in the present book is a model essay on a branch of children's tradition (unapproved by adults!) which has survived, with expectable change, till today. *What They Say in New England* (mentioned earlier) is an outstanding pioneer collection of Anglo-American signs, sayings, superstitions, rhymes, catches, songs, nursery tales and other old tales and legends. It has throughout the sound of verbal authenticity. There is much internal and external evidence, too elaborate to detail here, that the folktales (and other items) in this book were reported directly from oral tradition, without any essential alteration of incident or language. It appeared eight years after the American Folklore Society was founded in 1888.

Johnson saw in this new field an additional outlet for his interests and energy. He began to compile books of folktales for children. Following the pattern of Andrew Lang's enormously popular fairy-tale books (*The Blue Fairy Book, The Red Fairy Book*, etc.), Johnson created a series named for American trees: *The Oak Tree Fairy Book, The Birch Tree Fairy Book, The Elm Tree Fairy Book, The Fir Tree Fairy Book* (1905–1912). In them he followed the recommendation of the American educator Felix Adler, in *The Moral Education of Children* (1892), that "falsehood, gluttony, drunkenness and evil" should be lessened in folktales presented to children, and that "malicious stepmothers and cruel fathers should be excluded." In the Grimm Brothers' (and Lang's) "Little Red Riding Hood," the Wolf eats up the little girl; in *The Oak Tree Fairy Book*, the grandmother kills the wolf with an ax "and Little Red Riding Hood was not hurt at all." That Americans of Johnson's time felt it was necessary to soften *all* traditional and educational materials designed for children is not unrelated to the hardship and severity of our early educational history, as described in *Old-time Schools and Schoolbooks*. As compared to Lang, Johnson edited out of the stories he selected for his collections far more of the cruelties; in style, however, his versions sound more like oral, rather than literary, narratives. For the lucrative children's market, Johnson later produced a fifteen-volume series of Bedtime Wonder Tales "from the folklore of all nations," and "free from the savagery [and] distressing details . . . of their original forms." He also edited juvenile anthologies of verse, songs and Bible stories, and versions of many popular books, including *Don Quixote*, the Arthurian stories and the *Arabian Nights*. His *Mother Goose Rhymes My Children Love Best* (1917) omits familiar rhymes that contain harsh sentiments, but includes a number that had appeared in no previous collection.   They seem to have come from the New England folk tradition Johnson knew so well.

No effort has been made to mention *all* the books Johnson wrote, edited or illustrated during his forty-five productive years (1893–1938).   A number of them, like *Old-time Schools and School-books*, *What They Say in New England*, and *The Country School* are genuine classics, written with loving care from deep immersion in his material, and likely to return from time to time into print.   Other tastes in travel, and styles in travel reporting, have supplanted his travel books. Present standards regarding anthologies and the simplification of great literature and folktales for the children's book market are different from his (but only rarely better). His New England books and travel books, however, are mines filled with many treasures for researchers in social history, folkways and folklore.   Their texts and pictures combine admirably to depict, with great intimacy, many ways of life that have vanished forever.   We see people at home, at work, at recreation and at worship.   We hear them talk.   We see their villages, churches, schools, houses, wells, furniture, clothing, barns, domestic animals, tools, fields, gardens, conveyances—all the artifacts and objects surrounding daily life.   Johnson retouched his photographs (as he retouched folktales for children), but in this case accentuating, rather than diminishing, their essential truth and beauty.

New York   CARL WITHERS
  January, 1963

Introductory Note

THE contrast between the dainty picture books that are provided to entice the school children of the present along the paths of knowledge, and the sparsely illustrated volumes conned by the little folk of two or three generations ago, is very great; and yet the old books seemed beautiful to the children then, and the charm all comes back when a person of middle age or beyond happens on one of these humble friends of his youth. What an aroma of the far-gone days of childhood hovers in the yellow pages! The scenes in the schoolroom rise in the memory, one is young again, and has in gentle illusion the same feelings and the same juvenile companions as of old.

But the pleasure of seeing the books of our schooldays is seldom experienced; for, once their work was done, they received scant care, and most of the multitude that were printed have perished utterly. The wear and tear of use and the accidents and exigencies of time have made way with them, and to-day one could hardly find the books he studied as a child save by long and patient search, and perhaps some of them not at all. My own collection of school-books has been largely gathered by exploring the nooks and corners of the old bookshops from New England to South Carolina; but many things I could not get, and I have been greatly aided in compiling this volume by the collections of various individuals and institutions. I am especially grateful to the American Antiquarian Society of Worcester, the Essex Institute of Salem, the Deerfield Museum, the Connecticut Historical Society, and to Mr. Albert C. Bates of Hartford, and Mr. George A. Plimpton of New York. I also am much indebted to the Henry Barnard Collection, now at Hartford, but probably soon to be sold and transferred elsewhere — a collection which includes the American publications used in our schools from the beginnings down to 1850 more completely than any other in existence.

My readers will doubtless notice that I have dwelt on the educational history of Massachusetts rather than on that of any of its neighbors. This I have done because it seems to me to possess unrivalled interest. Massachusetts has always been a pioneer in educational experiments, and where it has led the way the sister states have followed. Its experience has been a constant aid to them, and the attention it has given to education has always been far above the average for the whole country.

CLIFTON JOHNSON.

HADLEY, MASSACHUSETTS.

Contents

Two Illustrations
selected from one hun-
dred and sixty similar
pictures in *Paul Pres-
ton's Book of Gym-
nastics*, 1847.

A Whale.   From Comly's *A New Spelling-book*, 1806.

List of Illustrations

NOTE. — The reproductions from old school-books are the same size as the originals unless otherwise stated beneath the engravings. All pictures not credited in the following list to individuals or societies are from the author's own collection.

Page

List of Illustrations

Page

Page

Page

List of Illustrations

A Melancholy Scene. From Town's *Second Reader*, 1848.

Old-time Schools and School-Books

I

IN 1642, twelve years after the settlement of
Boston, the General Court of Massachusetts,
"taking into consideration the great neglect of
many parents and guardians in training up their children in learning and labor which may be profitable
to the commonwealth," ordered that the selectmen
in every town should have power to take account
of all parents and masters as to their children's education and employment. Each town was to be
divided by its selectmen into sections — a section
to each selectman; and for the families in his
apportionment the selectman was responsible. He
must see that all the children learned to read, and
that they were taught to understand the principles
of religion and the capital laws of the country, and,
finally, he must make sure that they were put to
some useful work.

The education required could be provided by the
individual parents in their homes, or it could be
provided in any manner they chose to devise col-

lectively.   Nothing was said about schools, and the law which is the foundation of the school system of the state was enacted five years later.   The preamble starts with the premise that " It being one chiefe project of y^t ould deluder, Sathan, to keepe men from the knowledge of ye Scriptures," effort must be made to thwart this " ould deluder y^t learning may not be buried in ye grave of o^r fath^{rs} in ye church and commonwealth " : —

It is therefore ord^{r}ed, y^t ev^{r}y towneship in this iurisdiction, aft^r ye Lord hath increased y^m to ye number of 50 household^{rs}, shall then forthwth appoint one wthin their towne to teach all such children as shall resort to him to write & reade, whose wages shall be paid eith^r by ye parents or mast^{rs} of such children, or by ye inhabitants in gen^{r}all, by way of supply, as ye maior p^t of those y^t ord^r ye prudentials of ye towne shall appoint.

The law also made it obligatory that parents, where schools were lacking, should teach " their children and apprentices perfectly to read the English tongue"; and instances are not rare of persons brought before the courts and admonished for neglecting this duty.   Another provision of the law was that any town containing one hundred families should " set up a gramer schoole, ye master thereof being able to instruct youth so farr as they may be fited for ye university."   The university referred to was Harvard, for the establishing of which arrangements had been made in 1636.

In England a " gramer schoole " meant one where Latin was the staple.   English grammar, the study the name most suggests, was not taught in such a school at all. But in this country the grammar schools, with few exceptions, were Latin and English schools combined. Even in those of the early Boston schools which were distinctly " Latin Schools," there appears to have been an usher, as the master's assistant was called, who taught English. The grammar schools rounded out and completed the educational system of Massachusetts, and this colony was decidedly in advance of all the others in providing for a general distribution of knowledge.

The legislature of Connecticut soon followed the example of Massachusetts in enacting a system of school laws ; but in all the other colonies each parish or settlement was a law unto itself in educational matters, and the schools were mainly under the patronage and control of the church.

The claim has been made that New Amsterdam had a free school before Boston did ; but its first school, established in 1633, was a public school in only a very limited sense. It was maintained for the town's children of the Dutch Reformed Church and no others. The citizens were complaining fourteen years later that no schoolhouse had yet been built, and that " the school is kept very irregularly, by this one or that, according to his fancy, as long as he sees fit." Ten years more passed, and we find the Manhattan folk humbly representing to the Dutch West India Company, under whose auspices they were governed, that there was no school in the colony where their children could learn Latin ; that there was no such school nearer than New England ;

and they prayed the honorable company to send a man capable of teaching this language. Their request was granted, but by that time Massachusetts had half a score of flourishing Latin schools, and seventeen classes had been graduated from Harvard.

The early schools were supported partly by the subscriptions of the well-to-do, partly by the rentals of lands set aside for the purpose, partly by tuition fees, and partly by taxes. There was no uniformity in the methods the different towns had for meeting their school expenses. Some took one way, and some another, but most adopted a combination of several ways; and while there was usually a town rate, this was only to supplement the other sources of income. Each town in Massachusetts had full control of its own schools, and the people voted in their regular town meetings what they would spend on them, how raise the money, who should teach, and what should be the amount of compensation. All the details of the school economy were attended to by the town officers.

The pay received by the teachers was meagre, and not always easily collected. In Northampton the first teacher was a town farmer by the name of Cornish, who, in 1664, was voted "six pound towards the scoole & to tacke the benifet of the scollers provided that he teach Six months in the yeare together." The total expense was in this instance shared between town and pupils; but just what fees resulted to Farmer Cornish from being allowed to " tacke the benifet of the scollers " is uncertain. At best, the remuneration could hardly have sufficed for the support of the master and his family, and he must have continued largely dependent on agriculture. He was apparently a man of considerable ability and standing in the town, for the records give his name the prefix of " Mr.," which was then an honorable distinction. Yet he had a habit of profanity, and once was fined twenty shillings by the court for cursing.

A year or two later his successor received an annual ten pounds from the town, while the scholars paid " ffowre pence pr weeke for such as are in the primer & other English books and Six pence pr weeke to learne the Accidence wrighting Casting Accounts." The instruction was practically all rudimentary. Even in the " Accidence," by which was meant Latin grammar, probably only the slightest outlines were taught. It is doubtful if the pupils were generally supplied with books, and in " Casting Accounts " the master presumably imparted nothing but his own knowledge of the art.

In 1687 the town changed its method of paying the master. He was still to collect tuition fees, but whatever he lacked of getting forty pounds was to be made up by the town. There was always much delinquency in paying on the part of those who sent children to school, and when the teacher was thus relieved from any absolute necessity for following up his debtors, it can easily be imagined that the amount collected dwindled. The result was that the town voted shortly afterward to allow " the Scholers to go free."

It was customary to pay the early masters in produce, agreement being made in hiring the teacher just what this should be. An old Dedham contract calls for two-thirds in wheat and the other third in corn ; and Deerfield, in 1703, covenants to pay the master

Twenty and five pounds in manner following : y^t is to say They have by bargin liberty to pay him ye one 3d part of s^d sum in Barley and no more : ye other two 3ds in other grain y^t is to say in indian corn : peas : or Rye in any or all of them : all these afore mentioned to be good and merchantable.

The net salary of the schoolmasters in most towns, after allowing a moderate sum for board, is estimated to have hardly exceeded, as expressed in modern terms, sixty or seventy dollars.

I have spoken of tuition fees. They were an accepted part of the educational financing in nearly all the old towns, and free schools were many years discussed before the majority of the towns adopted them. Free schools found favor with the poorer classes, but were opposed by the wealthy, especially the wealthy who had no children to send ; and they did not become the rule until long after the beginning of the eighteenth century. Indeed, school support by taxation was not made compulsory in Massachusetts until 1827.

The first town to have a school supported by general taxation — that is, by a tax on all the property holders of the community — was Dedham. The date of the innovation was 1649. The town records show that the schoolhouse was " built together with a watch house, the length 18 foote, the wideness,

15 foote; two convenient windows in the lower room & one in the chamber." The watch house was "a leanto set at the back of the chimney sixe foote wide" and it projected beyond the corner of the house on either side two and one-half feet. It had a fireplace and it had "open windowes so that the watch might have an aspect 4 severall wayes." The building stood in the centre of the village on the borders of the parish green near the meeting house. In the schoolroom the scholars labored dur-

Schoolhouse erected in 1649 at Dedham, Mass.

ing the day, and in the lean-to a sentinel watched from the windows during the night. The master was permitted to keep the school in his own home in extreme weather; and during the heat of summer he might use the meeting-house, provided he kept it clean and mended all the windows that his boys broke.

For a hundred years we find frequent mention of keeping schools in the meeting-houses. Those early churches were never invested with the religious sanc-

tity that is attached to a church now. They were
designed not only for places of worship, but for all
gatherings as the people had need. Until after the
beginning of the nineteenth century, meeting-houses
were in some communities used for town meetings and even for sessions of the law courts. Occasionally the building was outgrown as a church
and was then devoted to school use exclusively.
This happened in 1664 in one of our Connecticut
valley towns, and what had been the first meeting-
house sheltered the master and his pupils for thirty
years. The structure had been erected about a decade
previous to its becoming a schoolhouse, and was " of
Sawen Timber, 26 foot long and 18 foot wide, 9
foot high from the lower p^t of ye cell to the upper
part of the raisens."

It was decidedly superior to the log houses which
sheltered the people, for most of the pioneer dwell-
ings were of round logs, and the finest of them had
nothing better in their walls than hewn logs. The
meeting-house, however, was of material that could
only be obtained by great manual labor. Saw-mills
had long before been introduced in the vicinity of
the settlements on the coast, but many years elapsed
before any were possessed by the new towns inland,
and the only means of sawing logs into timbers or
boards was by use of a long heavy saw operated by
two men, one standing on the log and the other in a
pit below.

The meeting-house had a single doorway, two
windows, and a chimney. The roof was of thatch.
Probably the edifice never had a pulpit or pews.

Backless benches served for seats, and the change to a schoolroom was very easily made.

Most schools had to be content with buildings far less substantial than this one; yet the worst trouble was that the structures seldom received the attention they should have had when they began to get out of repair. We are given a rather startling impression of what these conditions might be by a master who, writing in 1681 of the "inconveniences" of his schoolhouse, describes

the confused and shattered and nastie posture that it is in, the glass broke, and thereupon very raw and cold; the floor very much broken and torn up to kindle fires, the hearth spoiled, the seats some burned and others out of kilter, that one had well-nigh as goods keep school in a hog stie as in it.

A very prolific source of annoyance to the school-master was the supply of firewood. The parents were required to bring a certain quantity of wood to the schoolhouse for each of their children attending. Thus, in 1699, we find one of our New England towns ordering " that all and every Scholler bring one load of wood though they goe but two months, that is two months from the beginning of October to yᵉ first of Aprill." During the other portion of the year little or no fire was needed. Those who failed to do their duty in this matter of fuel were to pay a fine of four shillings. A penalty of some sort was a necessity; and it is explained that many who " sent their children to Schoole were too negligent in bringing of wood for want whereof the Schoole oft times was omited." An enormous fireplace was the sole means of warming the schoolrooms of that day, and in sharp weather it consumed the wood most ravenously. The vote mentioned above was intended to remedy the chronic vanishing of the school woodpile, but it was not wholly effective, and the next year the selectmen were directed to prosecute delinquents.

Such an experience was not at all exceptional, and most of the towns passed special acts applying to the case. Sometimes the children of parents who did not do their part in keeping up the woodpile were turned out of the school. Sometimes they were refused " the benefit of the fire," and the master saw to it that they sat in the schoolroom's bleakest corner. Another rule was that the schoolboys of households whose parents sent the wood in sled length must cut it up where it lay in the school-yard.

Many of the towns provided a grammar school before they did an elementary. It seems to have been generally understood that children would be taught to read before attending the grammar schools. Thus in an agreement with a teacher of the Roxbury grammar school we find he is to " use his best skill and endeavor, both by precept and example, to instruct in all scholastical, moral, and theological discipline the children of the proprietors of the school — all a-b-c-darians excepted."

We get suggestive glimpses of the routine of the early schools in the Dorchester school rules of 1645, which provided that for seven months in the warmer

part of the year the master should every day begin
to teach at seven o'clock in the morning and dismiss
the scholars at five in the afternoon, while in the
colder and darker months of the remainder of the
year he was to begin at eight and close at four.
There was to be a midday intermission from eleven
to one, except on Monday, when the master

shall call his scholars together between twelve and one of
the clock to examine them what they have learned, at
which time also he shall take notice of any misdemeanor
or outrage that any of his scholars shall have committed
on the sabbath, to the end that at some convenient time
due admonition and correction may be administered.

He shall diligently instruct both in humane and good
literature, and likewise in point of good manners and dutiful behavior towards all, especially their superiors. Every
day of the week at two of the clock in the afternoon, he
shall catechise his scholars in the principles of the Christian religion.

He shall faithfully do his best to benefit his scholars,
and not remain away from school unless necessary. He
shall equally and impartially teach such as are placed in his
care, no matter whether their parents be poor or rich. (A
necessary warning, for the well-to-do and influential were
given a preference in most affairs of the times.)

It is to be a chief part of the schoolmaster's religious
care to commend his scholars and his labors amongst them
unto God by prayer morning and evening taking care that
his scholars do reverently attend during the same.

The rod of correction is a rule of God necessary sometimes to be used upon children. The schoolmaster shall
have full power to punish all or any of his scholars, no
matter who they are. No parent or other person living in
the place shall go about to hinder the master in this. But

if any parent or others shall think there is just cause for complaint against the master for too much severity, they shall have liberty to tell him so in friendly and loving way.

The emphasis laid on religious instruction in these rules was very characteristic of the colonial period. The children were perpetually enveloped, week-days and Sundays, in an atmosphere saturated with religious forms, services, ideas, and language. To illustrate how omnipresent this religious atmosphere was, I cannot do better than to cite the occasion when Judge Sewell found that the spout which conducted the rain water from his roof did not perform its office. After patient searching, a ball belonging to the Sewell children was discovered lodged in the spout. Thereupon the father sent for the minister and had a season of prayer with his boys, that their mischief or carelessness might be set in its proper aspect and that the event might be sanctified to their spiritual good. Powers of darkness and of light were struggling for the possession of every youthful soul, and it was the duty of parents, ministers, and teachers to lose no opportunity to pluck the children as brands from the burning.

The efforts to make the children religious were not by any means uniformly successful. No doubt the insistence of the elders on the solemnities often deadened their charges' sensibilities. At any rate, character and conduct among the young people were far from perfect. A committee appointed to see if the instruction at Harvard remained true to its early adopted motto, *For Christ and the Church*, reported that the Greek Catechism was recited regularly by the freshmen, and that Wollebius's *System of Divinity* was diligently pursued by the other classes, while on Saturday evening, in the presence of the president, the students repeated the sermon of the foregoing Sabbath. " Yet the committee are compelled to lament the continued prevalence of several immoralities, particularly stealing, lying, swearing, idleness, picking of locks, and too frequent use of strong drink."

Boys began to attend the grammar schools when they were seven or eight years of age, and now and then a youngster entered the Boston Latin School no older than six and one-half. Not infrequently the boys had by that time made considerable progress in Latin, and sometimes the merest infants were taught by doting parents to read this learned language as soon as they were taught to read English. Precocity was encouraged, not alone by intelligent parents, but by leading writers and thinkers. A good example of what was expected of the little ones is furnished by Isaac Watts's *The Young Child's Catechism*. The first half of it was designed for learners of " Three or Four Years Old," and the questions for these beginners included such as

Have you learnt to know who God is?

What muſt you do to eſcape God's Anger, which your Sins have deſerved?

What muſt become of you if you are wicked?

The answer to the last is, " If I am wicked, I ſhall be ſent down to everlaſting Fire in Hell among wicked and miſerable creatures."

The text-book equipment of the old schools was exceedingly meagre, and the average schoolboy had only a catechism or primer, a Psalter, and a Testament, or a Bible. For Latin students this list would have to be extended, but ordinarily it comprised all a boy ever used as long as he attended school. Still, scattered copies of the school-books put forth in England were possessed, and these were not without influence in the schools and on the attainments of the pupils. The text-books were practically all of foreign authorship. Indeed, I believe the only school-book of American origin prior to the Revolution was a little Latin grammar by Ezekiel Cheever. Cheever was one of the most notable of the early schoolmasters. He taught in New Haven and some smaller places; but for the last thirty-eight years of his life was master of the Boston Latin School. He died at his post in 1708, at the age of ninety-four, after having given seventy years of continuous service to the New England schools. His death was widely mourned, and he was long held in affectionate remembrance, for he was more patient with the slow boys and less severe and brutal with all boys than schoolmasters of that age were wont to be.

Full to the brim with Puritan theology, he wrote a book called *The Scriptural Prophesies Explained*, and he was unflagging in earnest endeavors to help his boys to become Christian men. The text-book of his authorship to which I have referred was, *A Short Introduction to the Latin Tongue*, generally known as "Cheever's Accidence." It enjoyed for over a century immense popularity. The first edi-

Orbis Senſualium Pictus.

A World of Things Obvious to the Senſes Drawn in Pictures.

Invitation.   I.   *Invitatio.*

The Maſter and the Boy.	*Magiſter & Puer.*
M. Come Boy, learn to be wiſe.	M. Veni Puer, diſce ſapere.
P. *What doth this mean, to be wiſe?*	P. *Quid hoc eſt, Sapere?*
M. *To underſtand rightly,*	M. Omnia, quæ neceſſaria, rectè

First Lesson Page of Comenius's *Visible World.*

tion appeared in 1645, and the book was republished as late as 1838. In the grammar schools Cheever's was usually the first Latin book, and after the boys had worked their way through that they plunged into the dreary wilderness of " Lily's Grammar " with its twenty-five kinds of nouns, its seven genders, and other things in proportion — all to be wearisomely committed to memory. The purgatory of this grammar was early recognized, and Cotton Mather said of it, " Persisting in the use of Lily's book will prolong the reign of the ferule." The only copies I have seen have been revisions of the original, yet the one I own, dated 1766, states that the unrevised is still printed and for sale. The author of the work died in 1523, and one would think that in the two centuries and a half since the book first appeared it would have been entirely supplanted.

A more attractive book to the Latin boys was John Amos Comenius's *Visible World* which was published in 1658. Aside from A B C primers, this was the first illustrated school-book ever printed. Comenius, born in 1592, was a Moravian bishop, and the most distinguished educational reformer of his time. He wrote a number of books, but the one that attained the widest circulation was this "*Vifible World:* or a Nomenclature, and Pictures of all the chief things that are in the World, and of Men's Employments therein; in above an 150 Copper Cuts." Every subject treated had its picture, and below the engraving was a medley of explanatory little sentences in two columns, one column in Latin,

Cornix cornicatur, *á á*	A a
The Crow crieth.	
Agnus balat, *b é é é*	B b
The Lamb blaiteth.	
Cicáda ſtridet, *ci ci*	C c
The Graſhopper chirpeth.	
Upupa dicit, *du du*	D d
The Whooppoo ſaith.	
Infans ejulat, *é é é*	E e
The Infant crieth.	
Ventus flat, *fi fi*	F f
The Wind bloweth.	
Anſer gingrit, *ga ga*	G g
The Gooſe gagleth.	
Os halat, *háh háh*	H h
The mouth breatheth out.	
Mus mintrit, *i i i*	I i
The Mouſe chirpeth.	
Anas tetrinnit, *kha kha*	K k
The Duck quaketh.	
Lupus ululat, *lu ulu*	L l
The Wolf howleth.	
Urſus murmurat, *mum mum*	M m
The Bear grumbleth.	

Felio

Part of an Illustrated Alphabet in the *Visible World.*

c

the other in English.   By such means the pupil was
supposed not only to learn Latin, but to absorb a
large amount of general knowledge concerning the in-
dustries and other "chief things that are in the World."
It was a crude effort to interest the child, and was
encyclopædic, dry, and verbal, having more the
character of an illustrated dictionary than a child's
reading-book ; yet for one hundred years this was the
most popular text-book in Europe, and it was translated into fourteen languages.

Other Latin books in common use were Æsop,
Eutropius, and *The Colloquies of Corderius ;* and for
the older boys Cæsar, Ovid, Virgil, and Cicero.   In
Greek they had the grammar, the Testament, and
Homer.   Thus they fitted themselves for the university, which made very exacting requirements in
the dead languages, but paid little attention to the
progress its prospective students had made in science, mathematics, or anything else.   The Harvard
terms of admission were these : —

Whoever shall be able to read Tully, or any other such-
like classical author at sight, and correctly, and without
assistance to speak and write Latin both in prose and
verse, and to inflect exactly the paradigms of Greek nouns
and verbs, has a right to expect to be admitted into the
college, and no one may claim admission without these
qualifications.

The classical requisites noted above become quite
impressive when it is remembered that the law
ordered every town in Massachusetts of a hundred
families to provide this knowledge.

The Barbers Shop. LXXV.   *Tonſtrina.*

75.

The Barber, 1.	*Tonſor,* 1.
in the Barbers-ſhop, 2.	in *Tonſtrina,* 2.
cutteth off the Hair	tondet *Crines*
and the Beard	& *Barbam*
with a pair of Sizzars, 3.	*Forcipe,* 3.
or ſhaveth with a Razor,	vel radit *Novaculâ,*
which he taketh out of his	quam è *Theca,* 4. depromit.
Caſe, 4.	
And he waſheth one	Et lavat
over a Baſon, 5.	ſuper *Pelvim,* 5.
with Suds running	*Lixivio* defluente
out of a Laver, 6.	è *Gutturnio,* 6.
and alſo with Sope, 7.	ut & *Sapone,* 7.
and wipeth him	& tergit
with a Towel, 8.	*Linteo,* 8.
combeth him with a Comb, 9.	pectit *Pectine,* 9.
and curleth him	criſpat
with a Criſping Iron, 10.	*Calamiſtro,* 10.
Sometimes he cutteth a Vein	Interdum Venam ſecat
with a Pen-knife, 11.	*Scalpello,* 11.
where the Blood ſpirteth out, 12.	ubi Sanguis propullulat, 12.
	The

A Page showing the Method of Teaching in the *Visible World.*

Most of the teachers of the early Latin schools had received a college education in England, and were men of more than ordinary capacity and experience. Our own Harvard, too; sent forth many graduates who found places in the schools as well as in the pulpits. The teachers were all deeply imbued with that religious spirit which characterized

THE

ENGLISH

SCHOOL-MASTER.

Teaching all his Scholars , of what
age foever, the moft eafy, fhort, and perfect order of diftinct Reading , and true Writing our Englifh-tongue , that hath ever yet been known or publifhed by any.

Portion of the Title-page of a popular Text-book first published in 1596.

the Puritan epoch, for this was the trend of their whole training. Their college studies were the studies of a divinity school. There was some arithmetic and geometry, physics and science, but as for the rest — it was grammar, logic, and rhetoric; politics and ethics ; Chaldee, Hebrew, and Syriac; biblical and catechetical divinity.

The earliest spelling-book was Coote's *The English School-Master*, a thin quarto of seventy-two

Frontispiece to a Speller entitled, *A Rational Way of Teaching*, 1688.

pages, first published in 1596. It continued to be extraordinarily popular for over a century. According to the title-page, " he which hath this Book only, needeth to buy no other to make him fit from his Letters to the *Grammar-School*, or for an *Apprentice.*" Besides spelling, it contained arithmetic, history, writing lessons, prayers, psalms, and a short catechism. To add to the intricacy, much of the text was printed in old English black letter.

Another ancestral speller was *England's Perfect School-Master*, by Nathaniel Strong, London, 1676, of the editing and use of which the author says in his

The Epiſtle to the Reader

UPon conſideration of the bad reading of many, who know not how ſcarcely to spell any word rightly : I have ſorted all the words I could think of and ranked them in particular Tables. By this Book a Lad may be taught to read a Chapter perfectly in the Bible in a quarter of a years time. I have likewiſe added unto this Book certain other neceſſary Inſtructions, and uſeful Varieties, as well for writers as Readers. The whole I crave God's Bleſſing upon, and leave it to thy candid acceptance; Remaining

Thine to ſerve thee or thine,

NAT. STRONG.

One curious department, covering fifteen pages, consists of " Some Obſervations of Words that are alike in ſound, yet of different ſignification, and ſpelling." Their use and meaning are indicated thus : —

I Saw one *ſent* unto the Hill's *aſcent*,
Who did *aſſent* to me before he went.

Above thy reach a *Spire*-ſteeple ſtands,
Aſpire not high, thou *Spyer* out of Lands.

The latter portion of the book is ·devoted to Latin exercises, " Forms of Letters," and arithmetic. From the arithmetic I quote these two bills, the items of which have a strangely unfamiliar look : —

A Shoomaker's Bill.

1 pair Cloth Shooes and Golfhoes, with Ferry Boots
2 pair of Shaſhoons for Boots
9 dozen of Wooden-heel'd Shooes
For waxing a pair of Boots
2 pair of Women's Lac'd Shooes and Slaps

A Taylor's Bill.

Mr. *John Saddler*, his bill.

For a Set of Gold and Silver Buttons
For Tabby for lining the Coat
For ſeiſing Flap
For Cottoning for the Hoſe and Pockets
For canvas for Stays and Stiffenings
For Belly-Pieces, Hooks, Eyes, and Stay-Tape
For Silk and Galloon

The lessons in the book are supplemented by several prayers, and then at the bottom of the final page there is this " Advertiſement," in which the author says he has a school

where Youth may be fitted for the Univerſity : Alſo taught to write all manner of Fair Hands, with Arithmetick :

Likewiſe Boarded with a great conveniency. My encouragement where I am b'eing as yet but ſmall; If any Perſon
can adviſe to any Place or Pariſh wanting a School-maſter;
upon aſſurance of a competent livelihood, I ſhall ſoon quit
my preſent concerns, and readily accept it.

The ministers had much to do with the public
schools in all places, large and small. Their supervision was constant and vigilant. The church was
then supported by the whole town, and its affairs
regulated in the town meetings; and the minister
was a town officer. He was employed for the religious instruction of the people; and as the children
were an important part of his charge, his visits to
the schools were frequent. He examined the children in the catechism and in their knowledge of the
Bible, and sometimes questioned them on the sermon of the preceding Sunday. In 1710 we find it
was expected of the Boston ministers that they
would, on their school visits, pray with the pupils,
and "entertain them with some instructions of
piety specially adapted to their age and education"; and something of this sort continued to be
the duty of the ministers in our rural towns until
the middle of the last century. The rural minister
also often rendered service as a teacher, especially as
a teacher of Latin in towns that had no grammar
school. Many ministers boarded several students,
as well as taught them.

When other means of education were lacking, the
laws ordered that the parents themselves should impart instruction to their children. But most communities contrived at least to have a dame school.

The School Dame.

There was always some woman in every neighborhood who, for a small amount of money, was willing
to take charge of the children and teach them the
rudiments of knowledge.   The older and larger
towns had these dame schools as well as the pioneer
villages, and they were everywhere a chief dependence
for elementary instruction; yet they were seldom at
first town schools, and none of them were free for
a long time.   The dame school was an English
institution, and the description of it by the poet
Crabbe as it existed across the Atlantic would very
well fit it here : —

> . . . a deaf, poor, patient widow sits
> And awes some thirty infants as she knits;
> Infants of humble, busy wives who pay
> Some trifling price for freedom through the day.
> At this good matron's hut the children meet,
> Who thus becomes the mother of the street.
> Her room is small, they cannot widely stray,
> Her threshold high, they cannot run away.
> With band of yarn she keeps offenders in,
> And to her gown the sturdiest rogue can pin.

The school dame did not usually find the labor of
teaching very onerous.   While she heard the smaller
pupils recite their letters, and the older ones read
and spell from their primers, she busied her fingers
with knitting and sewing, and in the intervals
between lessons sometimes worked at the spinning-
wheel.   An interesting instance of school-dame
industry occurs in the annals of Northfield, Massachusetts.   The first teacher in the town was a woman hired
to care for a class of little ones twenty-two weeks in

the warm season. Besides the neighbors' children
she had four of her own to look after, yet her en-
ergies were by no means exhausted, and the semi-lei-
sure of the school-room allowed her to work quite steadily
making shirts for the Indians at eight pence each.

The beginner's chief aid in starting on the road to
learning was a hornbook — not really a book at all,
but simply a bit of printed paper about three by four
inches fastened on a thin piece of board. The name
"hornbook" origi-nated in the fact that the printed
slip was covered with a translucent sheet of horn,

A Typical Hornbook.

"To save from fingers wet the letters fair." A
light strip of metal, usually brass, was fastened with
several short nails or tacks around the edges of the

horn to keep it in place. The board had a handle
at one end, and occasionally this handle was pierced
with a hole so that a string could be attached and
the toddling owner of the hornbook could carry it
suspended from his neck. At the top of the paper

Revolving Alphabet.
Diameter of the original, five inches.

was printed the alphabet, capitals, and small letters;
and then in orderly array the vowels, then double
lines of ab, eb, ibs, and the benediction, "In the
name of the Father, and of the Son, and of the Holy
Ghoſt. *Amen.*" The remaining space was devoted
to the Lord's Prayer, unless, as was sometimes

the case, this was supplemented at the bottom by the Roman numerals.

A curious successor to the hornbook was produced by a Hartford publisher in 1820. It was called "The Revolving Alphabet or Child's Instructive Toy," and consisted of two wooden disks about five inches in diameter with a circular sheet of paper between them. On one side of the paper was printed the alphabet; on the other side a series of little syllables. By turning a thumb-piece the paper inside the disks could be made to revolve, and an aperture near the edge of one of the disks allowed you to see the printing, a short column at a time. I imagine this educational toy never had much vogue, and that few people have ever seen one.

II

COLONIAL SCHOOLS OF THE EIGHTEENTH CENTURY

THE early Massachusetts school laws decreed that any town neglecting to provide a schoolmaster should be subject to a penalty of ten pounds. In 1701 the General Court, after declaring that the observance of this decree was "shamefully neglected by divers towns, and the penalty thereof not required, tending greatly to the nourishment of ignorance and irreligion, whereof grievous complaint is made," doubled the penalty, and enjoined all justices of the peace and grand juries to vigilantly attend to the law's execution. As a result, at nearly every session of the court there were towns "presented" for not maintaining the schools required by law, especially the grammar schools. Many excuses were offered — sometimes poverty, sometimes inability to secure a teacher. The poverty was often very real, for the colony had passed through King Philip's War, 1675–78, on which it had spent more than half a million dollars. Besides the expense, there had been great loss of life, twelve out of the ninety towns had been utterly destroyed, and forty others had been the scene of fire and massacre. A number of communities were so reduced that their share in the colony tax was remitted.

For a long time the fear of Indian invasion had a tendency to hold the settlers closely together, and in some of the towns it was forbidden to build beyond

A Salem Schoolhouse with Whipping-post in the near Street.
From a drawing made about 1770.

a fixed distance of one or two miles from the meeting-house.   But now that the savages had been thor-oughly subdued, the people began to push out into the wilderness, and new towns were planted and added to the commonwealth in quick succession. Many of them had no village nucleus. They either consisted of widely scattered farms, or of several isolated hamlets.   The old towns, too, sent forth new shoots, and developed outlying neighborhoods. Thus the schooling of the children presented new conditions and problems.   All the children must be taught, and to reach them "moving schools" were devised — that is, the towns voted that a school should be kept for a part of the year in each of several vicinities.   The Massachusetts town of Scituate ordered the school to be kept one-third at each end of the town and one-third in the middle ; Yarmouth decided to have the school in five places varying from one to four months each ; and in Sutton, where a more scanty education was provided, the school was kept at the discretion of the select-men in four places, one month to each.   It was permissible in some of the towns for the scholars to follow the schools, but this privilege was probably not much used.   The various divisions of the town were called " angles " or " squadrons " at first, and later " districts."   For a long period few of them had schoolhouses, but presently the school was made conditional on the district's erecting a building.   By the middle of the century the towns began to allow the districts to draw their proportion of the school money and spend it as they liked.   The schools ceased to be town schools, and the choice of teachers, their pay, and the time the schools should keep, was taken out of the hands of the selectmen.

The early dame schools had been privately sup-ported, but they were gradually absorbed into the public school system, and we find such entries on the town records as : —

Paid Widow Walker ten shillings for schooling small children.

Paid for boarding schooldame, at three shillings per week.

However, in some towns no public provision was made for the youngest children until after the Revolution.

I have been describing educational conditions more particularly as they were in New England. Though far from ideal, these conditions were nevertheless better than in any other part of the country. Especially in the South, with its widely separated houses and few villages, the environment was in every way unfavorable for maintaining public schools. The children of wealthy planters were usually taught by private tutors, or sent to England to be educated; yet once in a while a planter would start a little school for the benefit of his own children and the other white children who chanced to live on or near his plantation. The teachers of such plantation schools were apt to be redemptioners and exported convicts. In Europe at this time the lot of the poor was extremely hard, and many persons came across the Atlantic solely to escape the inevitable misery at home. The captain of the ship that brought over a penniless man of this class was allowed to sell him for four years to pay his passage. It was also customary to transport men who had been convicted of small crimes and sell them for periods of greater or less length. When one of these unfortunates could read and write, he sometimes was purchased for a schoolmaster, and teachers of this kind were common both in the Southern and the Middle colonies. Not infrequently they were coarse and degraded, and they did not always stay their time out as is witnessed by advertisements like the following in the newspapers of the period : —

Ran away : a Servant man who followed the occupation of a Schoolmaster, much given to drinking and gambling.

Among those who bought a bondsman for educational purposes was George Washington's father, and this bondsman was Washington's first schoolmaster. He was a slow, rusty old man by the name of Hobby. Besides doing duty as dominie he served as sexton, and in the intervals of teaching swept out the church and now and then dug a grave. The schoolhouse in which he taught is said to have stood in an "old plantation field"—a field exhausted by successive tobacco crops, and allowed to grow up to pines. Tradition relates that Hobby lived long enough to see his pupil rise to distinction. He was very proud of his own services as the boy's teacher, and was wont to boast it was he "who between his knees had laid the foundation of Washington's greatness."

After Hobby had laid this "foundation," his pupil attended another school for four or five years presided over by a Mr. Williams. If we are to believe one of Washington's early biographers, Mr. Williams "knew as little as Balaam's ass." Under him the boy in playtime became expert in running and wrestling, but in his studies failed to acquire either correct spelling or the commonest rules of English grammar. The book he perhaps learned most from at this time was one entitled *The Young Man's Companion,* which apparently came into his

D

possession when he was about ten.   It claims to teach a boy without a tutor " a fhort and eafy Method of Book-keeping," how to " fpell, read and write true Englifh, indite Epiftles or Letters in a familiar ftile," how to make out papers such as deeds, bonds, and wills, how to measure timber, and do other useful things.

Facsimile of Washington's Schoolboy Handwriting.
Reduced one third.

Blank-books are still preserved into which the boy Washington copied various legal forms, some poor poetry, and a list of one hundred and ten " Rules of Civility and Decent behavior in Company and Conversation."   The handwriting is round, fair, and bold, the letters large like the hand that formed them, and the lines run straight and even. Sometimes he made ornamental letters with scroll work such as clerks were accustomed to use.   The Rules of Civility were probably taken down from the lips of the teacher.   They sound rather stiff now, but it was a common thing then to set such precepts before children, and Washington very likely committed them to memory.   They touch on things great and small, and in certain instances throw a rather curious light on the rude habits of the times. How strange, for example, is the admonition, " Kill no Vermin as Fleas, lice, ticks, etc., in the Sight of Others."

The Virginia schools long continued to have much the same desultory character they had in

One of the Log Schoolhouses still to be found in the South.

Washington's youth.   A master who kept a plantation school in 1800 for a few months tells of one of his pupils who was a man thirty years of age. Another pupil persisted in coming with two huge

mastiffs at his heels, and the dogs would uncere-
moniously enter the schoolroom "bringing with
them myriads of fleas, wood-lice and ticks." Then
there were two sisters who rode on a single horse to
the schoolhouse door, followed by " a running foot-
man of the negro tribe with their food in a basket."
The building was of logs.   It stood on blocks about
two and a half feet from the ground, and the space
underneath formed a convenient rendezvous for
hogs and poultry.   The interior had neither ceiling
nor plastering.   When it stormed, the rain was excluded by going outside and propping a square board
against the window opening with a broken rail—and
yet the farmers of the neighborhood referred to this
rude structure as " The Academy."

    The first schoolhouses in the Middle colonies were
of logs almost exclusively.   Such school buildings
were common in many sections for at least fifty
years after the Revolution, and among the mountains they have lingered in use until quite recently.
The earlier ones had a rough puncheon floor, if they
had any floor at all.   Often there was only the bare
earth which the children's feet soon rendered very
dusty.   On occasion the youngsters would purposely
stir up this dust in clouds to annoy the teacher and
amuse their fellows.   Sticks were inserted between
the logs around the sides of the room at a convenient
height, and boards were nailed on them to serve as
desks.   Roofs were of bark, and at one end of the
building was a chimney of short logs laid up cob-
house fashion and daubed with clay.   Many of the
school-houses, even to the borders of the nineteenth

century, had no glass in their windows.   The paper that served instead was greased with lard to make it transparent and less easily affected by wet.

Inkstand, Sandbox, and Bunch of Uncut Quills.

The colonial schools had no blackboards and no maps, but once in a while a schoolroom in the more flourishing communities would possess a globe.

Slates did not come into general use until about 1820, and lead pencils not for a good many years after that. In filling the pages of their manuscript "sum-books" and "copy-books," the children were in the habit of using pen and ink exclusively. A favorite book of instructions of the period in its "Directions to Beginners in Writing" says that the necessary implements are

a pen-knife, quills, paper, good and free ink; likewiſe a flat Ruler for Sureneſs; and a round one for Diſpatch; with a leaden Plummet or Pencil to rule Lines: Alſo Gum Sandrich Powder with a little Cotton dipped therein, which rub gently over the Paper to make it bear Ink the better.

The pens were goose-quills, and one of the schoolmaster's most essential accomplishments was the ability to make and mend these pens. Even if he was very expert in the art, the making and repairing for a large school consumed a good deal of time. Each family was its own ink manufacturer. The usual process was to dissolve ink-powder; but many of the country folk gathered the bark of swamp-maple, boiled it in an iron kettle to give it a more perfect black color, and when the decoction was thick added copperas. These home-made inks were often weak and pallid, and sometimes they dried up. Again they were spoiled with grease that got into the inkstands at the schoolhouse; for when there were evening meetings in the school building it came handy to use the inkstands as candlesticks.

The paper ordinarily bought for school purposes was rough and dark. Its cost, and the scarcity of money, led the scholars to use it sparingly, and in the newer and poorer communities children frequently

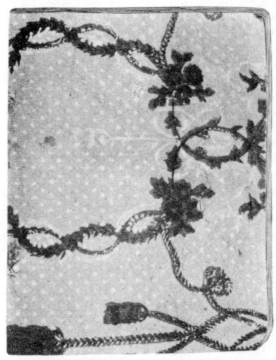

A Homemade Copy Book with a Wall-paper Cover.
Size of original about 10 × 12 .

ciphered on birch bark. The paper came in foolscap size, unruled. For the copy and sum books each sheet was folded to make four leaves or eight pages. Then enough of these folds were slipped within each

other to form a book of the desired thickness.
Lastly a cover of coarse brown wrapping-paper, or
possibly of wall-paper, was cut out, and the whole
was carefully sewed into shape.   In preparation for
writing, the children ruled the paper themselves with
lead plummets.   Some plummets were merely pieces
of sheet lead, but oftener the lead was melted and
run into a wooden mould and later smoothed with a
jack-knife.   The most popular shape was that of a
tomahawk.   When properly finished and sharpened
and drilled with a hole at one end, the plummet was
tied with a string of tow to the owner's ruler.

The handwriting of the colonial children, judging
from the copy-books that have been preserved, was
admirably legible and uniform — much better than
that of the young people of the present.   In fact, it
was a chief requisite of the old schoolmasters that
they should be good teachers of penmanship.   The
spelling mattered little, if only the " wrighting " was
clear and fair ; and as a logical result of this view a
very large proportion of the early chirography is
handsome and dignified, and easy to read.

Some particularly interesting glimpses of education
in the score of years preceding the Revolution are to
be found in the biography of John Trumbull, who
attended one of the best schools of the period in the
little town of Lebanon, Connecticut.   For thirty
years the master of the school was Nathan Tisdale,
a man whose assiduity and fidelity became so widely
known that he not only had pupils from the New
England and Northern colonies, but from those of
the remotest South and from the West India Islands.

A Colonial Schoolmaster.

From Judd's *Margaret*.

It was the rule of the school to have no vacations, and because of this rule, or in spite of it, Trumbull, who became a pupil as a very small child, could read Greek at six years of age, and at twelve was sufficiently advanced to be admitted to college.

There is, perhaps, no better record of the appearance of a typical colonial schoolmaster than is to be found in Judd's *Margaret* : —

He wore a three-cornered hat.   His coat descended in long, square skirts, quite to the calves of his legs.   He had on nankeen small-clothes, white silk stockings, paste knee and shoe buckles.   His waistcoat was of yellow embossed silk with long lappels.   The sleeves and skirts of his coat were garnished with rows of silver buttons.   He wore ruffle cuffs; on his neck was a snow-white linen stock. Under his hat appeared a gray wig falling in rolls over his shoulders.   He had on a pair of turquoise-shell spectacles. A golden-headed cane was thrust under his arm.

I also wish to quote from the reminiscences of Alexander Graydon a graphic description of the methods of discipline adopted in the school he attended in Philadelphia, about 1765.   His master, an Englishman by the name of Dove, was a humorist, and it was his practice to substitute humiliation for corporal punishment.   His birch was rarely applied in the usual way,

but was generally stuck into the back part of the collar of the unfortunate culprit, who, with this badge of disgrace towering from his nape, was compelled to take his stand upon the top of the form for such a period of time as his offence was thought to deserve.   He had another contrivance for boys who were late in their morning attendance. This was to dispatch a committee of five or six scholars for them, with a bell and lighted lantern; and in this odd equipage, in broad daylight, the bell all the while tingling, were they escorted through the streets to school. As Dove affected a strict regard to justice in his dispensations of punishment, and always professed a willingness to have an equal measure of it meted out to himself in case of his transgressing, the boys took him at his word; and one morning, when he had overstaid his time, he found himself waited on in the usual form. He immediately admitted the justice of the procedure, and, putting himself behind the lantern and bell, marched with great solemnity to school, to the no small gratification of the boys and entertainment of the spectators.

Later, Graydon entered the Latin School presided over by a Scotchman of diminutive figure, named Beveridge. Of this master, Graydon says: —

He was diligent and laborious in his attention to his school; and had he possessed the faculty of making himself beloved by the scholars, and of exciting their emulation and exertion, nothing would have been wanting in him to an entire qualification for his office. Though not, perhaps, to be complained of as intolerably severe, he yet made a pretty free use of the rattan and the ferule, but to very little purpose. He was, in short, no disciplinarian, and consequently very unequal to the management of seventy or eighty boys. He was assisted by two ushers, who eased him in the burden of teaching, but who, in matters of discipline, seemed disinclined to interfere. I have seen them slyly slip out of the way when the principal was entering upon the job of capitally punishing a boy, who, from his size, would be likely to make resistance.

Various were the rogueries that were played upon him; but the most audacious of all was the following. At the hour of convening in the afternoon (that being the most convenient, from the circumstance of Mr. Beveridge being usually a little beyond the time) the bell having rung, the ushers being at their posts, and the scholars arranged in their classes, three or four of the conspirators conceal themselves without for the purpose of observing the motions of their victim. He arrives, enters the school, and is permitted to proceed until he is supposed to have nearly reached his chair at the upper end of the room, when instantly the door and every window-shutter is closed. Now, shrouded in utter darkness, the most hideous yells that can be conceived are sent forth from at least three score of throats; and Ovids and Virgils and Horaces, together with the more heavy metal of dictionaries, are hurled without remorse at the astonished preceptor, who, groping and crawling under cover of the forms, makes the best of his way to the door. When attained, and light restored, a death-like silence ensues. Every boy is at his lesson: no one has had a hand or a voice in the recent atrocity. What, then, is to be done? and who shall be chastised?

This outrage, from its succeeding beyond expectation, and being entirely to the taste of the school, had a run of several days, and was only put a stop to by the interference of the faculty.

The ferule was the standard implement for reforming the erring pupil, but some masters used a rattan or a cowhide. Even a cat-o'-nine-tails was not unknown. It was a time when young men were publicly whipped in colleges, and the severity of the treatment meted out to the pupils in the minor schools is not at all surprising. One New York

master had a short ladder beside his desk, and when
he called forth a culprit for punishment, the boy
had to step up on the ladder to receive his caning.
It is related of a certain rustic schoolmaster that he
kept a long birch rod with the butt-end resting on
his chair, so that he could use it without rising.
Another master would sit with his feet on the table
and call up all the boys to march around the table
in single file. As they passed in front of him he
hit them each in turn with his ruler. In this way,
though some of the innocent may have suffered, he
made sure that none of the guilty escaped. But not
all the discipline in the old schools was muscular.
Instances are recorded of an offender's being ordered
out to cut a small branch from a tree, and when he
returned with it, the teacher squared and partially
split the larger end and fitted the cleft on the culprit's
nose. Pinched and ridiculous, the boy was forced
to stand in full sight of the school until the teacher
relented.

In the dame schools premiums of gingerbread
were now and then bestowed for good behavior, but
these were not a chief reliance in the cultivation of
virtue. Most dames had great faith in a thimble
tapped sharply on the delinquents' craniums. Whis-
perers were sometimes compelled to silence by having inserted in their mouths a short stick, like the
bit of a bridle, with strings at the ends which could
be tied at the back of the head. There were schools
where transgressors were made to stand on the
benches and wear dunce caps, or huge leather spectacles; or they might have pinned to their persons

large labels lettered, "Lying Ananias," or "Idle Boy," or whatever the teacher thought was appropriate to the case. Occasionally a child rebelled when punished and attempted revenge. Thus, in a Boston dame school, where the teacher had a habit of pinning haughty pupils to the cushion of her chair, one rogue, while fastened in this way, contrived to pin the dame's gown to the same article. When she rose she carried cushion and boy with her, to the great consternation of all concerned.

THE

HISTORY

OF

GENESIS.

BEING

An Account of the Holy Lives and Actions of the Patriarchs; explained with Pious and Edifying Explications, and illuftrated with near Forty Figures.

Fitted for the Ufe of Schools, and recommended to Teachers of Children, as a Book very proper for the learning them to read Englifh, and inftructing them in the right underftanding of thefe Divine Hiftorys.

Part of the Title-page of an Early Religious School-book.

Reduced one-third.

Books written especially for school use increased in number with the passing years; but almost without exception they were of English authorship, and most were of British printing.

A text-book with an individuality all its own was *The History of Genesis*, published in 1708. It was made up of short narratives retold from the first book of the Bible. To add to its attractiveness there were numerous illustrations. What the volume aspired to do for youthful students can best be shown by an extract from the Preface.

This Book of Genefis (the antienteft Writing now extant) is juftly ftiled the Epitome of all Divinity. It is indeed a great Blefling of God, That Children in England

Noah's Ark, as depicted in *The History of Genesis.*

have liberty to read the holy Scriptures, when others abroad are denied it. And yet alas! how often do we fee Parents prefer *Tom Thumb, Guy of Warwick,* or fome fuch foolish Book, before the Book of Life! Let not your Children read thefe vain Books, profane Ballads, and filthy Songs. Throw away all fond and amorous Romances, and fabulous Hiftories of Giants, the bombaft Atchievements of Knight Errantry, and the like; for thefe fill the Heads of Children with vain, filly and idle imaginations.

The Publisher, therefore, of this History of Genesis, being sensible how useful a Work of this Nature might be for Schools, hopes it will meet with a general Acceptance.

One of the earliest elementary books of the century was entitled *The Child's Weeks-work*. It was a compilation of lessons for each day of four weeks. Among other things there were proverbs; fables, a section devoted to "Behavior," and "A Short Catechism fitted for the Use of Children after they have said their Prayers." But the oddest feature was the insertion here and there of conundrums and anecdotes. Several

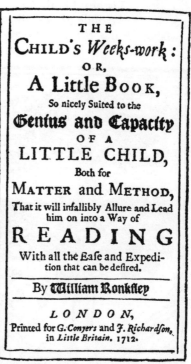

THE
CHILD'S *Weeks-work*:
OR,
A Little Book,
So nicely Suited to the
𝕲𝖊𝖓𝖎𝖚𝖘 𝖆𝖓𝖉 𝕮𝖆𝖕𝖆𝖈𝖎𝖙𝖞
OF A
LITTLE CHILD,
Both for
MATTER and METHOD,
That it will infallibly Allure and Lead him on into a Way of
READING
With all the Ease and Expedition that can be desired.

By 𝖂𝖎𝖑𝖑𝖎𝖆𝖒 𝕽𝖔𝖓𝖐𝖘𝖑𝖊𝖞

LONDON,
Printed for *G. Conyers* and *J. Richardson*, in *Little Britain*. 1712.

Title-page of *The Child's Weeks-work*.
Reduced one-third.

of the former and one of the latter follow : —

Quest. What's that which is higher sitting than standing?

Answ. It is a Dog.

Queſt. A long Tail, a Tongue and a Mouth
    Full fifty feet above the Ground,
'Tis heard both *Eaſt, Weſt, North* and *South*,
    A mile or two all round.
Anſw. *It is a Bell in a Steeple.*

Queſt. I never Spoke but once.
Anſw. *It is* Balaam's *Aſs.*

A Countryman being preſt for a Soldier, was engaged in a Fight, and at his return was aſk'd, what Manly Acts he had done, he anſwer'd he had cut off one of the Enemy's legs. Oh! ſaid the other, you had done much more like a ſtout Man, if you had cut off his Head: Oh! ſaid he, that was off before.

A Tree of Knowledge Frontispiece.
From *The London Spelling-Book.* 1710.

Somewhat allied to the two books just described, in their distinctly religious character, was "*The Protestant Tutor*, instructing Youth and Others, in the compleat method of *Spelling*, *Reading*, and *Writing*, True Englifh: Alfo difcovering to them the Notorious *Errors*, Damnable *Doctrines*, and cruel *Maffacres* of the bloody *Papifts*, which *England* may expect from a Popifh SUCCESSOR: Printed by and for *Tho. Norris*, and fold at the Looking-glafs on *London-Bridge*." The title-page from which this is

An Illustrated Alphabet in *The London Spelling-Book*.

taken is dated 1715, but there were earlier editions, and the book apparently enjoyed a considerable circulation. The lessons included the alphabet, a few

E

pages of spelling words and easy reading lessons,
but mostly were made up of rabid anti-Catholic
matter illustrated with dreadful pictures of persecu-
tions and of heaven, hell, death, and the judgment.

A bird in the hand is worth two in the buſh.

FABLE XII. *Of the Fiſherman and the Fiſh.*

The Fisherman with "a bird in the hand."
From Dilworth's *A New Guide to the English Tongue.*

Only infrequent copies of the text-books I have
mentioned wandered to our shores; nor were any
school-books imported in quantity until the publication of Dilworth's *A New Guide to the English
Tongue,* in 1740. This was the most popular speller
of the eighteenth century. A portrait of Dilworth
with a scholastic cap on his head and a pen in his
hand served for a frontispiece; and, in truth, as the

He that will not help himfelf, fhall have help from
nobody.

FABLE I. *Of the Waggoner and Hercules.*

AS a waggoner was driving his team, his waggon funk into a hole, and ftuck faft.

The poor man immediately fell upon his knees,
and prayed to Hercules, that he would get his waggon out of the hole again.

Thou fool, fays Hercules, whip thy horfes, and
fet thy fhoulder to the wheels; and then if thou
wilt call upon Hercules he will help thee.

The Interpretation.

Lazy wifhes never do a Man any fervice; but if he would
have help from God in time of need, let him not only implore
his affiftance, but make ufe of his own beft endeavours.

From Dilworth's *A New Guide to the English Tongue.*

Evil be to him that evil think. Alſo, give a
    cruſt to a ſurly dog, and he will bite you.

FABLE X. *Of the good natured Man and the Adder.*

A Good natured man being obliged to go out
    in froſty weather, on his return home found
an adder almoſt frozen to death, which he brought
home with him and laid before the fire.

As ſoon as the creature had received freſh life
by the warmth, and was come to herſelf, ſhe began to hiſs, and fly about the houſe, and at length
killed one of the children.

Well, ſaid the man, if this is the beſt return
that you can make for my kind offices, you ſhall
even ſhare the ſame fate yourſelf ; and ſo killed
her immediately.

The Interpretation.

Ingratitude is one of the blackeſt crimes that a man can be
guilty of: It is hateful to God and man, and frequently brings
upon ſuch a graceleſs wretch all that miſchief which he either did
or thought to do to another.

From Dilworth's *A New Guide to the English Tongue.*

greatest school-book author of his time he was not unworthy of the honor. The spelling words were interspersed with much religious reading and dismal moralizing, but as an offset to this matter there was "A Select Number of Fables, adorned with proper Sculptures."

Two of the fable pages are reproduced entire. The other illustration, delineating the fisherman, is accompanied by the following story : —

A Fiſherman having caſt his line into the water preſently drew up a Fiſh.

The little captive intreated the fiſherman that he would ſpare her (ſhe being but ſmall) till ſhe was grown larger ; and then ſhe would ſuffer herſelf to be taken by him again.

No, no, replied the fiſherman, I am not to be ſo ſerved. If I let you go, I muſt never ſee you any more : I was always of that temper that whatever I could catch I had rather take it away than leave it behind me.

The Interpretation.

Never let go a certainty for an uncertainty.

The only speller to seriously rival Dilworth's in circulation during the remainder of the colonial period was Fenning's, which appeared in 1755. Besides " Tables of Words," this contained " Leſſons both moral and divine, Fables and pleaſant Stories, and a very eaſy and approved Guide to Engliſh Grammar." There was also some minor material including a chronology of " the moſt remarkable Occurrences in Sacred and profane History," that had in it items like : —

THE Creation of the World .   .   .   B.C. 4047
    Noah's Flood   2350
Walls of *Jericho* fell down   1454
Eleven Days fucceffive Snow   .   .   .   A.D. 1674
A very great Comet   1680
A terrible high Wind, *November* 26   .   .   .   1703
The furprifing Meteor and Signs in the Air   .   1719

Here is one of the " Fables " : —

The Town in Danger.

From Fenning's *The Universal Spelling-Book.*

THERE was a Town in Danger of being befieged, and
it was confulted which was the beft Way to fortify
and ftrengthen it ; and many were the different Opinions
of the Town Folks concerning it.

A grave fkilful Mafon faid, there was nothing fo ftrong

Frontispiece to Fenning's *The Universal Spelling-Book*.

nor fo good as *Stone*. A Carpenter faid, that Stone might do pretty well; but, in his Opinion, good ftrong *Oak* was much better.

A currier being prefent, faid, Gentlemen, you may do as you pleafe; but to have the Town well fortified and fecure, take my Word, there is nothing like *Leather*.

MORAL.

'Tis too common for Men to confult their own private Ends, though a whole Nation fuffer by it.

Then here is one of the " pleafant Stories ": —

THERE were feveral Boys that ufed to go into the Water, inftead of being at fchool; and they fometimes ftaid fo long that they ufed to frighten their Parents very much; and though they were told of it Time after Time, yet they would frequently go to wafh themfelves. One Day four of them, *Smith*, *Brown*, *Jones* and *Robinfon*, took it into their Heads to play Truant, and go into the Water. They had not been in long before *Smith* was drowned: *Brown's* Father followed him, and lafhed him heartily while he was naked; and *Jones* and *Robinfon* ran Home half dreffed, which plainly told where they had been. However, they were both fent to Bed without any Supper, and told very plainly, that they fhould be well corrected at School next Day.

By this time the News of *Smith's* being drowned, had reached their Mafter's Ear, and he came to know the Truth of it and found *Smith's* Father and Mother in Tears, for the Lofs of him; to whom he gave very good Advice, took his friendly Leave, and went to fee what was become of *Brown*, *Jones* and *Robinfon*, who all hung down their Heads upon feeing their Mafter; but more fo, when their Parents defired that he would correct them the next Day, which he promifed he would; though, fays he, (by the bye) it is rather your Duty to do it than mine, for I cannot anfwer for Things done out of the School.

Do you, therefore, take Care to keep your Children in Order at Home, and depend on it, fays the Mafter, I will keep them in Awe of me at School.   But, fays he, as they

The Truant Boys.
From Fenning's *The Universal Spelling-Book*.

have been naughty difobedient Boys, and might indeed have loft their Lives, I will certainly chaftife them.

Next Day, *Brown*, *Jones* and *Robinfon* were fent to School, and in a fhort time were called up to their Mafter; and he firft began with *Brown*. — Pray, young Gentleman, fays he, what is the Reafon you go into the Water without the Confent of your Parents? — I won't do fo any more, fays *Brown*. — That is nothing at all, fays the Mafter, I cannot truft you.   Pray can you fwim? — No, Sir, fays *Brown*. — Not fwim, do you fay!   Why you might have been

drowned as well as *Smith*. — Take him up ſays the
Maſter. — So he was taken up and well whipt.

Well, ſays he to *Jones*, can you ſwim? — A little, Sir,
ſaid he. — A little! why you were in more danger than
Brown, and might have been drowned had you ventured
much farther. — Take him up, ſays he.

Now *Robinſon* could ſwim very well, and thought as
Brown and *Jones* were whipt becauſe they could not ſwim,
that he would eſcape. — Well, *Robinſon*, ſays the Maſter,
can you ſwim? — Yes, Sir, ſays he, (very boldly) any where
over the River. — Pray, Sir, ſays his Maſter, what Buſineſs had you in the Water, when you ſhould have been at
School? — Take him up, ſays he; ſo they were all ſeverely
corrected for their Diſobedience and Folly.

Virtuous Tommy gives Naughty Harry some Good Advice.
From Fenning's *The Universal Spelling-Book*.

The next story is a most vivid contrast of good
and evil as personified by virtuous Tommy and

Frontispiece to *The British Instructor;*

"Being a Plain and Eafy Guide to the Englifh Language on a Plan Entirely New."
London, 1763.

naughty Harry.   The latter was " A fullen perverfe
Boy from his Cradle," while Tommy was " good-

natured, pleafant and mannerly." Hence Tommy becomes a great and rich man while Harry sinks to poverty and wretchedness and crime. Finally,

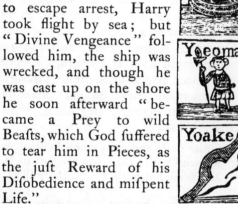

Selections from a series of Alphabet Illustrations in *The British Instructor*.

to escape arrest, Harry took flight by sea; but "Divine Vengeance" followed him, the ship was wrecked, and though he was cast up on the shore he soon afterward "became a Prey to wild Beafts, which God fuffered to tear him in Pieces, as the juft Reward of his Difobedience and mifpent Life."

In the miscellany of the latter part of the book are directions for making both black and red ink. The red ink recipe is:—

TAKE Half a Pint of Water, and put therein Half an Ounce of Gum Senega; let this diffolve in a Gallipot, and then add one Pennyworth of the beft Vermilion, ftirring it well for two Days.

That stirring for two days makes it sound like a weary process. In some books the ink recipes were supplemented by a paragraph like this : —

IN hard frofty weather, Ink will be apt to freeze ; which if it once doth, it will be good for nothing; it takes away all its Blacknefs and Beauty. To prevent which put a few Drops of Brandy into it, and it will not freeze. And to hinder its moulding put a little falt therein.

One of the handsomest spellers of colonial days was "WATTS's Compleat SPELLING–BOOK." Its contents included, besides the ordinary spelling-book matter, " Praxes on Words of different Syllables ; Portions of Scripture ; a Short History of England ; and Directions for writing the Round Hand, and Round Text, and the *Italian* Hand." In connection with the writing directions there are two or three pages of sentences designed for copies. I quote from these several maxims in a list of " Moral Inftructions, beginning with every Letter of the Alphabet."

> Grow quiet and eafy, when Fools ftrive to tieze ye.
> Remember the Liar, has his Part in Hell–fire.
> X Excufe but with Truth, the Follies of Youth.

Concerning the last a foot-note says : —

The Letter X begins no Englifh Word fo that we might begin that line with EX, unlefs the Reader will choofe this inftead of it, viz.

X is fuch a crofs Letter, balks my Morals and Metre.

The quotations which follow are portions of lessons in a book that was made up from a number

GEORGE III. by the Grace of
GOD, of GREAT-BRITAIN,
FRANCE and IRELAND, King,
Defender of the Faith.

In ev'ry Stroke, in ev'ry Line,
Does some exalted Virtue shine;
And *Albion*'s Happiness we trace,
In every Feature of his Face.

Frontispiece to *Watts's Compleat Spelling-Book*, 1770.

of English spellers and published in Boston in 1770 under the title, *The Youth's Inftructor in the Englifh Tongue, Or the Art of Spelling Improved.* It claimed to be "a more plain eafy and regular Method of teaching young children than any other Book of this kind and Bignefs extant."

The Defcription of a good Boy.

THE boy that is good
    Does mind his book well;
And if he can't read
    Will ftrive for to fpell.

His fchool he does love;
    And when he is there,
For plays and for toys,
    No time can he fpare.

Of taking God's Name in vain.

TO mention God, no man has juft pretence,
    But to his honour, or the truth's defence.
In common talk, where trifles moft abound,
God, Chrift or Lord ftrikes horror with the found.
Nor fhould we dare appeal to him on high,
To gain belief, or to atteft a lie,
Thus to abufe that name, if man prefume,
The third Commandment loudly fpeaks their doom.
Yet fome, alas! in every trivial caufe,
To ftop a gap in fpeech, or for a paufe;
Or to fill up the fentence, at each word,
From mouths unhallow'd, breathe, Chrift, God or Lord.
Good Lord, if e'er fuch monfters I come nigh,
From their ill ways give me the grace to fly.

The Inside of the First Leaf of *A New Battledoor.*
Reduced one-third.

Againſt Songs or Ballads.

HATE vulgar impious ſongs, a wretched chime,
Where fulſome nonſenſe jingles into rhyme.

An American Reprint of *A New Battledoor*.

Size of original, 4 × 6½ inches.

Of Man.

Lord what is man! a dunghill blanched with fnow, or a
May game of fortune, a mark for malice, a butt for envy;
He is born crying, lives laughing and dies groaning!

For acquiring the elements of education the
hornbook still held its humble place among the
school publications.   Another help somewhat related
to the hornbook was the "battledore" — a folded
card of two or three leaves with a little flap like an
old-time pocket-book.   The battledores were essentially little illustrated primers ; the price was from a

A Heading from a Manuscrlpt Arithmetic of Colonial Days.
Reduced one-half.

penny to fourpence, and they found ready sale.
One English publisher in ten years sold upwards
of a hundred thousand, and many other firms were
issuing them at the same time.   They are said first
to have been put on the market in 1746.   The
earlier ones were covered outside with Dutch gilt
embossed paper, and the inner, printed side was
varnished.   Later the varnish and the fancy outer
pasting of gilt paper were omitted and the entire
folder, outside and in, was printed.   Battledores were

comparatively little used in this country after the Revolution, but in England they were common for fifty years longer.

The colonial teachers usually taught arithmetic

Page from a Manuscript Arithmetic of Colonial Days.
Reduced one-half. The original book is a quarto of one hundred pages with a cardboard cover.

without text-books.   They gave out to their scholars
rules and problems from manuscript sum-books
which the schoolmasters had themselves made
under *their* teachers.   It was such a sum-book that

Frontispiece and Title-page of a Colonial Arithmetic.
Reduced one-half.

the boy Abraham Lincoln copied while he was learning arithmetic; for even at that date the old method
of teaching without a text-book survived here and
there.   Many scholars in the seventeenth and
eighteenth centuries never saw a printed arithmetic,

F

and when a master chanced to own a copy, most of it was likely to be quite incomprehensible to the average pupil. One of the earliest to attain favor was *Cocker's Arithmetic:* "Being a Plain and familiar Method, fuitable to the meaneft Capacity, for the underftanding of that incomparable Art." It was first printed in 1677. Later came *Hodder's,* and in 1743 *The Schoolmafter's Affiftant* by Thomas Dilworth. Dilworth's book was still in use to some extent at the beginning of the last century.

Frontispiece to *The Schoolmaster's Assistant.*
Reduced one-third.

One can judge from the fact that it makes no allusion to decimal currency it could not by then have been very well adapted to American requirements.

Among the books concerned with the dead languages, Bailey's *English and Latin Exercises for School-Boys* was very popular. It was made up sandwich fashion from cover to cover of alternating paragraphs of English·and Latin, one a translation of the other. Some of the material would hardly find place in a school-book of to-day, as, for instance : —

Joan is a nafty Girl.

Ugly Witches are faid to have been black Cats.

The Report of the great Portion of an unmarried Virgin is oftentimes the Sound of a great Lye.

Greedy Gluttons buy many dainty Bits for their ungodly Guts.

Children drink Brimftone and Milk for the Itch.

If we fhould compare the Number of good and virtuous Perfons to the Multitude of the Wicked, it would be but very fmall.

Toward the close of the book are several of those excessively polite conversations between Master and Scholar such as were frequently inserted in the early school-books. From Dialogue III in this Latin book I take enough to show the manner of them.

Scholar. Sir, I entreat, that you would be pleas'd to grant me my requeft.

Mafter. If my grant may profit thee, I will not deny ; if thou afk thofe things, that tend to thine own Hurt, I muft refufe.

Scholar. I only beg, Sir, that you would repeat to me thofe Inftructions that you gave to our Form Yefterday.

Thus they go on through a number of pages, and at the conclusion the Scholar says, " I thank you, honored Sir."

4. *Of* ZAARA, *or the* DESART.

Tyro. How is this *Defart* fituate?
Philo. Zaara is bounded on the N. by *Bildulgerid*, on the E. by *Egypt* and *Nubia*, on the S. by *Negro-Land*, and on the W. by the *Atlantic Ocean*.

Portion of Page from Fenning's *A New and Easy Guide to the Use of the Globes*, 1760.

The ordinary binding of all these colonial school-books was full leather, even when the books were small and thin. Illustrations were used sparingly, and the drawing and engraving were very crude. The volumes of English manufacture were as a rule well printed on good paper; but 'the American editions were quite inferior, and they continued to make a poor appearance as compared with the trans-Atlantic books until after the middle of the nineteenth century. The most marked typographical contrasts to the present that one observes is the use of the long *s*, that looks like an *f*, and the habit of printing beneath the final line of each page the first word of the page following. The catchwords and long *s* were employed up to 1800, but within the first decade of the new century they were entirely abandoned.

III

ORIGINALLY a "primer" was a book of private devotions. The earliest books thus named contained devotions for the hours, the Creed, the Lord's Prayer, the Ten Commandments, a few psalms, and some simple instruction in Christian knowledge. They date back almost to the time when type-printing was invented. Before that time the only way of producing books had been by laboriously copying them with brush or pen, letter by letter. Learning, and even knowledge how to read, were confined to the very few. But type-printing reduced the cost of books so materially that they were possible in the homes of the people, and it at once became desirable that the rudiments of language should be put within reach of the many who now wished to learn to read. In consequence an alphabet was often included in the little devotional primers, and this led presently to giving the name "primer" to all elementary books for the use of children.

The contents of the old-time primers changed, but for hundreds of years the teaching of religion and reading continued united in them. No other way could have been devised to mould the religious thought of the people so effectively. The need of guiding public sentiment on this subject was plainly apparent; for those who studied the Bible did not understand its teachings alike, and printing no sooner gave the Scriptures a wide distribution than divergent opinions multiplied. The Bible itself does not contain a distinct creed, nor does it tell us what to think about it — hence the importance of setting forth the simple tenets of religion in a form for general distribution. The primers were an especially valuable medium, because they went to the fountain head. Their precepts were instilled in minds as yet unformed, and the children were drilled to believe what they were to think out for themselves when they were more mature.

One trouble, however, was that primers from different sources did not present the truth alike, and successive rulers from Henry VIII down tried to control their teachings. The unauthorized books were seized and burned, and preachers and printers guilty of preparing and distributing them were whipped, imprisoned, and put to death. But their production could not be stifled, and after the reign of James II, the people were allowed to have such primers and catechisms as they chose.

No doubt the early settlers of New England possessed primers that they brought across the ocean with them. The family Bible and primer occupied the same shelf in the pioneer homes, and from the primer the children were faithfully catechised every Sabbath day. The exact date of the first issue of the " New England " primer is not known, but

below is the earliest mention that has been dis-
covered of a primer with that name. It is from a
Boston "Almanack for the year of the Chriſtian
Empire, 1691."

ADVERTISEMENT.

There is now in the Preſs, and will ſuddenly
be extant, a Second Impreſſion of *The New-England Primer enlarged*, to which is added, more
DireEtions for Spelling : the *Prayer of* K. *Edward*
the 6*th*. and *Verſes made by Mr.* Rogers *the Martyr, left as a Legacy to his Children.*

Sold by *Benjamin Harris*, at the *London Coffee-
Houſe* in *Boſton*.

The Earliest Mention known of *The New England Primer*.

From Newman's *News from the Stars*. Boston, 1690.

This Harris had formerly been a printer in London where he brought out many tracts and broad-
sides of a religious or political character. He was
a man of considerable enterprise and ingenuity and
wrote both in verse and prose much of what he
printed. In 1681 a " Protestant Petition " he put
forth got him into trouble with the government,
which at that time was inclined toward Catholicism,
and he was fined five hundred pounds and condemned to stand in the pillory. This apparently
ruined his business, and we hear no more of him
till 1686, when he arrived in Boston and became the
proprietor of a book and coffee shop. Soon he
was publishing pamphlets and circulars, and among

other ventures he started a newspaper under the title of *Public Occurrences*, which was the first newspaper printed in America.

The general plan of the primer sent forth by Harris was old, but the compilation had new features, and its name lent it an aspect of originality. In New England and the neighboring colonies it promptly became an institution. Every home possessed copies, and they were for sale at all the town and village bookshops. Occasionally printers changed the title, and called it *The New York Primer*, or *The American Primer*, or *The Columbian Primer;* but the public preferred the New England title. For a hundred years this book beyond any other was the school-book of American dissenters. Its power waned rapidly later. The cities abandoned it first, and gradually it was neglected in the villages. Still, even in Boston, it was used in the dame schools as late as 1806. Its total sales are estimated to have been not less than three million copies. Astonishingly few of these have been preserved, and early editions are among the rarest of school-books. All issued previous to 1700 have vanished, and only a few score have survived of those that were published during the next century when it was in the zenith of its popularity. The oldest perfect copy known is one printed in Boston in 1735. This was picked up by a Pennsylvania teacher at a farm-house auction in 1893 for twelve cents. Ten years later he sold it to a New York dealer for $2500.

The newspapers heralded this sale throughout the

country, arousing much interest in the old primers, and giving to the average owner a fabulous idea of

A Characteristic Binding.

Showing the oak sides, with portions of the blue paper which was pasted over the wood still adhering.

the value of his possession.   As a matter of fact the chances are that five to twenty dollars is as much

Children, like tender oziers, take the bow,
And as they first are fashioned always
   grow.
For what we learn in youth, to that
   alone,
In age we are by second nature prone.

Frontispiece to a Brookfield, Mass., edition
of 1828.

Published by the firm which later became famous
as the publishers of *Webster's Dictionary.*

as could be realized even for copies antedating 1800. Anything more recent is seldom worth over a dollar or two.

The covers of the New England primers were usually of thin oak, that cracked and splintered badly with use, in spite of the coarse blue paper which was pasted over the wood. The back was of leather. Neither back nor sides had any printing on them. Most editions of the primer contained a frontispiece. For this a rudely engraved portrait of the reigning English monarch was customary until the Revolution, when one or another of the American patriots had the honor. After the war Washington was the favorite frontispiece character. Sometimes a school scene was substituted, as in the cut reproduced from the Brookfield edition. This same picture is to be

found in a Boston book of 1791, but the verse
underneath it was —

> The *School-Mam*, fee, whofe only care,
>   Is to inftruct her tender youth,
> How they may vice's ways beware,
>   And tread the fteps of peace and truth.

Every primer had a page devoted to the alphabet, followed by two pages of those curious word fragments, " ab, eb, ib, ob, ub," etc., which the book itself calls " Easy syllables for Children." Then came three pages of words grading up from those of one syllable to "a-bo-mi-na-ti-on" and a few others of six syllables. The rest of the book is almost entirely a religious and moral miscellany of verse and prose gathered from all sorts of sources. Prominent in this miscellany is a picture alphabet —a series of twenty-four tiny pictures, each accompanied by a two or three line jingle. Apparently two of the letters are slighted, but not really — for it was customary to teach that J was simply I with another name, and that U and V were likewise identical. One must grant that the pictures are expressive in spite of their diminutive size. The artist took care to get everything he could into them that would help the text.

Easy syllables for Children.

Ba	be	bi	bo	bu
ca	ce	ci	co	cu
da	de	di	do	du
fa	fe	fi	fo	fu
ga	ge	gi	go	gu
ha	he	hi	ho	hu
ja	je	ji	jo	ju
ka	ke	ki	ko	ku
la	le	li	lo	lu
ma	me	mi	mo	mu
na	ne	ni	no	nu
pa	pe	pi	po	pu
ra	re	ri	ro	ru
sa	se	si	so	su
ta	te	ti	to	tu
va	ve	vi	vo	vu
wa	we	wi	wo	wu
ya	ye	yi	yo	yu
za	ze	zi	zo	zu

In the first series reproduced, notice the apple tree
in the garden of Eden.   It is all there, and you can
plainly see the apples among the leaves.   The tree
that Zaccheus did climb is also shown practically
entire; and how effectively Noah's Ark is brought
out sailing on the flooded world while in the background the forked lightning plays in the black clouds.
Then there are Felix and Paul with the judgment as
distinct before them as if it was in the same room;
and opposite the letter *T*, how horrid sin is made to
appear! — no wonder that young Timothy flies!

This rhyming method of teaching the alphabet
is much older than *The New England Primer*, but
the little book gave the old idea fresh expression.
The primer rhymes are thought to have originated
with the Boston printer Harris, as the poetry he
was in the habit of manufacturing had much the
same character.   They were always being changed,
however, sometimes merely in wording, sometimes
in subject, and the only one of the twenty-four that
remained unaltered was —

> In Adam's Fall
> We finned all.

That seemed to find general acceptance as a desirable
fact to promulgate in exactly those words.   The new
features in the jingles were in part casual changes
made by the printers, and in part were a result of
the feeling that many of the rhymes earlier adopted
were too earthy in their sentiment.

> The Cat doth play,
> And after flay,

G As runs the Glass,
Our Life doth pass.

H My Book and Heart
Must never part.

I JOB feels the Rod,
Yet bleffes GOD.

K Proud Korah's troop
Was fwallowed up

L LOT fled to *Zoar*,
Saw fiery Shower
On *Sodom* pour.

M MOSES was he
Who *Israel's* Hoft
Led thro' the Sea.

A In ADAM's Fall
We finned all.

B Heaven to find,
The Bible Mind.

C Chrift crucify'd
For finners dy'd.

D The Deluge drown'd
The Earth around.

E ELIJAH hid
By Ravens fed.

F The judgment made
FELIX afraid.

Picture Alphabet of Religious Jingles.

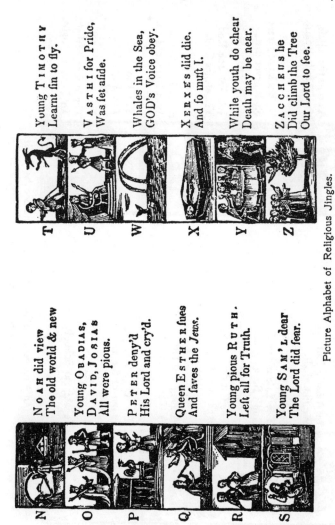

N NOAH did view
   The old world & new

O Young OBADIAS,
   DAVID, JOSIAS
   All were pious.

P PETER deny'd
   His Lord and cry'd.

Q Queen ESTHER sues
   And saves the Jews.

R Young pious RUTH.
   Left all for Truth.

S Young SAM'L dear
   The Lord did fear.

T Young TIMOTHY
   Learnt fin to fly.

U VASTHI for Pride,
   Was fet afide.

W Whales in the Sea,
   GOD's Voice obey.

X XERXES did die.
   And fo muft I.

Y While youth do chear
   Death may be near.

Z ZACCHEUS he
   Did climb the Tree
   Our Lord to fee.

Picture Alphabet of Religious Jingles.

In Adam's Fall
We ſinned all.

Thy Life to mend,
God's Book attend.

The Cat doth play,
And after ſlay.

A Dog will bite
A Thief at Night.

The Eagle's Flight
Is out of Sight.

The idle Fool
Is whipt at School

As runs the Glaſs,
Man's life doth paſs.

My Book and Heart
Shall never part.

Job feels the Rod,
Yet bleſſes God.

Proud Korah's troop
Was ſwallow'd up.

The Lion bold
The Lamb doth
hold.

The Moon gives light
In Time of Night.

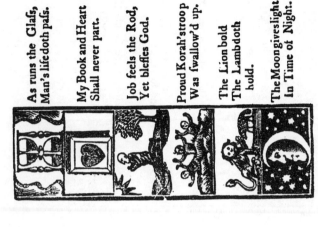

An Alphabet including both Religious and Secular Jingles.

From a primer printed in Boston about 1800.

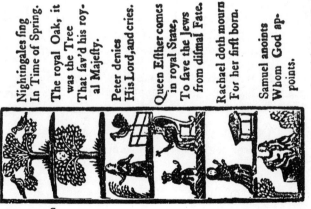

Time cuts down all,
Both great and small.

Uriah's beauteous
Wife
Made David seek
his life.

Whales in the Sea
God's Voice obey.

Xerxes the Great
did die,
And so must you
and I.

Youth forward slips,
Death soonest nips.

Zaccheus, he
Did climb the Tree,
His Lord to see.

Nightingales sing
In Time of Spring.

The royal Oak, it
was the Tree
That sav'd his roy-
al Majesty.

Peter denies
His Lord, and cries.

Queen Esther comes
in royal State,
To save the Jews
from dismal Fate.

Rachael doth mourn
For her first born.

Samuel anoints
Whom God ap-
points.

G

An Alphabet including both Religious and Secular Jingles.
From a primer printed in Boston about 1800.

and the similar couplets, were gradually rewritten and given religious significance.

Another curious change found in some of the primers was connected with the *K* rhyme.   At first this read : —

> King Charles the Good
> No Man of blood.

But by the time of the Revolution praise of royalty was not as acceptable as it had been, and rhymes like the following were substituted : —

> Kings fhould be good
> No men of blood.

> Britain's King in fpleen
> Lost States thirteen.

> Queens and Kings
> Are Gaudy Things.

In addition to the picture alphabet there was an unillustrated one of " Leffons for Youth."   Three of the short precepts will suffice to show what stern stuff was put into these lessons : —

FOOLISHNESS is bound up in the Heart of a Child, but the Rod of correction fhall drive it from him.

LIARS fhall have their Part in the Lake which burns with Fire and Brimftone.

UPON the Wicked God fhall rain an Horrible Tempeft.

The letter *X* presented difficulties that were gotten around in this way : —

E X HORT one another daily, while it is called To
   Day, left any of you be hardened thro' the
Deceitfulnefs of Sin.

The feature of the primer that perhaps aroused most interest was an illustration depicting Mr. John Rogers burning at the stake, with his wife and ten children looking on. Every youthful primer owner counted those children to make sure the statement of the text as to their number was correct. Of course the readers never suspected that the scene in the engraving was at all fictitious — yet history only records of Rogers's wife and children that they " met him

MR. JOHN ROGERS, minifter of the gofpel in *London*, was the firft martyr in Queen MARY's reign, and was burnt at *Smithfield, February* 14, 1554.—His wife with nine small children, and one at her breast following him to the ftake ; with which forrowful fight he was not in the leaft daunted, but with wonderful patience died courageoufly for the gofpel of JESUS CHRIST.

The Rogers Page.

From the Webster edition of 1843.

by the way as he went toward Smithfield," his place of martyrdom.   In connection with this tragic picture is printed a long poem of practical and spiritual exhortation that purports to be of Rogers's authorship.

Some few Days before his Death he writ the following Advice to his Children,

says the heading, but in truth the composition was the work of another martyr who met his death a year later than Rogers.   The poem attained considerable popularity among the Puritans before it was included in the primer.

A Rude Primer Cut purporting to show John Rogers being burned at the Stake.

An officer stands on the right, and Mr. Rogers's wife and ten children on the left.

Another long poem to be found in most primers was *A Dialogue between Christ, Youth, and the Devil.*   It starts with a declaration on the part of the Youth that —

> Thofe days which God to me doth fend,
> In pleafure I'm refolved to fpend.

The devil applauds, remarking among other things that —

If thou my counſel wilt embrace,
And ſhun the ways of truth and grace,
And learn to lie, and curſe and ſwear,
And be as proud as any are;
And with thy brothers wilt fall out,
And ſister with vile language flout;
Yea, fight and ſcratch, and alſo bite,
Then in thee I will take delight.

Christ pleads with Youth to leave his folly, until at length Youth wavers; but he cannot make up his mind to yield. He is promising to reform at some time in the future, when to his surprise and dismay Death appears and says: —

Youth, I am come to fetch thy breath,
And carry thee to th' ſhades of death,
No pity on thee can I ſhow
Thou haſt thy God offended ſo.
Thy ſoul and body I'll divide,
Thy body in the grave I'll hide,
And thy dear ſoul in hell muſt lie
With Devils to eternity.

In minor matters the primers varied greatly, but you could usually depend on finding the Apostle's Creed, Dr. Watts's *Cradle Hymn*, and several prayers, including the Lord's Prayer and *Now I lay me down to sleep;* and there was a page of " Inſtructive *Queſtions and Anſwers*," beginning with " Who was the firſt man? — *Adam*," and continuing in the same tenor with such items as —

The Butterfly and Crocodile.
From an edition of about 1785.

Who was the oldeſt Man?	*Methuſelah.*
Who was the patienteſt Man?	*Job.*
Who was the meekeſt Man?	*Moſes.*
Who was the hard heartedeſt Man?	*Pharaoh.*
Who made iron ſwim?	*Eliſha.*
Who was in the Whale's Belly?	*Jonah.*

A primer published by E. Draper about 1785 has five pages of natural history, consisting of two pictures to the page with a couplet below each like : —

> The Afs, tho' mean, will by his Bray,
> Oblige your Horfe to run away.

The Nightingale and Cuckow.
From an edition of about 1785.

The C O C K.

T HE *Cock* doth crow to let you know,
  If you be wife, what Time to rife.

There is no Bird treat-ed with fo much Cru-
el-ty as the *Cock* ; for he, poor Thing (with-out
the leaſt Of-fence) is ti-ed to a Stake, and thrown
at by a ſet of i-dle, wick-ed, bar-ba-rous Fellows, until he is beat in Pie-ces.   This is a Cuſ-
tom the very Hea-thens would bluſh at ; and
there-fore I hope you, who are a Chriſt-ian, will
nev-er be guilt-y of any Thing fo in-hu-man,

One of Several Similar Pages of Illustrated Rhymes and Comments in
The Royal Primer, Worcester, Mass., 1787.

In an edition of 1771 we find what at first sight
promises to be an entertaining story, but it proves
only a description of one of the priggish little good
boys that abound in the juvenile literature of the
period.

THE HISTORY OF MASTER TOMMY
FIDO.

A S Goodneſs and Learning make the Child a Man, ſo
    Piety makes him an Angel.   Maſter *Tommy Fido*
not only loved his Book becauſe it made him wiſer, but becauſe it made him better too.   He loved every Body, and

could not fee a Stranger hurt, without feeling what he fuffered, without pitying him, and wifhing he could help him.
He loved his Papa and Mamma, his Brothers and Sifters
with the deareft Affection; he learnt his Duty to God,
thanked him for his Goodnefs, and was glad that he had
not made him a Horfe or a Cow, but had given him Senfe
enough to know his Duty, and every Day when he faid his
Prayers, thanked God for making him a little Man.   One
Day he went to Church, he minded what the Parfon faid,
and when he came home afked his Papa, if God loved him;
his Papa faid Yes, my Dear.   O! my dear Papa, faid he,
I am glad to hear it; what a charming Thing it is to have
God my Friend! then nothing can hurt me; I am fure I
will love him as well as ever I can.   Thus he every day
grew wifer and better.   Every Body was pleafed with him,
he had many Friends, the Poor bleffed him, and every one
Strove to make him happy.

A Philadelphia edition of 1797 "much improved"
indulged in some similar fiction that took the form
of eighteen little reading lessons, one of which was
the following: —

Har-ry! fays Bil-ly, what do you think the world ftands
on? I don't know, fays Har-ry; but I can tell you what
our Tom fays: Old Tom fays the world ftands on a great
tur-tle; but he could not tell me what the tur-tle ftood on.
Well, fays Bil-ly, I will tell you what my pa-pa fays; My
pa-pa fays the world don't ftand on a-ny thing; but is
ba-lanc-ed on its own cen-tre, and goes round the fun,
in the o-pen fpace, once e-ve-ry year.

Another story is this from *The Royal Primer*,
Worcester, Massachusetts, 1787: —

The Rewards of VIRTUE.

Mifs *Goodchild* had the advantage of fuch Inftructions in her youth that fhe could reafon juftly on the Being, Provi-

The Rewards of Virtue.

dence and Perfections of God; whom fhe admired, loved, and reverenced, from a Conviction of his infinite Excellence; and to whom every Morning and Night, fhe offered up her Prayers for Protection, and for Advancement in ufeful Knowledge, and good Difpofitions, the chief object of her Pur-

fuit! Her Papa and Mamma foon died; and fhe had no other Portion left her but her undiffembled Piety, a decent Modefty, which fhowed itfelf in her Actions, an innocent Simplicity and a Heart full of Goodnefs. Thefe raifed her Friends; they admired her, they loved her, they ftrove to make her happy. A Gentleman of Underftanding and Virtue became fenfible of her Merit, and married her. It was the Bufinefs of their Lives to make each other happy, and as their Fortune was large fhe was enabled to

Illustration to "The Hufbandman's Prayer" in a New England Primer of about 1785.

gratify the generous Difpofitions of her Heart, in relieving any diftreft honeft Man; and in promoting the fubftantial Benefit of all about her.

Here are a few morsels showing the kind of material that was used in the primers to fill space between the more important portions : —

Good children muſt

Fear God all day,　　　　　　Love Chriſt alway,
Parents obey,　　　　　　　In ſecret pray,
No falſe thing ſay,　　　　　Mind little play,
By no ſin ſtray,　　　　　　Make no delay

In doing good.

F A I T H.

THE Father of the Faithful ſaid,
　　At God's firſt calling, " Here am I ;"
Let us by his example ſway'd,
　　Like him ſubmit, like him reply.

Then let us imitate the Seer,
　　And tender with compliant grace
Ourſelves, our ſouls, and children here,
　　Hereafter in a better place.

Poem from a Charlestown, Mass., Edition of 1802.

He that loves God, his school, and his book, will no doubt do well at last; but he that hates his school and book, will live and die a slave, a fool, and a dunce.

☞ Children, obey your parents in the Lord : for this is right.   Honour thy father and mother, (which is the first commandment with promise,) that it may be well with thee, and thou mayest live long on the earth.

The Sum of the Ten Commandments.
WITH all thy soul love God above,
And as thyself thy neighbour love,

Our Saviour's Golden Rule.
BE you to others kind and true,
As you'd have others be to you,
And neither do nor say to men,
Whate'er you would not take again.

A Page from an Edition of about 1810.

Ancient Proverb.

Young folks think old folks to be fools;
but old folks know young ones to be so.

Human Frailty.

OUR days begin with trouble here,
    Our life is but a ſpan;
And cruel death is always near,
    So frail a thing is man!

Believe in Jeſus Chriſt while young
    Then when thou com'ſt to die,
Thou ſhalt ſing forth that pleaſant ſong,
    "Death, where is thy victory?"

Acts 13:11.   John 4:5—7.

Two Pictures.
From Emerson's *The Evangelical Primer.* 1810.

A modification of *The New England Primer* that
continued to enjoy a wide circulation for many years
was Emerson's *The Evangelical Primer.* It was a
little larger and thicker than *The New England
Primer* and contained considerable more matter but
less variety. Among those who vouched for its
value and recommended its use in families and
schools were Noah Webster, Jedidiah Morse, and
the president of Yale College. The contents were

a "minor doctrinal catechism, a minor historical catechism," — which however only covered Bible history, — and *The Westminster Assembly's Shorter Catechism* with explanatory notes and Scripture proofs and a few hymns. Like all books of its kind it did not fail to set forth the terrors of hell with definiteness and detail, and the closing paragraphs of the doctrinal catechism were these : —

What will be your condition in hell ? I shall be dreadfully tormented. — What company will be there ? Legions of devils, and multitudes of sinners of the human race.

Will company afford me any comfort in hell ? It will not, but will probably increase my woes.

If you should go to hell, how long must you continue there ? For ever and ever.

If you should die in your sins, and God should make you miserable, should you have any reason to complain of him ? Not the least. I must be speechless.

Amidst our cheer
DEATH may be near;

All shortly must
Be laid in dust.

From a Picture Alphabet in Fisher's
A Youth's Primer, 1817.

A similar book was *The Youth's Primer* " by Jonathan Fisher, A.M., Minister of the Gospel at Bluehill, Maine, 1817." It contained " a series of short verses in alphabetical order, each followed by religious, moral, or historical observations," and it contained the catechism. The verses and accompanying illustrations were reminiscent of the picture alphabet in *The New England Primer* and occasionally treated the same subject. Thus, the first jingle was—

By ADAM came   Our Parents fell
Our sin and shame.   And we rebel.

For the letter *Y* there was this : —

Take ye my YOKE   Borne with delight
So Jesus spoke   'Tis easy quite,

and the picture shows Christ carrying an ox yoke in his hand while two oxen stand in the field in the background.

The EARTH must burn,   What then will hide
And Christ return;   The sons of pride?

From a Picture Alphabet in Fisher's *A Youth's Primer*.

The " observations " that went with the verses were often very lugubrious, as the extract below will indicate.

There is a very pretty little hymn, and a true one, which parents often teach their children, and that very fitly : I will here insert it : —

I in the burying place may see
    Graves shorter there than I;
From death's arrest no age is free,
    Young children too may die.
My God, may such an awful sight
    Awakening be to me!
Oh! that by early grace I might
    For death prepared be.

Young people may very soon learn that they are dying

KINDNESS appears, | And from her store
Dissolv'd in tears | Relieves the poor.

From a Picture Alphabet in Fisher's *A Youth's Primer.*

creatures. This dying is the parting of the soul from the body, so that the body is left without thought, or motion; being thus left, it soon putrefies and becomes loathsome, so that it is necessary to bury it under ground, out of our sight, where it moulders away to dust. This is the consequence of sin, by reason of which God said to Adam, *Dust thou art, and to dust shalt thou return.* If man had not sinned, he would have lived for ever.

The backbone of *The New England Primer* was *The Westminster Assembly's Shorter Catechism,* which Cotton Mather called a "little watering pot to shed good lessons." He urged writing masters to set sentences from it to be copied by their pupils, and he advised mothers to "continually drop something of the Catechism on their children, as Honey from the Rock."

This Catechism was the work of the great Westminster Assembly called together by parliament in 1643 — an Assembly composed of one hundred and twenty-one clergymen, thirty of the laity, and five special commissioners from Scotland. It held 1163 sessions and lasted six years. The 107 questions and answers printed in the primer were entitled *The Shorter Catechism*, but the children who were expected to memorize all the ponderous answers could discern no sign of condensation or abbreviation, and they sometimes wondered what a longer one could be like. They were drilled in the Catechism constantly, both in the church and at school. Ministers preached about it, and it was much in every one's mind. Its importance in the thought of the time is suggested by the fact that the largest book printed in New England previous to the nineteenth century was Samuel Willard's *Complete Body of Divinity in Two Hundred and Fifty Expository Lectures on the Assembly's Shorter Catechism;* and this enormous volume of nearly a thousand pages had marked popularity.

Many primers contained a second catechism — *Spiritual Milk for American Babes*, it was called — which in general was of the same type as the Westminster Assembly's, only it had not much more than half as many questions and the answers were shorter.

Public interest in the primer was kept up in

H

country communities by the custom of " Saying the Catechism " yearly in church.   Three summer Sundays were set apart for the purpose, and a portion was recited each Sunday at the close of the afternoon service.   It was a momentous occasion, and when the parson announced from the pulpit that, " Sabbath after next, the first division of the Catechism will be recited here," a thrill of excitement ran through the congregation.   In this recitation all the children between eight and fifteen years took part. There were fortnight intervals between the three Sundays to allow the children to perfect their memory of the next lot of questions.   They must know every answer, and old primers were looked up, new ones bought, and the young folk got to work in earnest.

When the first of the great days came, and the other exercises of the day were concluded, the children, arrayed in their " Sabba'day clothes," gathered in two long lines in the broad aisle, the boys on one side, the girls on the other.   The lines began near the deacon's seat under the brow of the pulpit, and very likely extended the full length of the broad aisle and around into the aisles at the rear.   Parents and relatives crowded the pews and galleries, all watching the scene with solemn interest — an interest that was tinged on the part of the mothers with anxiety lest their children should not acquit themselves with credit.

The minister, standing in the pulpit, gave out the questions.   Each child, in order, stepped forth into mid-aisle, faced the pulpit, made his manners, answered the questions put to him, and stepped back. To be "told" — that is, to be prompted or corrected by the minister — was a dire disgrace, and brought one's ability and scholarship into ill repute. Many were the knees that smote together, and many were the beating hearts and shaky voices among the little people in those two conspicuous lines.

When the second division of the Catechism was recited, the smaller children had dropped out, and, on the third Sunday, reserved for the long and knotty answers in the last portion of the Catechism, only a meagre squad of the oldest children lined up in front of the pulpit.

The Catechism was treated scarcely less seriously in the schools than it was in the churches, and the teachers drilled their pupils in it as thoroughly as they did in spelling or any other lesson. With the primer so constantly used in church, school, and home, the people could not help but be saturated with its doctrines, and no book save the Bible did more to form New England character. In short, this humble little primer was a chief tool for making sure that the children, or, as Jonathan Edwards called them, "young vipers and infinitely more hateful than vipers to God," should grow up into sober and Christian men and women.

IV

THE DISTRICT SCHOOLS

THE years after the Revolution, till about 1840, form the most picturesque period in our educational history. This was preëminently the period of the district school; and while I refer especially, in what follows, to the experiences of Massachusetts, these experiences did not differ essentially from those of the states neighboring. At first the prevailing poverty and rusticity and loose government made it difficult to maintain any school organization that was at all adequate. Many communities had no schoolhouse until the beginning of the nineteenth century, but hired a room in some dwelling and furnished it with desks and benches.

In colonial times, either the town in its meetings chose the master, fixed his salary, and determined the conditions on which pupils were admitted, or else this business was turned over to the selectmen. Now, however, the control of school affairs in each division of the town was delegated to a " prudential committeeman " elected by the people of his own district. The amount of money to be raised for school support was still determined by the town and was assessed with the other taxes, but after its distri-

A Vacation Visit from the Committeeman to consider Repairs.

bution among the districts there was no responsibility to the town for its expenditure.

Yet it is to be noted that the Massachusetts law of 1789 required supervision. This supervising was done by a committee that usually included the ministers of the gospel and the selectmen in their capacity as town officials. They were obliged to visit and inspect the schools at least once in six months and inquire into the regulation, discipline, and proficiency of the scholars. Their visitations were very formal and solemn affairs. The whole delegation, composed of the community's chief priests and elders — sometimes to the number of more than twenty — went in stately procession to the schools in turn. They heard the classes read in the primer, Psalter, Testament, etc., examined the writing and ciphering books, and addressed the children in short speeches of the customary school-committee style. Just before departing, they entered on the school records their testimony to the good behavior and proficiency of the pupils, and the fidelity of the master. " The school may be said to flourish like the palm tree " is the way one such visitation closed its commendation in the records of old Nicholas Pike's school at Newburyport.

Supervision waned as time went on, until nearly all real power in the affairs of each local district was vested in the prudential committeeman. This individual received no pay and little honor, and there was seldom any rivalry for the position. It went to the man who was willing to serve, and had ability enough to look after the repairs of the building

and other material needs of the school.   His educational qualifications were likely to be meagre,
and some· of the local committeemen were very
rude and ignorant.   The district system resulted
in many a tea-pot tempest, for every person had
decided ideas as to how affairs in his or her own
neighborhood should be managed, and whatever
action the committeeman took, he had to run a
gauntlet of criticism that was often far from judicial
or gentle.   To settle the question of where one of
the little frame schoolhouses should stand has been
known to require ten district meetings scattered over
a period of two years; and the meetings would be
attended by men from the mountain farms for miles
around.   Some of these men had no children to be
schooled, and some of them were not interested
enough in national affairs to vote in a presidential
election.   The one point on which all could agree
was that the schoolhouse should be built where the
land was as nearly valueless as possible.   Any spot
was good enough, provided it was in the geographical centre of the district.   If the schoolhouse was
not thus centrally located, and the rights, real or
fancied, of individuals were set aside for the convenience of the majority, then there was trouble that
might smoulder almost interminably, ready to blaze
forth at any time.

Most of the buildings were erected close to the
highway, and they encroached on the adjoining field
very little.   Usually they formed a part of the line
fence.   A favorite situation was at the meeting of
two or more roads, and sometimes the building

would be so near the wheel tracks that a large stone
was set up at the most exposed corner to protect
the structure from being injured by passing vehicles.

An Old-time District Schoolhouse.

The schoolhouses seldom had enclosures or shade
trees, and the summer sun and the winter winds had
free play.

The number of pupils to be accommodated in a
district was likely to be large, for the children in the
old-time families were numerous, and the farm regions
had not yet begun to be depopulated by the city-
ward migration destined to drain them later. Nevertheless, no matter how many the scholars, there was
never any thought of providing more than a single
teacher. The main purpose of the constructors of
the buildings seems to have been to see into how

small a space the children could be crowded, and
some schoolrooms not over thirty feet square accommodated a hundred pupils.   The structure was generally roughly clapboarded, and it might possibly
receive a coat of red or yellow paint, but more likely
paint was lacking both outside and in.   The school-

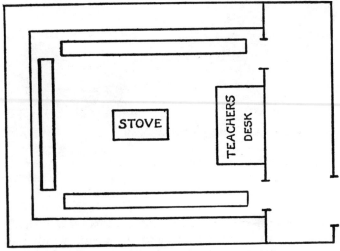

Plan of a Characteristic Schoolroom of 1840.

room was lathed and plastered, and was lighted by
five or six small windows of twelve panes each.
The glass in the windows was often broken, and
during school hours, in cool weather, the place of
the missing panes was apt to be supplied with hats.

Just inside, next to the entrance, was a fireplace,
and at this same end of the room was the master's
desk or table — usually a table in the early days;

but later a desk specially contrived by the carpenter,
on a slight platform, was customary.   Besides serv-

A Teacher's Desk.

ing the ordinary purposes of a desk, it was a reposi-
tory for confiscated tops, balls, penknives, marbles,
jewsharps, etc., and was frequently a perfect curiosity-
shop.

Against the walls on the remaining three sides of
the room was built a continuous sloping shelf, about
three feet from the floor.   Long, backless benches

One of the Benches for the Older Pupils.

accompanied it, on which the older scholars sat,
facing the wall.   While they were studying, they
leaned against the edge of the shelf, and when they
wrote or ciphered they rested their exercise books
and slates on it.   Under it, on a horizontal shelf
that was somewhat narrower than the upper one, the
pupils kept their books and other school belongings
when not in use.   A line of lower benches for the

One of the Benches for the Smaller Pupils.

smaller children was set within the three-sided square
formed by those of the big scholars.   The number
of children the schoolhouse would hold depended on
how closely they could be packed on the benches.
In the middle of the room was a limited open space.
Here the classes stood while reciting, at which time

they were expected to faithfully " toe the crack " —
a particular crack between the floor boards chosen
for the purpose of keeping them in line.

The schoolroom walls were dismally vacant except
for weather-stains, and grime from the fire which
had an annoying tendency to smoke.   There were
no maps or pictures, and even blackboards were not
common until about 1820.   The earliest reference
I have seen to a school blackboard is in the preface
to an arithmetic published in 1809, in Philadelphia.
Evidently the use of such a thing as a school aid
was an innovation.   A footnote explained that " the
Black Board should be about 3 feet square, painted
or stained with ink, and hung against the wall in a
convenient place for a class to assemble around it."

Seats and desks were of pine or oak, rudely fashioned by some local carpenter.   Their aspect was not
improved by the passing years ; for the unpainted
wood became more and more browned with the
umber of human contact, and every possessor of a
jack-knife labored over them with much idle hacking
and carving.

Ordinarily there was a narrow entry running across
the front of the building that was mostly filled by
a big chimney.   The boys were supposed to hang
their hats in the entry, but the diminutive space and
few nails in the wall did not accommodate all the
extra apparel, and much of it would lie on the floor
to be trampled on.   The fireplace which warmed
the schoolroom was large and deep, and in severe
weather it consumed not far from a cord of wood a
week.   The wood was always burned green.   No

one thought of getting the school wood ready long enough beforehand to allow it to season. Most of what was used was standing in the forests at the time the winter term began. When it was presently delivered in the schoolyard, it lay there exposed, and it was often wet by rain and buried in snow. In summer the place of the woodpile was marked by scattered chips and refuse.

The children usually played around outside for a while before school began in the morning, but at length a sudden outcry would arise, "There he is — the master's coming!" and they would all start pell-mell for the schoolroom and clatter noisily into their seats, girls on one side of the room, boys on the other. In below-zero weather, however, there was no lingering in the open air, and if the lad who made the fire was not prompt, the little children stood about the room crying with cold, while the big boys blew the flickering flames and coaxed them into a brisk blaze. Later in the morning the fire gradually waxed hotter and hotter until the heat was a real trial to those nearest the fireplace. But at the rear of the room the atmosphere might still be frigid, and the back-seat scholars would be asking, "Master, may I go to the fire?" at the same time those in front were complaining, "Master, I am too hot."

In a winter school of forty pupils there might be a dozen young men and women who were practically grown up. On the other hand, quite a group of the youngest could not read, and several had not mastered the alphabet. The little scholars were most of the time "busy" keeping still. The backless benches they occupied were commonly far too high for them, leaving their feet dangling in mid air. Of course they would get to knocking the shins of one another, a whiffet of laughter would escape, and the noise would increase

An Illustration from Jenkins's *Art of Writing*, 1813.

until it attracted the attention of the master. Then down would come the pedagogue's ferule on his desk with a clap that sent shivers through the little learners' hearts to think how it would have felt had it fallen somewhere else. "Silence!" commanded the master, and he gave them a look that swept them into utter stillness.

The usual routine of a school day began with reading from the Testament by the "first class." Next came writing and its accompanying preparation of pens and copies, and possibly thawing and watering of ink. Huntington's *American*

Penman, 1824, gives these directions for writing pupils : —

The ink should be the best British ink-powder. The paper should be of the first quality, folded in a quarto form,

Slate, Inkstand, Writing-sand, and Ink-powder.

and stitched across the narrowest side, that the lines may be ruled the longest way of the paper. Where blank writing books, ready ruled, can be procured, they would be preferable, and of less trouble than to rule by hand.

For each writer the master set a copy at the top of a page in the pupil's copy-book   This copy in the case of a beginner would be simply straight lines; but a little practice on these sufficed, and then the master changed the copy to " hooks and trammels " — that is, to curved lines which received their name from their resemblance to the kitchen fireplace implements on which pots and kettles were hung from the crane.   For the more advanced pupils the

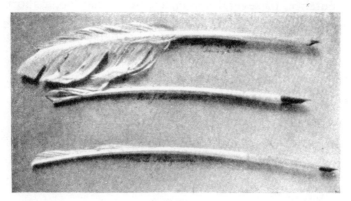

Quill Pens.

master wrote, in a large round hand, " Procrastination is the thief of time," " Contentment is a virtue," or some other wise saw.   Every writer was expected to fill out a page daily in imitation of the master's copy.   Occasionally a master had narrow slips of engraved copy that he could distribute among the writers.   The first series of these copy slips put forth in this country was prepared and published by the celebrated Boston schoolmaster, Caleb Bingham, in 1796.

If the end of the term was near, the writing scholars, instead of using their copy-books, made exhibition pieces to pass around among the visitors on the last day. Ordinarily they did the work on a sheet six by eight, or eight by ten inches in size; but some of the more ambitious used paper four or five times larger. The sheet would contain a sentence, or several sentences, or, it may be, a short essay on such subjects as Happiness, How to Get Riches, Spring, Resignation, Friendship; and there

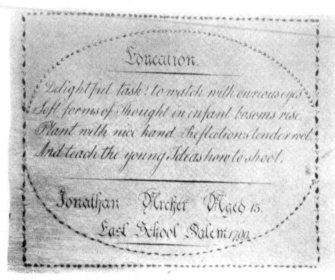

Exhibition Piece of a Writing Student.

Size of original, 6 × 8.

was a decorative border and flourishes, and often colored drawings of birds, flowers, pens, houses, ships, or other objects.

Another Exhibition Piece.
Size of original, 8 × 10.

After writing, the second and third classes read from the Testament, and the smallest children were called out to repeat a few easy sentences from their primers or spelling-books.

About half-past ten the teacher said, " You may go out." The recess was short, but the scholars

I

A Schoolroom Corner.

made the most of it till the instructor appeared at
the door and rapped sharply with his ferule on the
door-post as a signal for them to come in. Just
inside the schoolroom near the door was a pail of
water and a cup, and the children helped themselves
as they entered. Some drank large quantities — in
part to quench their thirst and in part to make an
exhibition of their capacity. Work was resumed,
and the rest of the session was spent chiefly in a
general "spell," the teacher giving out the words
from a spelling-book and the pupils spelling them
at the top of their voices.

The afternoon began with reading by the first
class from a reading-book, and then the other classes

recited in turn until recess. The final hour was devoted to spelling once more with some minor instruction in abbreviations, currencies, weights, measures, etc. Then there was a roll-call, and the boy whose turn it was to make the fire next morning was reminded of the fact. As the scholars prepared to leave, the master gave positive orders for them to "go straight home and be civil to everybody they might meet."

"Peter Parley."

An interesting description of a school about the beginning of the last century is found in the autobiography of Samuel G. Goodrich, or "Peter Parley," as he preferred to call himself on the title-pages of his numerous books. He was born in 1793 in the little farming town of Ridgefield, Connecticut, and the school he attended was typical of those in all the older Northern states; for the city population of the nation in 1800 was only three per cent of the whole. Hence, nearly all the young people received their educational training in the rural schools. Parley says that the immediate surroundings of the schoolhouse to which he went were

. . . bleak and desolate. Loose, squat stone walls, with innumerable breaches, inclosed the adjacent fields. A few tufts of elder, with here and there a patch of briers and pokeweed, flourished in the gravelly soil. Not a tree, however, remained, save an aged chestnut. This, certainly, had not been spared for shade or ornament, but probably because it would have cost too much labor to cut it down; for it was of ample girth.

The schoolhouse chimney was of stone, and the fireplace was six feet wide and four deep. The flue was so ample and so perpendicular that the rain, sleet, and snow fell directly to the hearth. In winter the battle for life with green fizzling fuel, which was brought in lengths and cut up by the scholars, was a stern one. Not unfrequently the

School in Connecticut.

From *The Malte-Brun School Geography*, 1831.

wood, gushing with sap as it was, chanced to let the fire go out, and as there was no living without fire, the school was dismissed, whereat all the scholars rejoiced.

I was about six years old when I first went to school. My teacher was " Aunt Delight," a maiden lady of fifty, short and bent, of sallow complexion and solemn aspect.

We were all seated upon benches made of slabs — boards having the exterior or rounded part of the log on one side. As they were useless for other purposes, they were converted into school benches, the rounded part down. They had each four supports, consisting of straddling wooden legs set into auger holes.

The children were called up one by one to Aunt Delight, who sat on a low chair, and required each, as a preliminary, " to make his manners," which consisted of a small, sudden nod. She then placed the spelling-book before the pupil, and with a pen-knife pointed, one by one, to the letters of the alphabet, saying " What's that ? "

I believe I achieved the alphabet that summer. Two years later I went to the winter school at the same place kept by Lewis Olmstead — a man who made a business of ploughing, mowing, carting manure, etc., in the summer, and of teaching school in the winter. He was a celebrity in ciphering, and Squire Seymour declared that he was the greatest " arithmeticker " in Fairfield County. There was not a grammar, a geography, or a history of any kind in the school. Reading, writing, and arithmetic were the only things taught, and these very indifferently — not wholly from the stupidity of the teacher, but because he had forty scholars, and the custom of the age required no more than he performed.

The voters decided in town-meeting how much money should be expended for school purposes and how it should be distributed. Some towns apportioned it to the districts according to the number of families they contained; others according to the number of children of school age; or the money received in taxes was returned. The last two methods were very unfavorable to the poorer and more

thinly populated districts, and most towns distributed a part of the money in equal sums among the
districts, and the rest according to valuation or
number of school children.   That there were great
inequalities is shown by the fact that as late as 1844
several Massachusetts districts were reported to receive less than ten dollars with which to provide
schooling.   Each district aimed to get the most for its
money, and quality was apt to be sacrificed for quantity.
The cheaper the teacher, the more weeks of school.

In the larger towns school kept almost continu-
ously, but as a rule the towns were content with
a master's winter school of ten or twelve weeks
attended by the older children, and a summer term
of equal length taught by a woman, chiefly for the
benefit of the little ones.   The poorer communities
had to get along with a single term of two or three
months, or possibly of only a few weeks.

The winter term invariably began the Monday
succeeding Thanksgiving Day, and preparations
were made for it by giving the schoolroom a
thorough cleaning, and getting fuel ready.   The
cleaning was done by the local women with the
help of the older boys and girls.   None of
the scanty school money was spent for janitor's
work.   The big boys took turns during the
term in opening and heating the schoolhouse,
and the larger girls alternated in sweeping out.
Attendance was irregular, there was much tardiness,
and many scholars did not come for some time after
the term began because they had to wait until shoes
or other articles of clothing were ready.

Darley invent et sculp'

Ichabod Crane's School.

A considerable proportion of the masters of the winter schools were men whose pedagogic earnings helped them to work their way through the academy and the college. Others, during the larger part of the year, were engaged in farming or labored in the village shops, and took up the task of teaching each recurring winter, reckoning on the wages as a regular part of their annual income. They bargained for a term at a time, and change of place was common, so that they were likely to teach in nearly all the towns neighboring their homes. Some of them with a more pronounced roving disposition wandered far and wide. One of these wanderers was Ichabod Crane who reigned in Sleepy Hollow a few years subsequent to the Revolution. He was a native of Connecticut.

His schoolhouse was a low building of one large room, rudely constructed of logs. It was most ingeniously secured at vacant hours by a withe twisted in the handle of the door, and stakes set up against the window-shutters. The schoolhouse stood just at the foot of a woody hill, with a brook running close by. From hence the low murmur of his pupils' voices conning over their lessons might be heard in a drowsy summer's day, like the hum of a bee-hive; interrupted now and then by the authoritative voice of the master, in the tone of menace or command; or, peradventure, by the appalling sound of the birch, as he urged some tardy loiterer along the path of knowledge.

When school hours were over he had various ways of rendering himself both useful and agreeable. He assisted the farmers occasionally in the lighter labors of their farms. He laid aside, too, all the dominant dignity with which he lorded it in his little empire, the school, and found favor in

the eyes of the mothers, by petting the children, particularly the youngest; and he would sit with a child on one
knee, and rock a cradle with his foot for whole hours
together.

In addition to his other vocations, he was the singing
master of the neighborhood, and picked up many bright

Ichabod Crane at his Boarding-place.

shillings by instructing the younger folks in psalmody.   It
was a matter of no little vanity to him, on Sundays, to take
his station in front of the church gallery, with a band of
chosen singers; where, in his own mind, he completely carried away the palm from the parson.   Thus, by divers little
makeshifts, the worthy pedagogue got on tolerably enough,
and was thought, by all who understood nothing of the labor
of headwork, to have a wonderfully easy life of it.

Generally the teacher was young, sometimes not more than sixteen years old; but if he was expert at figures, if he could read the Bible without stumbling over the long words, if he could write well enough to set a decent copy, if he could mend a pen, if he had vigor enough of character to assert his authority, and strength enough of arm to maintain it, he would do.

Pluck was indeed of superlative importance, for according to the old-time educational ideal, the lesson of all others to be impressed on the scholars was obedience, and there were pretty certain to be big boys among the pupils, whose love of knowledge was far exceeded by their love of mischief and spirit of insubordination. A muscular clash with them was all but inevitable, and the master who lacked courage or athletic vigor was likely to meet with ignominious disaster. When the boys had "put out" two or three masters in succession, the school got the name of being "hard," and the prudential committeeman was obliged to offer liberal wages and seek out a teacher who could overpower the young savages. That this warfare between the teachers and taught was common is shown by a record of over three hundred Massachusetts schools broken up in the year 1837 by the mutinous pupils or by the incompetence of the teachers.

Severity was held to be a virtue in a teacher rather than the contrary. Some parents were uneasy if the master was backward in applying the rod, and inferred that the children could not be learning much. The means the average schoolmaster employed to tame and discipline his pupils were extremely primitive.   He depended chiefly on a ruler,

A Salem Reward of Merit.

or on what was called "the heavy gad," by which expression was designated five feet of elastic sapling. These two implements were applied with force and frequency.   An appropriate share of the chastisement was visited on the girls, and the older ones were not allowed to escape justice any more than the younger ones; for it was thought that a youth of either sex who was not too old to do wrong was not too old to be punished.

We get a suggestive impression of what the discipline could be from the fact that a Sunderland, Massachusetts, schoolhouse erected in 1793 con-

tained a whipping-post set firmly in the schoolroom
floor. To this post offenders were tied and whipped
in the presence of their mates. It is also related
that the schoolroom walls, as time went on, became
marred with dents made by ferules hurled at mis-
behaving pupils' heads with an aim that sometimes
proved untrue.

Occasionally a teacher did not punish at all by
main strength, but resorted to moral suasion. Horace
Greeley tells of attending a New Hampshire district
school of sixty or seventy pupils about 1815, the
master of which rarely or never struck a blow. He
governed instead by appeals to his scholars' nobler
impulses. When the master left at the close of his
second term, a general attendance of parents on his
last afternoon, and a rural feast they provided of
boiled cider and doughnuts attested the emphatic
appreciation of his worth. Another master of this
gentler type held sway in Belchertown, Massachusetts, a little earlier. If his scholars became noisy,
he would stamp his foot and cry out, " Children,
if you do not behave better, I will go right off and
leave you ! " and the children would be frightened
into orderly quiet.

To turn again to Horace Greeley's reminiscences,
a still more curious bit of school lore is his description of the custom of barring out.

At the close of the morning session of the first of January, and perhaps on some other day that the big boys chose
to consider or make a holiday, the moment the master left
the house in quest of his dinner, the little ones were

Whipping-post formerly in a Sunderland, Mass., Schoolroom.
Height of original, about five feet.

started homeward, the doors and windows suddenly and
securely barricaded, and the older pupils, thus fortified

William Biglow.

Who taught for many years in Salem and Boston during the latter part of the eighteenth century and the early part of the nineteenth. From a portrait in wax.

against intrusion, proceeded to spend the afternoon in play
and hilarity. I have known a master to make a desperate
struggle for admission, but the odds were too great. If he

appealed to the neighboring fathers, they were apt to advise him to desist, and let matters take their course. I recollect one instance, however, where a youth was shut out who, procuring a piece of board, mounted from a fence to the roof of the schoolhouse and covered the top of the chimney nicely with his board. Ten minutes thereafter, the house was filled with smoke, and its inmates, opening the doors and windows, were glad to make terms with the outsider.

The usual sum paid to a master was ten or twelve dollars a month, though a wealthy district might, in exceptional cases, give twenty dollars to retain a man of culture and experience. Women earned from four to ten dollars. Even after the middle of the nineteenth century the standard pay for a woman teacher in many districts was one dollar a week. Instances of still lower wages can be found a few decades earlier. Thus a "qualified woman teacher" in a Connecticut town in 1798 received a weekly stipend of sixty-seven cents, and some masters of that period were paid no more. Besides the money remuneration, the districts boarded the teachers. Otherwise, the salary would have loomed much larger, and the town appropriation would have quickly melted away. The teacher "boarded round" among the homes of the pupils, spending at each house a length of time proportioned to the number of school children in the family. The custom was common until after 1850. The following paragraphs from what purports to be a schoolmaster's diary written early in the last century give a very spirited account of a week's experience of—

Boarding Round in Vermont.

Monday. Went to board at Mr. B's; had a baked gander for dinner; suppose from its size, the thickness of the skin and other venerable appearances it must have been one of the first settlers of Vermont; made a slight impression on the patriarch's breast. Supper — cold gander and potatoes. Family consists of the man, good wife, daughter Peggy, four boys, Pompey the dog, and a brace of cats. Fire built in the square room about nine o'clock, and a pile of wood lay by the fireplace; saw Peggy scratch her fingers, and couldn't take the hint; felt squeamish about the stomach, and talked of going to bed; Peggy looked sullen, and put out the fire in the square room; went to bed, and dreamed of having eaten a quantity of stone wall.

Tuesday. Cold gander for breakfast, swamp tea and nut cake — the latter some consolation. Dinner — the legs, &c., of the gander, done up warm — one nearly despatched. Supper — the other leg, &c., cold; went to bed as Peggy was carrying in the fire to the square room; dreamed I was a mud turtle, and got on my back and could not get over again.

Wednesday. Cold gander for breakfast; complained of sickness, and could eat nothing. Dinner — wings, &c., of the gander warmed up; did my best to destroy them, for fear they should be left for supper; did not succeed; dreaded supper all the afternoon. Supper — hot Johnny cake; felt greatly revived; thought I had got clear of the gander, and went to bed for a good night's rest; disappointed; very cool night, and couldn't keep warm; got up and stopped the broken window with my coat and vest; no use; froze the tip of my nose and one ear before morning.

Thursday. Cold gander again; much discouraged to see the gander not half gone; went visiting for dinner and supper; slept abroad and had pleasant dreams.

Friday.   Breakfast abroad.   Dinner at Mr. B.'s; cold gander and potatoes — the latter very good; ate them, and went to school quite contented.   Supper — cold gander and no potatoes, bread heavy and dry; had the headache and couldn't eat.   Peggy much concerned; had a fire built in the square room, and thought she and I had better sit there out of the noise; went to bed early; Peggy thought too much sleep bad for the headache.

Saturday.   Cold gander and hot Indian Johnny cake; did very well.   Dinner — cold gander again; didn't keep school this afternoon; weighed and found I had lost six pounds the last week; grew alarmed; had a talk with Mr. B. and concluded I had boarded out his share.

In the newer and thinner populated portions of the country education was much neglected. Communities either had a poor school or none at all. We get some idea of the difficulty of obtaining an education on the frontier from the life of Abraham Lincoln. The schools he attended between 1814 and 1826 in Kentucky and Indiana were held in deserted log cabins with earthen floors. The windows were small holes cut through the logs; and in some of the schoolhouses sheets of paper greased with lard served in the window holes instead of glass. Lincoln never was able to go to any school regularly and had less than a year's schooling in all. He was seventeen when he attended his last school. It was four and a half miles distant from the home cabin, and no doubt the long daily walk back and forth seemed a waste of time to most of his relatives. The region was still new and but little subdued, with many bears and other wild animals in the woods, and

Lincoln has said of the schoolmasters that " No qualification was ever required beyond ' readin', writin', and cypherin' to the Rule of Three.' If a straggler supposed to understand Latin happened to sojourn in the neighborhood, he was looked upon as a wizard."

Teaching offered no rewards sufficient to attract men of education or capacity, and it sometimes seemed as if a master's chief reason for taking up teaching was inability to earn anything in any other way. Lincoln acquired much of his early education at home. In the evening he would pile sticks of dry wood into the brick fireplace. These would blaze up brightly and shed a strong light over the room, and the boy would lie down flat on the floor before the hearth with his book in front of him. He used to write his arithmetic sums on a large wooden shovel with a piece of charcoal. After covering it all over with examples, he would take his jack-knife and whittle and scrape the surface clean, ready for more ciphering. Paper was expensive, and he could not even afford a slate. Sometimes when the shovel was not at hand, he did his figuring on the logs of the house walls and on the doorposts, and other woodwork that afforded a surface he could mark on with his charcoal.

An interesting sidelight on education in the district schools is furnished by an official report of 1838 concerning the three thousand school buildings of Massachusetts. Their estimated value was little above a half million dollars. To-day the state has single school structures which have cost more than

K

that.   The report says " there is no other class of buildings within our limits, erected for the permanent

Box Desks and Cast-iron Stove.

or temporary residence of our native population, so inconvenient, so uncomfortable, so dangerous to health by their construction within, or without, abandoned to cheerlessness and dilapidation." In one town, for a series of years, all the money annually appropriated for repairs on its eight schoolhouses was five dollars — an average of sixty-two and a half cents each.

Conditions in the schools of other states were no better. Thus the local reports in Connecticut between 1840 and 1850 make frequent mention of

A Schoolboy.

A Schoolgirl.

the small size of the schoolrooms as compared with
the number of pupils they had to accommodate.
Some of the rooms were less than seven feet high;
often they had broken windows, clapboards hanging

At Work.

loose, props up at the blinds to keep them in place, stoves without doors, leaky roofs, patches of plastering missing and the rest of the plastering much marred and begrimed ; crevices in the floor admitted any quantity of cold air, while the woodwork of the desks and walls was cut and marked " with all sorts of images, some of which would make heathens blush."

The required studies now were reading, spelling, writing, arithmetic, geography, and grammar. Algebra and even Latin and French were attempted in an occasional school if the teacher was equal to them. Yet with all this broadening in studies and all the advances in school-books, and in spite of the correct English the books were supposed to impart, the scholars in their daily conversation continued to use the vernacular. Had they been reproved for so doing, they would have felt affronted.

One handicap to effective teaching was the fact that it might happen no two pupils were equally advanced in their studies — possibly did not have the same text-books. The books were often much worn and defaced, for they were family heirlooms and continued in use as long as they held together. One scholar would bring a volume used by some member of the family of the preceding generation ; another a book procured many years before for an elder brother or sister, and a third would appear with a copy just bought.

Some one has said, " It seems to me that we may learn everything when we know the letters of the alphabet ;" and it is unquestionably true that the capable and aspiring youth can make a very slender educational foundation serve to give an opportunity for great development. In most of the old district schools little was imparted beyond a few bare rudiments, the teachers were often ignorant, and sometimes brutal, the methods mechanical and dreary. Notable men have come from " the little red schoolhouses," but this was because of their own native energy and thrifty acquisitiveness, and was not due to any superlative virtues of the schools themselves.

On the Way Home.

V

THE old-time summer schools were nearly always kept by women. A man would have been considered out of place — would have had an unnatural appearance presiding over a school at that season. The women teachers were usually young, ambitious girls, eager to earn enough to

A Summer School as pictured in Bolles's *Spelling Book*, 1831.

allow them to attend an academy for a term or two. Most of them married later; but others lived on as schoolmarms, " sometimes sweetening as they ripened, sometimes quite the contrary."

The law ordered that the teachers should have good moral character and competence to teach the

135

The End of Recess.

required branches. What furnished a woman, however, the surest passport to employment was to be related to some prudential committeeman. He was all-powerful in his district, and while his daughters or sisters, of course, had first chance, if none among these closer relatives had anxiety for the place, there was opportunity for the more remotely connected. The partiality of the prudential committeeman in this respect was proverbial, and no little friction resulted from the family arrangements he was wont to make. Occasionally the discus-

sion would split a school in two, and a portion of the
families in the district would secede and set up a
school of their own in some dwelling or shop; but as
a rule nothing was done until the next annual meeting, when another committeeman might be chosen
and a new dynasty substituted.

The employment of women in the public schools
had become general, and coincident with this recog-
nition of their value as teachers came the enlarging
of the educational opportunities of the girls; but it
was not until the nineteenth century was well advanced that they had anything approaching the same
advantages as the boys.   Books had nearly always
been considered outside the feminine sphere from
the most ancient times.   When Françoise de Saint-
onges, in the sixteenth century, wished to establish
girls' schools in France, she was hooted in the
streets, and her father called together four doctors
of law to decide whether she was possessed of a
devil in planning to teach women.   In like manner,
early in the last century, when Mary Somerville's
father discovered that she was engaged by herself in
mathematical and other studies, he said to his wife,
" Peg, we must put a stop to this, or we shall have
Mary in a strait-jacket one 'of these days."

Instruction in household duties was the essential thing, and if a girl had that, she could do very
well without book-learning; yet there was a time
in England about the period of Queen Elizabeth
when English girls studied Latin and Greek, and
the wisest masters were glad to teach them.   However, this state of affairs passed away, and educated

women came to be regarded with marked disfavor by English gentlemen.

In our own country, also, while the seventeenth-century girls to some extent attended the public schools, they gradually dropped out. The early school laws did not recognize them at all, expressly stating that "the word 'children' is to be interpreted to mean 'boys.'" There was no controversy on the subject. It simply seems to have been thought unnecessary that girls should be instructed in the public schools. Nevertheless, either at the dame schools or at home, they nearly all learned at least to read and sew. Writing was held to be much less important, and not by any means an essential accomplishment for females in common life. Scarcely one in a dozen women could write in 1700, and of those whose names appear in the recorded deeds of the early part of the eighteenth century less than forty per cent sign their names. All the rest make their mark. Even at the time of the Revolution many of the patriot wives and mothers could not write.

As an example of feminine disadvantages it is worthy of note that the town of Northampton, now one of our most famous educational centres, voted in 1788 to be at no expense for the schooling of girls, and they were not admitted to its public schools until 1802. President Quincy of Harvard College, in his history of Boston, says that in 1790 Boston girls were allowed to attend the public schools in the summer months only, and not then unless there were seats left vacant by boys. This semi-exclusion lasted until 1822, when Boston became a city. The girls were then given free access to the common schools, and presently another innovation was made, whereby a high school was established for them with a three-year course, though Latin and Greek were not included in the curriculum ; but this school was such an " alarming success " that it was abolished after eighteen months' trial. The school authorities were apparently dismayed at the way the girls crowded into the new high school, and Mr. Quincy says of the pupils, " Not one voluntarily quitted it, and there was no reason to suppose that any one admitted to the

A Little Girl of the Eighteenth Century.
From a pastel.

school would voluntarily quit for the whole three years, except in case of marriage."

Boston was very conservative in this respect.

Throughout the country as a whole there began
to be a considerable change in public sentiment
regarding feminine education immediately after the
Revolution, and within a decade or two, most places
allowed the girls to attend all the town schools. Yet
the new advantages were accorded only gradually
and in the face of a good deal of opposition. At
first some towns were cautious enough to arrange
that the boys should be sent home earlier in the
forenoon and afternoon to give the girls a chance
to come in for the time remaining; but the girls
could attend all of Thursday afternoon, for that was
the boys' holiday. Even these slender schooling
privileges were cut off in the winter out of consideration for "the female health." Thus the summer district schools in many instances continued to
be, if not the only educational reliance of the girls,
at least a very important one. There they were
taught reading, writing, and spelling, and great attention was paid to polite behavior. The scholars
"made their manners"—that is, the girls dropped a

REWARD OF MERIT.

This certifies, that *Master Elijah Waters*
by diligence and good behaviour, merits the approbation of
his friends and Instruct*ress. Mary F. Davron*

A Reward of Merit, about 1820.

courtesy and the boys bowed, to the teacher when
they came into the schoolroom and when they left
it. They made their manners while out at play to

passing strangers ; and if the minister or some other
prominent person went by, they formed in line and

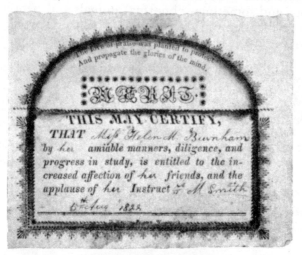

A Reward of Merit, 1822.

bowed and courtesied all together.   At the end of the
school day the teacher would tell them that as soon
as they reached home they must remember to make
their manners to their parents.

Besides studying their books, the girls did regular
stints at school of sewing and knitting, and each made
an elaborate sampler which was expected to be a
household treasure ever after.   The sampler was a
square or oblong of coarse linen, or possibly silk,
on which it was customary to stitch the alphabet in
capitals and small letters, the digits, a verse of sentiment appropriate to a child student, and the worker's

name, age, and place of abode.   There were also
decorations — borders, conventional trees, and flower-
pots, and sometimes abnormal animals and people —
all resplendent in many-colored silks or worsteds.
Not only was the sampler intended to be a thing of

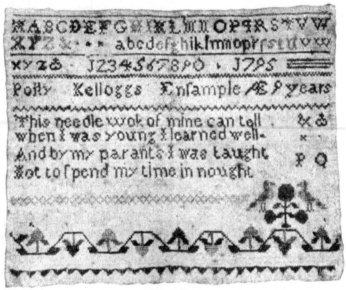

A Sampler.

Size, 10 × 12.

beauty, but the alphabet portion of it was useful for
reference to show the proper formation of the letters
when clothing was to be marked.   It was in fact this
reference feature that made the article a "sampler."
The smaller samplers were only about seven by
nine inches, but the larger ones were two or three

times those dimensions.   Some of the verses and inscriptions were very quaint, as is witnessed by the
two which follow : —

> Next Unto God Dear Parents I Address
> My Self to You in Humble Thankfulness
> For All Your Care And Pains on me Bestow'd
> The Means of Learning Unto Me Allow'd
> Go on I Pray And Let me Still Pursue
> Those Golden Paths the Vulgar Never Knew.

One of the More Elaborate Samplers.

Size, fifteen inches square.

Elizabeth Briggs is my Name And With my
Hand I Have Wrought the Same in the 10th year
Of my Age, Salem February 15th 1805

How should we scorn these clothes of flesh,
These fetters and this load,
And long for evening to undress
That we may rest with God.

Lower Half of a Sampler.

Showing a characteristic verse and some intricate and romantic designing.   Width of
original, fifteen inches.

When the girls began to go to the masters' schools,
the more aspiring of them adventured a little way
into geography, grammar, and mathematics.   The
ignorant derided them for so doing and, with regard

to the arithmetic, would ask them if they expected
to carry pork to market, else why should they want to
take up such a study. Some of the girls attended
private schools — "finishing schools," they were
called — which had been established at the dictate
of fashion to cultivate ladylike accomplishments.
All the larger towns had schools of this kind.
Boston gentlewomen were accustomed from very
early times to eke out their incomes by taking into
their homes little girls and misses from the country
and from the southern colonies and the Barbadoes
who wanted to attend the finishing schools of the
city. Salem and Newburyport were also favorite
towns for acquiring feminine polish. The finishing
schools taught a smattering of French, the art of
embroidery and other fancy needlework, considerable dancing, and many elegant manners. Dancing
seems to have had an especially important place
among the young misses' attainments, though in
early colonial days it was inveighed against by both
magistrates and ministers. Increase Mather loudly
proclaimed its evils just as he did the evils of wear-
ing wigs — "Horrid Bushes of Vanity," he called
those head adornments. But perverse human nature
adopted both wigs and dancing, and presently "or-
dination balls" were given when a new minister was
installed.

About the beginning of the last century, girls'
schools of genuinely serious aims and purposes
came into being, and their high character and the
success of their pupils, and the like success won
by the girls in the academies, were very effective in

L.

breaking down the opposition to feminine education. The higher institutions of learning for girls
established in those early years shone with added
lustre because their novelty attracted workers with
the enthusiasm of pioneers, and with a keenness of
appreciation and exhilaration that could be elicited
by no other circumstances. These schools were in
a marked way religious, their pupils absorbed moral
earnestness, and they had a deep and lasting influence on New England life. They furnished heroines
of the mission field and some of the most ardent
workers against intemperance. From them, too,
came such numbers of wives for the clergy that the
humorous appellation "ministers' rib factories" was
not wholly amiss. This nickname was the more
telling, owing to the fact that the buildings them-

"A Minister's Rib Factory."
Mary Lyon's Mt. Holyoke Seminary, built in 1837.

selves were apt to be great barren barracks with
very much of the factory look.

I have incidentally referred to the academies. Their waxing and waning form a curious phase of our educational development. In the eighteenth century the growth of the scattered villages, and the division of the towns into school districts, was attended by a gradual discontinuance of the grammar schools. Indeed, the law requiring grammar schools was relaxed, until we find in Massachusetts only seven towns where they were obligatory in 1824. The people preferred to spend all the money raised for education on the district schools; but some channel of more advanced instruction was a necessity, and there began to come into being many private schools and incorporated academies. The first of the latter was established in 1780 at Andover; others soon followed, and by 1840 the state had nearly one hundred of them. The purpose of the founders was primarily to provide a means by which young men could be fitted for college. They were imperatively needed. For instance, when Leicester Academy began its work, there was not in all Worcester County an educational institution higher than the district schools. The few boys who were determined to attend college conned their Latin and Greek by their own firesides, and recited to the parish ministers.

The standard studies in the academies were English, Latin, Greek, and French; writing, arithmetic, and geography; the art of speaking, logic, geometry, and philosophy. Some of the academies were little more than day schools for town pupils; others drew from a wide constituency, not alone in their own state, but from other states throughout the Union. They did excellent service in broadening the scope of education, but they fostered the idea of private schools. As a consequence there was a marked inclination among the well-to-do to withdraw their children from the common schools, which were thus left for the poorer families, the indifferent and careless, to get from them what little they could.

A typical academy was that at Deerfield, Massachusetts, formally opened in 1799. It had 269 pupils

An Old New England Academy.

the first year. The building was of brick, sixty by eighty feet, two stories high, and surmounted by a cupola. Ten years of prosperity encouraged the trustees to add another story and a wing, and a bell was bought and put in the cupola. Twelve rooms were fitted up for boarders, and rented at a weekly charge of from seventy-five cents to one dollar and a half. The latter sum was the standard price for board. It was ordered that "the preceptors and ushers, besides teaching the arts and sciences, should instil into the minds of the pupils moral and Christian principles, and form in them habits of virtue and the love of piety." The study of natural history, natural philosophy, and logic was encouraged, and "no person was suffered to attend to painting, embroidery, or any other of the ornamental branches to the neglect of the essential and fundamental facts of education."

For the regulation of the pupils' conduct there was a code of by-laws of thirty-six articles. Among other things, these provided that pupils of different sexes should not meet on the grounds or within the walls of the academy except at meals and prayers, nor walk or ride or visit together, under a penalty of one dollar. They were fined a dollar if they were absent from meeting Sunday, Fast Day, or Thanksgiving Day, and the same if they walked in the streets and fields or visited Saturday night or Sunday. They must forfeit a dollar if detected playing cards, backgammon, or checkers in the building. Ball and similar games near the academy were prohibited under a penalty of six cents, and a like sum was exacted from students found out of their rooms during study hours. The morning prayers were at five o'clock, or as soon as it was light enough to read; fine for absence, four cents — for being tardy, two cents. The appointed time for beginning to study was an hour later. Fines were imposed for damage to library books, or books belonging to fellow-students, at the rate of six cents for a blot, and six cents for each drop of tallow; while for every leaf torn, six cents an inch must be paid, and for every mark or scratch two cents. Separate schoolrooms were provided for the boys and girls, and separate entrances to the building, and the yard was divided by a high board fence to keep the sexes apart while at play.

The decay of the academies dates from about the middle of the nineteenth century, when Horace Mann began to urge the necessity of free high schools. These were rapidly established, and as they and the academies derived their students from the same source, the academies weakened. Most of them, after dragging out a lingering existence for a longer or a shorter time, finally succumbed. A few of the stronger ones adjusted themselves to the altered conditions and survived, but their students now came chiefly from the homes of the wealthy, and they were no longer the resort of the awkward rural youths and maids, to whom a short period in the academy was often their only opportunity for a glimpse of the broader world of culture and books.

VI

CHILDREN have always been prone to scrib-
bling, and the pupils in the old district schools
were no exception to the rule. They did not
by any means confine their chirography to their copy-
books. A fair surface of paper, no matter where
found, was a temptation to some of them, and all
had moments of mental ennui when the employment of the fingers in aimless, or at least unnecessary, whittling and writing was as natural as breathing.
Instances can be found where there was a genuine
ferment of literary or artistic inspiration, but mostly
the children produced only copies of what they had
seen their schoolmates do. Probably the young
folks of two or three generations ago scribbled less
in their school-books than their descendants; for the
majority of the old books that have survived the
wear and tear of use and the casualties of the passing
years are comparatively free from markings. Books
were rarer and far more valued in the early days than
later, and were treated with more respect, though it
must be admitted the comparative immaculateness
of such copies as are now extant is in part due to the
fact that the books most decorated were the soonest
to go to pieces, and they no longer exist. But

search and appeal to elderly people bring to light many curious bits of school-child lore.

The first thing the youthful proprietor of a book was likely to do was to mark it with his name. Usually he put his signature on the front fly-leaf, but he might write it on the final fly-leaf, or almost anywhere else in the book.   Sometimes he lettered

A Signature.

From a Dilworth's *Schoolmaster's Assistant.*

it outside on the cover, or even on the edges of the leaves.   Various common forms of name inscriptions are given below.   They exhibit considerable originality in spelling and in punctuation or the lack of it, and are transcribed just as they were written.

William Orne's 1779

Elisa Lee,s property
cost of it 3/   Hartford 10ᵗʰ Dec 1798

Allen m Shepherds
Book and pen the year
1831   augest 17

Jonathan Colton   owner   1807

Ella Morrill is my name   1828

Mifs Jane Elizabeth Smith   her book
Price 37 ½ Cnts   January 1ˢᵗ 1833
Mifs Nottinghams Seminary for Young ladies

'n an old Latin book I find this signature : —

> Andrew Hillyer Ejus Liber
> A D 1700 and frose to death.

The Latin students were fond of writing " Ejus
Liber," but the line which gives the date is the only
one of the kind I have seen.   Frequently the names
were accompanied by verses such as : —

Steal not this Book
For fear of Shame
For hear you read
The owners name
Asa Stobbins Book

A Warning.
From a Dwight's *Geography*, 1802.

If this book should chance to roam
Box its ears and send it home.

Steal not this book, for if you do,
Tom Harris will be after you.

Steal not this book for fear of strife
For the owner carries a big jackknife.

Steal not this book my honest friend
for fear the gallos will be your end
The gallos is high, the rope is strong,
To steal this book you know is wrong.

Let every lerking thief be taught,
This maxim always sure,
That learning is much better bought
Than stolen from the poor.
Then steel not this book.

Wise Advice in a Murray's *English Reader*, 1822.
Reduced one-half.

The longest and most impressive of these incantations against possible purloiners was the following:—

Whosoever steals this
Book away may
Think on that great
judgement day when
Jesus Christ shall
come and say
Where is that book you
stole away.
Then you will say
I do not know
and Christ will say
go down below.

The most dubious fly-leaf inscription that I have seen is this one : —

Francis Barton
is my name   a merica
is my nation
pitsfield is my
dweling place
and christ is my
salvation when
i am dead and
in my grave and
all my bones are
rotton its youl
remember me or else
i will be forgotten.

In a tiny volume published in Boston in 1685 entitled the *Protestant Tutor*, I find a quatrain of a very different character from the rough humor or the belligerent threatenings of the usual fly-leaf entries.   It runs thus : —

William Graham his Book
God grant him grace therein to look,
that he may run that blessed race
that heaven may be his dwelling Place.

A rhyme of similar gentleness was : —

This Book was bought for good Intent
pray bring it home when it is lent.

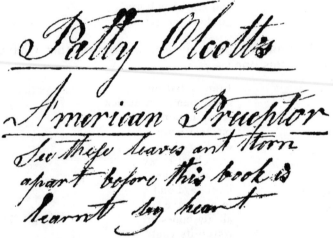

Patty Olcotts

American Preceptor

*See these leaves ant torn
apart before this book is
learnt by heart*

Lines from a Bingham's *American Preceptor*, 1803.

Sometimes a series of jingles was so arranged as
to lead the reader on a wild goose chase. At the
top of one of the early pages would be written : —

If my name you wish to see
look on page 103.

Turn to that page and you have : —

> If my name you cannot find
> look on page 109.

Again do as you are bidden, and you are rewarded with : —

> If my name you cannot find
> Shut up the book and never mind.

On occasion the poetry dealt with some incidental topic, as, for example, these lines in an Adams's arithmetic : —

> Oh may I learn with true submission
> Daniel Adams composition.

A ditty which was considered a fitting characterization to inscribe in the school histories was this : —

> If there should be another flood,
>   Then to this book I'd fly ;
> If all the earth should be submerged
>   This book would still be dry.

Among the schoolgirls attending the academies it was a fad to write sentimental verses of affection in each other's books, thus : —

> ### *To Miss Lottie*
>
> I always wish you happiness
> No sorrow veil your earthly bliss ;
> And when this little piece, you see
> Of friendship mine remember me.
>   Your friend and schoolmate
>   MARY ANN W.

To Ellen

> Many, many a voice will greet me,
> In a low and gentle tone
> But its music will not cheer me
> Like the cadence of thine own.

A FRIEND

The boys once in a while made similar declarations, but these were usually in prose, and evidently were not intended so seriously as those the girls produced.   Very likely the lad to whom the endearments were addressed would append joking comments.   Here are specimens of masculine handiwork : —

> You give your heart
> to me and I will give
> mine to you we will lock them
> up together and throw away the key

No Sir ee   Oh yes

I shall always think of you as a dear friend

S. GRAY

All right Gray ; only don't tell any one else about it

LEE

A school-book in my possession that is dated 1832 has pencilled inside the front cover these lines : —

Puzzle

writen over the commandments

P.RS.V.R.Y.P.RF.CTM.N
.V.RK..PTH.S.PR.C.PTST.N

No solution was offered, and I studied over the mysterious medley for some time before I saw that it made sense if an *E* was substituted for each of the dots.

In another of my books, published a dozen years later, is a fly-leaf assertion that

> 11 weeks will never go away
> never never never never

What repining and hopeless melancholy in looking forward to the long term just begun!

Some children would fill in with their lead pencils every letter *o* on the page they were studying, and they might even fill in the loops of the *b*'s, *d*'s, and other letters that had enclosed spaces suited to the whim. They delighted also to go over with pencil portions of the illustrations. If imaginative, they were apt to improve the pictures by putting in new features, and would run ropes to the ground from a sailing balloon, draw weather-vanes on the houses, etc.

Toward the end of the spellers was often a page of first names, male and female; and the owner of a book, recognizing some of these as belonging to his friends, was very likely inspired to write in the appropriate surnames, as follows: —

> *A'bel* Chapin
> *Alon'zo* Tyler
> *Eli'shä* Gunn
> *Ab'by* Bliss
> *Nan'cy* Steadman

I have a Webster's *Elementary Spelling Book* that belonged to S. Augusta Tinker. She must have liked her name, for it is found on page after page, and occasionally several times on the same page. The S. stood for Sarah or Sally, and occurs written in each of these ways. Evidently the book served for communication with other scholars, else why such pencillings as —

> you must go out of school if you dont be
>   have better
> lend me piece of paper
> you may tak it after recess

Here is an item which I suppose must be credited to one of the owner's schoolmates: —

> Augusta is goozey

Another interesting freak is the supplementing the short sentences of the book with comments in this fashion: —

> *The mason puts a layer of mortar between bricks.*   they dont
> *Intemperance is the grievious sin of our country.*   so it is
> *Boys like a warm fire in a wintery day.*   so do girles

A Fly-leaf Bird.
From a grammar of 1714.

Along with the writing in the old books there is more or less drawing. The very early books sometimes have fly-leaf sketches of Ind-

ians and log houses.   The later books have houses
of a more modern sort, and you find rude drawings of steamboats, houses; birds,
flowers, faces, and the like.   Often
a penny or other coin was slipped
under the fly-leaf and the surface
of the paper covering the coin was
rubbed with a piece of lead from
the schoolboy's pocket, or with the
blunt end of a pencil.   Usually
the boy was not satisfied till he got
a print of both sides of the coin.

Five characteristic school-book
decorations are shown on pages
162 and 163.   The first is a scroll
that could be lengthened out clear
across a fly-leaf or all down a
text-page border.   The second
is a flourish that frequently appeared beneath a signature.

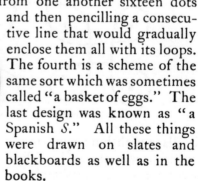

A Soldier.
Drawn in Webb's *The Common School Songster*, 1843.

The third was made by
drawing equidistant from one another sixteen dots

A Fly-leaf Rubbing from an
Old Medal.

M

and then pencilling a consecutive line that would gradually
enclose them all with its loops.
The fourth is a scheme of the
same sort which was sometimes
called "a basket of eggs." The
last design was known as "a
Spanish *S*." All these things
were drawn on slates and
blackboards as well as in the
books.

The children had numerous methods for defacing
their school-books, and they also had certain devices

Scroll Work.   A Diminishing Scroll.

for keeping them in good order. Many of the
older books are protected by an outer cover of
sheepskin neatly folded in at the edges and sewed

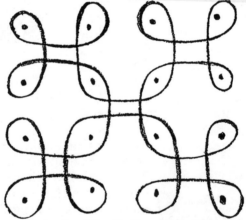

A Conventional Combination of Dots and Line.

in place with homespun tow. After 1825 this outer
covering was apt to be calico, and sometimes there
were tie strings attached at the sides. The girls

were addicted to the use of a "thumb paper," folded
and slipped in where the thumb rested when the

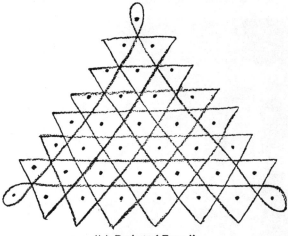

"A Basket of Eggs."

book was in use. This might be merely made of
a piece of newspaper or wrapping paper ; or it might
be nice new foolscap, or possibly
bright blue or red glazed paper.
Some children had their thumb
papers attached to the book by
a long thread, and they were particularly happy if instead of the
thread they acquired a bit of
gay-colored sewing-silk from the
mother's work-basket.

The most serious attention
the average boy gave to his books

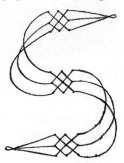

"A Spanish S."

had to do with the corners. When the leaves began to be dog-eared, he would get out his knife and carefully pare off the page corners of the entire book; and if he had an eye for beauty, he was not satisfied with a straight cut, but would round the corners. As soon as the leaves again showed a dog-eared tendency, the paring process was repeated.

For nearly fifty years after the Revolution the common text-book binding was either full leather, or was a leather back attached to sides of wood that were pasted over with blue paper. The full leather books, unless

A Protecting Cover of Leather stitched with Tow.
Reduced one-third.

quite thin, had the titles on the backs; the others had no lettering. Occasionally, instead of blue paper, there was marble paper or a fancy paper suggestive of wall-paper on the sides. The earliest book I have seen with printed sides is dated 1818, but within the next decade cover printing became common.   It soon was customary to print on the back cover a list of books issued by the publisher.   At first, however, the publisher, if he was also a bookseller and stationer, as he was pretty sure to be, used this space for advertising like the following : —

For Sale.

Bibles, Testaments, Spelling Books, Readers and Geographies, Atlases, Primers, Writing-paper, Inkstands, Ink-Powder, Slates, Pencils, Quills, Pen-knives, Wafers, Psalm Books, Writing Books, on the covers of which is printed a System of Writing.

There is a similar suggestion of primitiveness and rusticity in the way the publishers sometimes made known their location.   Thus, at the foot of the title-page of *The American Grammar* by Robert Ross, 1782, we find, " Hartford, Printed by Nathaniel Patten a few Rods North of the Court-House "; and on a *New England Primer* title-page of 1770, " Boston, Printed and Sold by William M'Alpine,

HARTFORD:
PRINTED BY *HUDSON* AND *GOODWIN*.
Sold by them, at their Book-ftore, oppofite the North Meeting-Houfe.   By *I. Beers*, New-Haven.   By *B. Tallmadge & Co.*
Litchfield,   By *T. C. Green*, New-London ;   and by
Andrew Huntington, Norwich.

1802,
A Title-page Imprint.
From Dwight's *A Short but Comprehensive System of the Geography of the World.*

about Mid-way between the Governor's and Dr. Gardiner's in Marlborough Street."

The publishing was not by any means confined to the large cities. In New England, the chief source of school-book supply, every town of any consequence and enterprise seemed to have its text-book publishers. The compilers were very apt to put forth their books from the town where they lived. Thus, Hartford, which was the home of an unusual number of prolific text-book authors, was for a time the most important educational publishing centre in America.

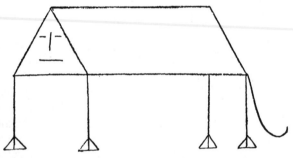

A Fly-leaf Animal.

VII

NOAH WEBSTER was born October 16, 1758, in Hartford, Connecticut, about three miles from the centre of the city. His father, Noah Webster, Sr., was a respectable farmer, a deacon in the church, and a justice of the peace. The boy worked on the home farm and attended the village school. When he had reached the age of fourteen, we find him beginning the study of the classics under the instruction of the parish clergyman, and two years later he was admitted to Yale College. The Revolutionary War seriously interrupted the college course, but he graduated with credit in 1778, and his father gave him an eight-dollar Continental bill, then worth about half its face value in specie, and told him he must henceforth rely on his own exertions.

It had been young Webster's intention to become a lawyer. The country, however, was impoverished by the war, and his first necessity was to make a living. So he resorted to school teaching. Pedagogy at that time was attended with unusual difficulties. Not only was the war still in progress, but the interruption of intercourse with Great Britain had made school-books very scarce. The need of a home source of text-book supply was evident, and in 1782, while in charge of a school in Orange County, New York, Webster compiled a spelling-book.   This was printed at Hartford the next year

Noah Webster.

and gradually won very wide acceptance — so wide, indeed, that during the twenty years its author was engaged in preparing his dictionary, 1807 to 1827, the profits from that one little school-book furnished the entire support of his family, though his copy-right receipts were less than a cent a book.   The sales went on increasing up to the time of Mr. Web-ster's death, at the age of eighty-four.   A million copies annually were then being called for and the total distribution had reached twenty-four millions.

In his person Webster was tall and slender.   To the very end he was remarkably erect, and his step light and elastic.   He was enterprising, self-reliant, and very methodical, and a most persevering worker. Besides the monumental labor of making his dic-tionary, he had much to do with newspapers and magazines, both as editor and contributor, and he wrote a great number of books and pamphlets on literary, historical, medical, religious, scientific, and political subjects, some of which were of very marked value in forming public opinion.   He taught school in his early manhood for about ten years, and then, from 1789 to 1793, was a lawyer in Hartford.   Dur-ing other periods, he served as an alderman in New Haven, as a judge in one of the Connecticut courts, and as a member of the Massachusetts legislature. His activity was astonishing in amount and variety, and it was unceasing.   Mental exertion seemed to be the native element of his soul.

Webster had originally intended to call his speller *The American Instructor*, but by the advice of the president of Yale College, the title was changed to *The First Part of a Grammatical Institute of the English Language*, the other parts being a grammar and a reader issued shortly afterward.   Profound names were to the liking of the old college presidents.

When Mary Lyon was starting her famous school for girls at South Hadley, President Hitchcock of Amherst proposed she should call it " The Pangy-naskian Seminary "; but she, wiser than Noah Webster in this matter, did not accept the suggestion, although the meaning of the name — that the whole woman was to be put to school — was exceedingly appropriate.

For a score of years Webster's spelling-book bore the ponderous title conferred on it, and yet survived. Then he changed the name to *The American-Spelling-book*, and still later to *The Elementary Spelling-book*. From almost the very first it took the leading place among books of its class and kept that place for many decades.   Webster, in a general way, compiled his book on the plan of Dilworth's, the most popular English speller of the century ; but radical divergencies were not lacking, for he aspired to reform the language and simplify the spelling.   Hitherto the spelling in the different text-books had been far from uniform ; and in letters, records, and other manuscripts of the time there was a curious variety in word construction.   Even men of high education often spelled the same word in several different ways ; but Webster presently became the American standard and brought order out of chaos.   He did not accomplish all that he at first planned in the way of reform, but some of his innovations, like the treatment of *tion* and *sion* as single syllables instead of two, as had formerly been the custom, found permanent acceptance, and he did very effective work in counteracting vulgarisms in pronunciation.

When the first edition of the spelling-book was printed, Webster had to give a bond to make good any loss that might result, but the copyright was soon very valuable.   Authors were in the habit of selling the printers the right to issue editions of their books for a certain number of years, and Webster sold his privilege to a firm in his home city, and to other firms in Boston, Albany, New York, and Philadelphia.   Such a multiplication of publishers would hardly do now, but the old-time difficulties of transportation afforded these firms ample protection from rival encroachment.   In 1817, when the speller was revised, one printer gave Webster three thousand dollars a year for his term of copyright, and another forty thousand for the privilege of publishing editions for fourteen years.

Each printer varied his issue in minor particulars to please his own fancy.   One edition appeared " embellished " with a portrait of " The Father of his Country," another with a dreadful woodcut that purported to show the features of " Noah Webster, Jun. Esq.," but which made him look like a porcupine.   This engraving and the absurd title of the book furnished vulnerable points of attack. Names like " Mr. Grammatical Institute," " Mr. Institutional Genius," and " Mr. Squire, Jun." were applied to the author, and one critic drew up a mock will, in which he bequeathed Webster " six Spanish-milled dollars, to be expended on a new plate of his portrait at the head of his spelling-book, that which graces it at present being so ugly it scares the children from their lessons ; but this legacy is to be paid only on condition that he leaves out the title of *'Squire* at the bottom of said picture, which is extremely odious in an American school-book, and must inevitably tend to corrupt the principles of the republican babies that behold it."

Webster was a good deal disturbed by the criticisms passed on his book, and in replying to one which especially irritated him, he challenged the writer to " meet him in the field." But the offender chose to shed ink instead of blood, and the warfare was confined to the columns of the newspapers. Fortunately this sort of thing proved good advertising and brought the speller thoroughly into notice.

One of the first effects of the publication of the *Grammatical Institute* was to make spelling a craze. Previously spelling had been little taught, but now it absorbed a large share of the student interest and enthusiasm, and the pupil who could " spell down the whole school" ranked second only to him who surpassed the rest in arithmetic. The child at the head of a class when the day ended had a credit mark, and perhaps was given a written certificate of good scholarship to carry home. There were instances, too, where the spelling classes had prizes — possibly a half dollar for the oldest class, a quarter for the next, and a " nine-pence " for the little ones. Each prize coin was drilled and hung on a string, and the winners in the afternoon spelling lessons were entitled to carry a coin suspended from their necks until the next morning, when these decorations were turned over to the teacher to be again contended for. A record was kept, and at the close

NOAH WEBSTER, JUN. ESQ.

The Portrait in " The Old Blue-back " that scared the Children.

of the term the child who had carried the coin home the greatest number of times was given permanent possession.

Once a week the school would choose sides for a spelling-match. This match took up half the afternoon and was frequently attended with efforts to defraud and exhibitions of envy. The side which spelled best was declared to have "beat" and usually manifested much triumph. The spelling-matches were also a common recreation of the winter evenings, and from time to time neighboring districts sent their champions to contend for orthographic honors in friendly combat. To these evening contests came not only the day pupils, but the older brothers and sisters and the rest of the community. Horace Greeley, when a tiny white-headed youngster of five or six years, had already become a famous speller, and had not an equal in his district. He was always the first one chosen at the spelling schools. Sometimes he fell asleep in his place before the evening was over and had to be nudged by his companions when his turn came. He would instantly be alert, spell his word, and then drop asleep again.

After the spelling came recitations of poetry, together with oratory and dialogues. The dialogues were inclined to buffoonery, but the oratory was entirely serious, though not infrequently it was high-flown to the point of grandiloquence. The speeches of the patriot leaders of the Revolution were always favorites, especially Patrick Henry's "Give me Liberty or Give me Death."

Until the *Grammatical Institute* became *The Elementary Spelling-book* in 1829, the usual binding consisted of a back of leather and sides of thin oaken boards pasted over with a dull blue paper. Blue paper of a somewhat brighter tint was used on the later editions, and the speller was often spoken of as "The Old Blue-back." Up to the time of the *Elementary*, the cover was entirely without lettering. The sheets were held together and fastened into the cover by means of two strands of tape that pierced the folds of paper a quarter inch from the back, and the book opened very stubbornly. In fact it could never be induced to be outspread flat unless the tape was severed. The paper was coarse, the ink poor, and the print varied from muddy blackness to a faint illegibility.

For the first two or three years that the children attended school, during the earlier decades of the Republic, Webster's speller was their chief textbook. Not only was it primer and spelling-book combined, but there was a formidable introduction containing an "Analysis of Sounds in the English Language," to be learned word for word. The Analysis begins with this definition : —

Language or speech is the utterance of articulate sounds or voices, rendered significant by usage, for the expression and communication of thoughts.

The rest of the explanations were in the same vein. Of course they failed to convey their meaning to the child mind, and the teacher offered no elucidation.

After the introduction there was a page devoted

to the alphabet.   The letters, Roman and Italic, large and small, were arranged in several columns, and opposite each letter in a final column was the letter's name. Webster called *r*, *er*, and *w*, *oo*, while in addition to the usual name for *h*, he gives *he*, and for *y*, *ye*. Authorities differed in naming the letters. Hale's speller, 1799, names *w*, *ew*, and says in a footnote : " Two words or two syllables make an awkward name for a letter.   *U* and *w* have the same sounds, and should have names as nearly alike as can be distinguished from each other."

A London speller of 1712 pronounced *w*, *wee*, and in another English speller *j* appears as *jee* or *jod*; still another colonial speller gives *j* as *iazh* and *z* as *zad* or *zed*.

In Webster's book the alphabet is succeeded by a page packed with " ab, eb, ib," and the rest of those meaningless word fragments.   Then come three-letter words, and orthoepy is fairly begun. The long columns march on without a break over to page 43 where we find a few " lessons of easy words to teach children to read, and to know their duty."   This first reading looks like poetry, yet when you test it, you discover it is a very prosaic prose.   The opening paragraph is

No man may put off the law of God ;
My joy is in his law all the day.
O may I not go in the way of sin !
Let me not go in the way of ill men.

Throughout the remainder of the book the reading breaks the spelling columns quite frequently.

The following selections will show how aptly the preface described the reading lessons when it said that they were planned " to combine, with the familiarity of objects, useful truth, and practical principles."

A good child will not lie, swear, nor steal. — He will be good at home, and ask to read his book ; when he gets up he will wash his hands and face clean ; he will comb his hair and make haste to school; he will not play by the way as bad boys do.

As for those boys and girls that mind not their books, and love not the church and school, but play with such as tell lies, curse, swear and steal, they will come to some bad end, and must be whipt till they mend their ways.

January begins the year, and the first day of that month is called New Year's day. Then people express to each other their good wishes, and little boys and girls expect gifts of little books, toys and plums.

There are five stages of human life, infancy, childhood, youth, manhood, and old age. The infant is helpless; he is nourished with milk — when he has teeth he begins to eat bread, meat, and fruit, and is very fond of cakes and plums. The little boy chuses some plaything that will make a noise, a hammer, a stick or a whip. The little girl loves her doll and learns to dress it. She chuses a closet for her baby-house, where she sets her doll in a little chair, by the side of a table, furnished with tea-cups as big as a thimble.

As soon as boys are large enough, they run away from home, grow fond of play, climb trees to rob birds' nests, tear their clothes, and when they come home their parents often chastise them. — O how the rod makes their legs smart. These are naughty boys, who love play better than their books.

N

One feature that appears rather queer in an elementary school-book is a lesson of " Precepts concerning the Social Relations." In this the " young man, seeking for a partner for life," is advised to " Be not in haste to marry," and the young women to —

Be cautious in listening to the addresses of men. Is thy suitor addicted to low vices? is he profane? is he a gambler? a tippler? a spendthrift? a haunter of taverns? and, above all, is he a scoffer at religion? — Banish such a man from thy presence, his heart is false, and his hand would lead thee to wretchedness and ruin.

Then for married people there are suggestions of this sort: —

Art thou a husband? Treat thy wife with tenderness; reprove her faults with gentleness.

Art thou a wife? Respect thy husband; oppose him not unreasonably, but yield thy will to his, and thou shalt be blest with peace and concord; study to make him respectable; hide his faults.

The reading which appealed most forcibly to the students who conned " The Old Blue-back " was undoubtedly a series of eight short fables, each with an illustration. One of the fables in particular made a profound impression, and no child ever forgot it or its picturesque telling. This was the story —

Of the BOY that stole APPLES.

AN old Man found a rude Boy upon one of his trees stealing Apples, and desired him to come down; but the young Sauce-box told him plainly he would not. Won't you ? said the old Man, then I will fetch you down ; so he pulled up some tufts of Grass and threw at him ; but this only made the Youngster laugh, to think the old Man should pretend to beat him down from the tree with grass only.

FABLE I.—*Of the* BOY *that ſtole* APPLES.
From a Webster's speller dated 1789.

Well, well, said the old Man, if neither words nor grass will do, I must try what virtue there is in Stones : so the old Man pelted him heartily with stones, which soon made the young Chap hasten down from the tree and beg the old Man's pardon.

MORAL

If good words and gentle means will not reclaim the wicked, they must be dealt with in a more severe manner.

The book ends with " A Moral Catechism " of about a dozen pages. The topics considered are "Of Humility, Of Mercy, Of Revenge, Of Industry," etc., and include such questions and answers as : —

2. Is pride commendable?
A. By no means.   A modest, self-approving opinion of
our own good deeds is very right — it is natural — it is
agreeable, and a spur to good actions.   But we should not
suffer our hearts to be blown up with pride ; for pride
brings upon us the ill-will of mankind, and displeasure of
our Maker.

The Elementary Spelling-book, which appeared in
1829, had a frontispiece and seven pictures in the

FABLE II.—*The* COUNTRY MAID *and her*
MILK PAIL.

From a Webster's speller dated 1789.

text.   There was also an illustrated edition containing the identical material that was in the other except
that every spelling page had a narrow cut added at
the top.   The lists of words in the Elementary were
newly arranged and were more comprehensive than
in its predecessors, but the most noticeable change

was in the reading matter. The Moral Catechism
was omitted, and so were the scattered religious and

Frontispiece to Webster's Elementary, 1829.

ethical lessons. Four of the little fables were re-
tained unaltered, but instead of the other four we

find " The Dog," " The Stag," and " The Squirrel " described, a paragraph to each.   Then there
was a half-page disquisition about time.   The read-

" A Virago is a Turbulent, Masculine Woman."
From the illustrated edition of 1829.

ing otherwise consisted of short disconnected sentences containing as a rule wise advice, or statements of interesting facts.   Nearly every page had

" An Orator makes Orations."
From the illustrated edition, 1829.

some of these sentences, and they numbered over
a thousand in all.   Below are selections from them,
beginning with the shortest and simplest : —

    an ox
    is it so
    I am to go in
    He has got a new tub

The man can put on his wig
I love the young lady that shows me how to read.
Vipers are bad snakes, and they bite men.
I saw a rill run down the hill.
Visitors should not make their visits too long.
Style not in verse is called prose.
The birds fly from branch to branch on the trees and clinch their claws fast to the limbs.
Wolves howl in the woods, in the night.
Never pester the little boys.
The lark will soar up in the sky to look at the sun.
Forks have two or three tines.
Shut the gate, and keep the hogs out of the yard.
The dysentery is a painful disease.
Our blood is often chilled at the recital of acts of cruelty.
When large hailstones fall on the house they make a great racket.
Pompions are commonly called *pumpkins*.
The chewing of tobacco is a useless custom.
Many kings have been thrown down from their thrones.
The rainbow is a token that the world will not be drowned again.
Christ is a mediator between an offended God and offending man.
A piece of cloth, if good, is worth what it will bring.
Friday is just as lucky a day as any other.
It is a mean act to deface the figures on a mile stone.
The ladies adorn their heads and necks with tresses.
Fiction is a creature of the imagination.
It is every man's duty to bequeath to his children a rich inheritance of pious precepts.
The love of whiskey has brought many a stout fellow to the whipping-post.
Large bushy whiskers require a good deal of nursing and training.

The little sentences make a curious medley, and are not at all childlike; yet they have a certain lively straightforwardness and are often picturesque and entertaining. They inculcate thrift, sobriety, and the other virtues, and considerable instruction is conveyed by them, though some of it is rather indigestible. All the editions of Webster's book from first to last have about them a certain crudity and primitiveness, but the book was suited to the times and regions when and where it most flourished. It did its work well, and it would have made Noah Webster's fame secure, had he produced nothing else. Its sway weakened first in New England, but its use continued to increase in the South and West until the Civil War began. Since then the sales have dwindled, yet there are schools where it is studied even at present, and "The Old Blue-back" stands unrivalled among American books in circulation and length of life.

The Bad Boy, as he appeared in the Illustrated Edition of 1829.

VIII

JOHN LOCKE, in 1690, said of elementary school education in England, "The method is to adhere to the ordinary road of the Horn-book, Primer, Psalter, Testament, and Bible; these are the only books used to engage the liking of children and tempt them to read." "The ordinary road" was the same here. There were three reading classes in the schools — "The Psalter Class" for beginners, next "The Testament Class," and thirdly "The Bible Class," which went through about two chapters at each school session and was expected to spell the words in the portions read. For a long time spelling-books were lacking, and they did not become common much before 1750; but after that time for fully three-quarters of a century the spelling-book was almost the sole resource of the school children for elementary instruction. Advanced readers were in the market in the early years of the republic, but readers for the beginners seem to have been thought unnecessary. Thus the spellers of the forefathers did double duty as spelling-books and primers, and were a much more important institution than they have ever been since.

185

During the years immediately preceding the
Revolution, Dilworth's speller was accepted almost
universally, but Noah Webster's book presently
supplanted it. The next American speller to take
the field was *The Child's Companion*, a small, thin
volume compiled by Caleb Bingham. As compared with most of the early text-books, *The Child's
Companion* was bright and attractive. Like all the

re-ply	fet-tee	tranf-late	un-wife
re-port	fe-vere	tranf-grefs	u-nite
re-prieve	fhal-loon	tranf-plant	un-feen

TABLE VI.

**Eafy Leffons, *confifting of* Monofyllables, *to
be* read *without* fpelling.**

LESSON I.

MY child, love God with all thy heart.
Let it be thy joy to do his will.
O do not go in the way of fin !
Turn thy feet from the road to death.

From Bingham's *The Child's Companion*.

older spellers, it contained fragments of rudimentary
prose and verse, and every few pages the " Eafy
Leffons " for reading made a pause in the column
of spelling words. The " Eafy Leffons " consisted
very largely of moral advice and reflections selected
from the Bible, but in the latter part of the book
were a number of fables and stories. Two of the
stories follow : —

The PRETTY BUTTERFLY.

BUTTERFLY, pretty butterfly! come and reft on the flower that I hold in my hand! Whither goeft thou, little fimpleton? Seeft thou not that hungry bird that watches thee? His beak is fharpened, and already open to devour thee. Come, come, then, hither, and he will not dare approach thee. I will not pull off thy wings, nor torment thee; no, no, no; thou art little and helplefs, like myfelf. I only wifh to look at thee nearer.

I will not keep thee long; I know thou haft not long to live. When the fummer is over, thou will be no more, and as for me I fhall only then be fix years old.

Butterfly, pretty butterfly! come and reft on this flower that I hold in my hand! Thou haft not a moment to lofe from enjoying this fhort life; but thou mayeft feed and regale thyfelf all the time that I look at thee.

A DIALOGUE *between Mifs* CHARLOTTE *and Mifs* SOPHIA.

Charlotte. MISS Sophia, why do you always carry your *Spelling Book* to fchool with you? I carry nothing but my *work*.

Sophia. Becaufe I mean to learn to *fpell* as well as learn to *work*.

Char. *I* mean to learn to fpell *too*. But what great matter is it if one is not always fo very *exact* about one's fpelling?

Soph. Why, if we don't fpell our words a little according to cuftom, people will not be able to make fenfe of them.

Char. But mamma fays if they do but know what we *mean*, that is enough. She fays, I may as well begin *pin-*

cuſhion with the *laſt* letter, and end it with the *firſt*, as any way, if I am but underſtood.

Soph. That is the very thing. If you ſhould begin it with an *n*, and end it with a *p*, you would be more likely to make *night cap* of it than *pincuſhion;* and that would be a ſad miſtake.

Char. Well now, I will tell you a little affair, if you will promiſe to keep it a *ſecret.*

Soph. You know I never reveal *ſecrets.*

Char. Last New Year's day, I wanted to make my couſin Sally Chapman a preſent of a pretty little hiſtory book. And ſo I wrote her name in it and ſent it. But, inſtead of writing it properly, I wrote *For Sale Cheap Mon.* My couſin opened it, and read it; but could make nothing more or leſs of it, than *For sale cheap for Money;* and immediately ſent back to know the loweſt price. Now, think how mortified I was.

Soph. We must expect that ſuch miſtakes will often happen, if we do not learn to ſpell in ſeaſon. I knew a man who had a great deal of money, and was about making a great feaſt, who ſent his ſervant to market with an order, the true meaning of which was, that he wanted a dozen of fowls, either ducks, turkies, or chickens. But it was written thus: " Send me a *doſe of fools — Dukes* will be preferred to *Turks;* but *Chittens* will be better than either." Gueſs the man's aſtoniſhment, at ſeeing his ſervant come home lugging a baſket full of *kittens !*

Char. I ſee that great miſtakes, and great injuries may ariſe from bad ſpelling. I am reſolved to learn to be a good ſpeller too; and will aſk mamma to let me carry my ſpelling book to ſchool every day.

Soph. I am glad you have come to that reſolution. You write a very handſome hand; and nothing looks more ſhameful than to ſee *good writing* and *bad ſpelling* together.

What philosophers the school-book children of that generation were — and how quickly the virtuous and industrious won over their less admirable mates! In this dialogue between the two "Miſſes" the glimpse we get of Charlotte's mother mirrors the general opinion of the times that it was hardly worth while to teach girls much except sewing and housework, and if they took their stitching to school, it did not matter if they left their spellers at home.

In the back part of Bingham's book is a "collection of vulgarisms" of which the author says that many more examples might have been added. I select rather freely, for the list gives an interesting impression of the language in everyday use. It fills twelve pages under this heading: —

APPENDIX.

IMPROPRIETIES *in* PRONUNCIATION, *common among the people of New-England.*

Afraid	*not*	Afeard	chimney	*not*	chimbly
afterwards		arterwards	cucumber		cowcumber
audacious		outdacious	confiſcate		confiſticate
awkward		awkid	cover		kiver
bellows		belluffes	drain		dreen
boil		bile	dandruff		dander
bachelor		bacheldor	eternity		etarnity
bonfire		burnfire	earth		airth

gown	*not*	gound	really *not*	raly
guardian		guardeen	rheumatiſm	rheumatiz
grudge		begrutch	ſervant	ſarvant
girl		gal	ſhook	ſhuck
his		hiſen	ſuch	ſich
however		howzever	ſomething	ſuthing
herbs		yerbs	ſpirit	ſperrit
hoof		huf	ſcarce	ſcaſe
hurricane		harricane	ſteady	ſtiddy
handkerchief		handkercher	ſpoonful	ſpumful
icicle		iſuccle	ſauſages	links
ideas		idees	ſtunned	ſtunded
january		jinuary	this	this-ere
linen		linning	that	that-are
medicine		medſon	tutor	tutorer
molaſſes		laſſes	umbrella	umberriller
muſquitoes		ſketers	value	valley
muſician		muſicianer	voyage	vige
novelty		newelty	vagabond	vagabone
nervous		narvous	widow	widder
ours		ourn	wreck	rack
potatoes		taters	walnut	warnut
quench		ſquinch	yonder	yender

The same subject is continued in sentence form, thus : —

I *gin* it to him.
I *dun* it myſelf.
He is the *moſt* wiſeſt man.
He *teached* a ſchool.
My *wives* ſiſter is ſick.
She *enjoys* a bad ſtate of health.
He *rid* and I walked.
Is your parents living?

I have *nary* one.
She ſpeaks very *proper*.
He *don't ought* to behave ſo.
What *does* I do but *goes* and *demands* the money.
I never *drink'd* better wine.
She died *of* a Tueſday.
About a year *agone*.

A speller very similar in size and makeup to Bingham's was " *The Child's Spelling-book :* calculated to render Reading Completely Eaſy to Little Children ; Compiled by a printer, Hartford, 1798." It is illustrated with a number of pictures and the text is unfailingly brisk and entertaining. The first reading starts off in this wise : —

Come hither, Charles, come, tell me your letters; do you know how many there are ?   Where is the pin to point with ?   Here is the pin.   Now read your book.

In the next extract we get more glimpses of old-time child life both at school and at home.

How cold it is !   Where are the little girls and boys ? Have they not yet come from ſchool ?
Here they come, here they come. — Who was at the head of the claſs to-day ?   Rachel.   And did ſhe get the bow ? Yes papa, here is the pretty bow.   And will papa give me a penny for bringing home the bow ?
Yes, Rachel ſhall have a penny.   No, pennies are out of date.   She ſhall have a cent.
Dinner is ready.   Come little frozen boys, come get ſome pudding.
Will mamma give Charles ſome beer ?   Yes, Charles ſhall have ſome beer.

Wipe your mouth before you drink.   Do not cough in the cup.

Thomas fhall I help you to a potato?   No, fir, I have dined.

Then go to the fcullery, and wafh your hands, your face, and your teeth.

*   *   *   *   *   *   *

This is winter.   Well never mind it.   We will fit by the fire, and read, and tell ftories, and look at pictures.

Take care, little boy, you ftand too near the fire.   You will burn your fhoes.

Do not fpit on the floor.   Spit in the corner.

It is dark.   Light the candle.   Shut the window-blinds. Bring in fome wood.

The fun is gone to bed.   The chickens are gone to bed; and little boys and girls muft go to bed.

Poor little boy is sleepy.   He muft be carried up-ftairs.

Pull off his thoes.   Pull off his frock and petticoat. Put on his nightcap.

Lay his head upon the pillow.   Cover him up.   Good night.

In 1799 appeared Caleb Alexander's *The Young Ladies' and Gentleman's Spelling Book*.   It was a well-printed, leather-bound twelve mo, and contained eight engravings, each illustrating a poem by that eminent divine, Isaac Watts, whose verse both for adults and children was the especial delight of New Englanders in the eighteenth century.

These illustrated poems were the book's most distinguished feature as can be imagined from the pictures and portions of text which follow: —

Againſt PRIDE *in* CLOTHES.

From Alexander's *Spelling Book*, 1799.

HOW proud we are! how fond to ſhew
  Our clothes, and call them rich and new!
When the poor ſheep and ſilkworm wore
That very clothing long before.

The tulip and the butterfly
Appear in gayer coats than I:
Let me be dreſt fine as I will,
Flies, worms, and flowers exceed me ſtill.

Then will I ſet my heart to find
Inward adornings of the mind;
Knowledge and virtue, truth and grace,
Theſe are the robes of richeſt dreſs.

No more ſhall worms with me compare;
This is the raiment Angels wear;
It takes no ſpot, but ſtill refines;
The more 'tis worn the more it ſhines.

o

Againſt EVIL COMPANY.

From Alexander's *Spelling Book.*

WHY ſhould I join with them in play,
　　In whom I've no delight;
Who curſe and ſwear, but never pray.
　　Who call ill names, and fight?

I hate to hear a wanton ſong;
　　The words offend my ears;
I ſhould not dare defile my tongue
　　With language ſuch as theirs.

My God, I hate to walk or dwell
　　With ſinful children here;
Then let me not be ſent to hell,
　　Where none but ſinners are.

THIS is the day when Chriſt aroſe
　　So early from the dead;
Why ſhould I keep my eyelids cloſ'd,
　　And waſte my hours in bed?

Today with pleaſure chriſtians meet,
To pray, and hear thy word;
And I will go with cheerful feet
To learn thy will, O Lord.

I'll leave my ſport and read and pray,
And ſo prepare for heaven;
O may I love this blessed day,
The beſt of all the ſeven.

For the Lord's Day Morning.
From Alexander's *Spelling Book*.

The Columbian Spelling Book, Wrentham, Massachusetts, 1799, was similar to Alexander's in size, but was more roughly made, and the cuts were marvels of crudity. Two of these queer engravings are here given with the fables they illustrated.

The Dove and the Bee.

A POOR Bee came to a brook to drink, but in her haſte ſhe fell in, and would have loſt her life, had it not been for a dove, who broke off a ſmall twig from a tree, and dropped it in, fo that the bee got on the top of it, and rode fafe to fhore.

In a few days time a man came with his gun, and would have fhot the kind dove; but the bee, who was clofe by, saw what he was at, flew to him, and ftung him on his hand.

The Dove and the Bee.
From *The Columbian Spelling Book*, 1799.

" For now, thought fhe bee is my time, and I will fave my friend, if I die for it." As foon as the man felt the fting, he made a ftart, and the good dove flew off, and got fafe to her neft.

MORAL.

Learn from hence to help thofe who are in need as much as you can.

The Old Knight *and his* Wig.

A CERTAIN Knight growing old, his hair fell off fo faft, that he foon became bald; and fo he was forced to buy a wig. But one day, as he was riding out a hunting with fome of his mates, they met with a fudden blaft of wind; and fo off fell his hat and wig. Thofe who were with him could not help laughing at the odd figure he made; and for his part, being a cheerful old blade, he laughed as loud as the beft of them. How could I expect faid he to keep the hair of other people on my head, when my own would not ftay on?

The Old Knight and his Wig.
From *The Columbian Spelling Book.*

MORAL.

The beft way to turn off the edge of a joke is to join in the laugh yourfelf.

A spelling-book with a title suggesting relationship to the one of which I have just been speaking was *The Columbian Primer* by H. Mann, Dedham, 1802. It was a small book of eighty-four pages, quite

Cc *Stands for* **Camel,** *who lives in the eaſt ;*

attractive typographically and containing many pictures.   The author thought the pictures would make
the lessons "a *pleaſure* rather than a *taſk,*" and that
the teacher would rejoice " in the ſatiſfaction of
ſeeing the animated looks and rapid progreſs of his
pupils."   Most of the pictures were used in illustrating a rhymed alphabet that began with: —

> Aa *Stands for* ADAM, *the firſt of our race ;*
> Bb *Stands for his* BRIDE, *with beauty & grace.*

Dd *Stands for* Drunkard, *a worſe looking beaſt.*
An Alphabet Rhyme.
From *The Columbian Primer*, 1802.

Q q Stands for a Queen, who looks very gay ;

Each line has its accompanying picture filling the upper third of a page, and the rest of the space is devoted to spelling columns. The spelling is scarcely interrupted until we get to the last twenty pages which are made up of "Lessons in Reading." Nearly half this final portion is occupied by a story called : —

The Little Wanderers.

IT was one of thofe fine days of fummer, when all nature fmiled with the feason, and feemed to invite

Rr *Stands for* **Robin,** *who fings on the fpray.*

An Alphabet Rhyme.

From *The Columbian Primer.* 1802.

every one abroad to feast among the great variety of beauties it afforded; when young *Edwin*, about four years old, and his little fifter *Eliza*, aged three, rambled off into the woods and could not find the way back.

We muft now conclude, that young *Edwin* and *Eliza* were filled with much fear and amazement.   We may fuppofe they recollected the many frightful ftories they had heard of huge, wild beafts and ferpents which frequent thefe abodes of folitude.

The LITTLE WANDERERS.
From *The Columbian Primer.*

At length there was a thunderstorm of such vio- lence that—

the whole foreft, at times, feemed on fire, and tumbling into ruins.   *Eliza* clung round her little brother, and tried to hide her face from the lightning, which every moment threatened to ftrike them lifelefs.

Behold, now, the fable curtains of the night fhrouding thefe unhappy innocents in the midft of this defolate foreft! Here was no mother to cherifh, and prepare for them a

wholefome fupper.   And inftead of the downy bed, and
the foft fong of the Whippoorwill and Nightingale to lull
them to repofe, naught, but a bed of leaves drenched with
rain, the wild wind which whiftled terror thro' the trees,
and the hoarfe note of the Owl, to frighten their ears!

Meanwhile, the father and all the neighbors had
been searching for the children, and the search continued unsuccessfully through the stormy night.
" At last, when the day had dawned, the father
happening to caft his eyes on a clufter of leaves —
who fhould he difcover but his fweet babes!   He
fprang to fold their cold bodies to his bofom : And
while he wiped the rain from their tender limbs, the
parental tear ran down his cheeks."

The mother and a daughter some years older than
the lost children were with the father.   Of this
older daughter the book says : " How could that
humane, delicate bosom, which always turned from
the cruel fcene where the lamb is led to the flaugh-
ter ; whofe foft hands could never indulge themfelves in the barbarous fport of depriving the robin
of her eggs, much lefs of her young neftlings ; I fay,
how could this amiable fifter endure the thought
that her little brother and fifter fhould thus perifh."

But she was spared the pain ; for while the
rescuers picked up the children and " were alternately preffing their clay-cold lips to their own, a
fmall breath was difcovered to proceed from their
mouths, and their little hearts faintly vibrated with
life," and shortly they recovered and the adventure
ended happily.

About a dozen years after this *Columbian Primer* was published at Dedham, a speller of the same title and very similar appearance was issued in New York. The text and illustrations, however, were new, though arranged just as in the earlier volume; but where the spelling pages of the Dedham book had single cuts at the top of each, the New York book had two. Beneath the pictures were jingling couplets such as : —

The blushing Flowers
bloom and spring,

Dick and Tommy go
to plough

The pretty Maids have
modest looks,

The Birds do in the
bushes sing.

And Caty milks the
brindled cow.

Good boys and girls will
learn their books.

The naughty Boy who
steals the pears,

Is whipt, as well as he
who swears.

The Captain boldly
draws his sword,

The Soldier marches
at his word.

Rhymes from *The Columbian Primer, or Ladder to Learning,* New York, 1827.

In the portion of a page given herewith from Fiske's *The New England Spelling-book*, Brookfield, Massachusetts, 1803, it seems a little odd to find

Words *frequently used in* Speaking *and* Writing, *which should be well learned by every Scholar.*

Ăxe	bright	Dămn	frăud
åught	broåd	dåwn	frâught
Bădge	brōgue	dĕad	frêight
bāize	bruĭſe	dĕarth	friēze
bâlk	bŭdge	dêign	fright
bàlm	bŭŏy	dew	fruĭt
bā,the	buȳ	dírge	Gāit
bâwd	Càlve	dōe	ˌgāol

Portion of a Page.

From Fiske's *New England Spelling-book*, 1803.

" Damn " included among the " words which ſhould be well learned by every Scholar." But words just as much out of place are not uncommon in the old spellers. To quote a text-book preface of 1828, " They contain words collected from all departments of nature, life, and action; from the nursery, the kitchen, the drawing-room, the stable, the bar-room, the gaming table, the seaman's wharf, the apothecary's shop; from the subtle pages of the metaphysician, and the rhapsodies of the pompous pedant."

The latter part of Fiske's speller, comprising the larger half, consists of the Constitution of the United States, the Declaration of Independence, the Constitution of Massachusetts, and Washington's Farewell Address. But preceding these profundities are a few short reading lessons of a more entertaining character including two " Moral Tales " which each have an illustration, the only pictures in the book. One of the tales was about—

MORAL TALES.

The CHILD *and the* SERPENT.

From Fiske's *The New England Spelling-book.*

A CHILD, playing with a tame ſerpent, ſaid to it, My dear little animal, doſt thou imagine I would be ſo familiar with thee if thy venom was not taken out; you ſerpents are the moſt perverſe, ungrateful creatures. I remember to have read, that a good natured countryman found a ſerpent under a hedge, almoſt dead with cold. He took it up and warmed it in his breaſt; but it was ſcarcely come to life when it ſtung its benefactor, and the too charitable peaſant died of the wound. This is aſtoniſhing ſaid the ſerpent: How partial are your hiſtorians! Ours relate this hiſtory in a different manner. Your charitable peaſant believed the ſerpent dead: Its ſkin was beautifully variegated with different colours; he took it up and was haſtening home in order to flay it.

Now tell me whether the ſerpent was ungrateful?

Hold your tongue, replied the boy. Where is the ingrate who cannot find ſome excuſe to juſtify himſelf?

Well anſwered, interrupted the boy's father, who had liſtened to the dialogue. Nevertheleſs, my ſon, if ever thou ſhouldeſt hear of an inſtance of ingratitude baſer than ordinary, forget not to examine every circumſtance to the bottom, and be extremely backward in fixing ſo foul a ſtain on any man's character.

Comly's *A New Spelling-book*, Philadelphia, 1806, has on nearly every page a few short paragraphs of reading in addition to the columns of words. The first of this reading starts off lugubriously with — "All of us, my son, are to die," and the tone of the reading lessons right through the book is very serious. If there is a pause for a bit of natural history about "The Wren," "The Camel," or some other creature, it is only momentary, and the text promptly reverts to its pedantic and melancholy moralizing, often with a touch of theology added. Here is one of the longer lessons : —

Joseph Harris, a child of eleven years old, during his last illness, gave the following advice to his sister. Dost

thou know that it is thy duty to pray to the Lord every
night, to return him thanks for his preservation through
the day, and to desire his protection through the night; also,
in the morning to return thanks to him for relieving thee
from darkness.

When thou sittest down to meals, recollect how many
there are that would be glad of the smallest morsel, while
thou hast full and plenty : return the Almighty thanks for
his bounty, and be good to the poor.

Mind the advice of thy uncles, aunts, and friends.   Love
every body ; even thine enemies.   Endeavour to assist thy
poor afflicted mother, who is struggling through the world,
with four children without a father, and her fifth going to
be taken from her.   Love thy little brother and sister, and
walk in the paths of truth, and the Almighty will be a father
to thee.

Among spellers of British origin Dilworth's, Fenning's, Murray's, and Perry's long continued in circulation, but in the early years of the nineteenth
century Perry's was by far the most popular.   It
was entitled *The Only Sure Guide to the English
Tongue,* although one would have difficulty in per-
ceiving wherein it was essentially better than some
of its contemporaries.   The thing in Perry's book
which most impressed those who studied it was the
frontispiece — a tree of learning.   This was growing
in a schoolyard, and groups of boys were playing in
its shadow.   A ladder reached from the ground up
into the branches, and several boys were ascending
with open books in their hands.   Another book boy
had stepped off the ladder into the tree and was preparing to climb higher, while three boys engrossed

in their books were perched among the loftiest
branches. To the average child this picture allegory
was very curious and incomprehensible.

The reading in Perry is decidedly moral and religious; but once in a while it reverts to such light-
some matter as the following : —

COME let us go forth into the fields; let us see how
the flowers spring; let us listen to the warbling of the
birds, and sport ourselves upon the new grass.

Toward the end of the book are several pages of
hymns, a number of illustrated fables, a chapter on
Manners, the Ten Commandments, and a morning
and evening prayer. Nearly all the old spellers
included material of this sort. I give two of the
fables : —

The naughty GIRL *reformed.*

From an 1803 edition of Perry's *The Only Sure Guide to the English Tongue.*

A CERTAIN little girl uſed to be very naughty; ſhe frequently ſtrayed away from home without the conſent of her parents; was often quarrelſome and was ſometimes ſo very wicked as to tell lies. One day ſhe went into an orchard, and, without leave, took ſome fruit and was carrying it off. A faithful dog obſerved her and purſued her, and would have bitten her, if a countryman had not at that inſtant been paſſing who very humanely reſcued her from the jaws of the furious animal. The danger ſhe was in cauſed her to reflect on her paſt bad conduct — ſhe repented of her folly, and became one of the beſt children in the neighbourhood.

The Complaisant Hermit.
From Perry's *Only Sure Guide*, 1818.

The Hermit.

A HERMIT, one morning, sat contemplating with pleasure on the various objects that lay before him. The woods were dressed in the brightest verdure; the birds carolled beneath the branches; the lambs frolicked around the meads; and the ships driven by gentle gales, were returning into their proper harbours.   In short, every object yielded a display either of *beauty* or of *happiness*.   On a sudden arose a violent storm.   The winds mustered all their fury, and whole forests of oak lay scattered on the ground.   Darkness instantly· succeeded; hailstones and rain were poured forth in cataracts; and lightning and thunder added horrour to the gloom.   And, now, the sea, piled up in mountains, bore aloft the largest vessels, while the horrid uproar of its waves drowned the shrieks of the wretched mariners.   When the whole tempest had exhausted its fury, it was instantly followed by the shock of an earthquake.

The poor inhabitants of a neighbouring village flocked in crowds to our hermit's cave, religiously hoping that his well known sanctity would protect them in their distress. They were, however, not a little surprised at the profound tranquillity that appeared in his countenance.   " My friends," said he, " be not dismayed.   Terrible to me, as well as to you, would have been the war of the elements we have just beheld, but that I have meditated with so much attention on the various works of *Providence*, as to be persuaded that his *goodness* is equal to his power.

The old-time school-book authors often attained a good deal of picturesqueness in the selections that went into their volumes, and some of these authors were hardly less picturesque in the arguments and opinions they addressed to the public in their prefaces.   Here is the way Joshua Bradley appeals for the acceptance of his " lessons in spellings " which he compiled in a square little volume of sixty-four pages, published at Windsor, Vermont, in 1815.

The author was led to lay this small work before the publick, for the benefit of beginners; who are apt to wear

P

out a large book, without gaining any more knowledge than they would from one of this description.

Should parents, instructors and the benevolent encourage the introduction and continuance of this little work among children, they may be instrumental in guiding millions to a true knowledge of the rudiments of our language and *receive their reward at the resurrection* of the just.

To such patrons of learning the author wishes to tender his unfeigned thanks and to subscribe himself their sincere and affectionate friend.

The Wolf accuses the Lamb of Muddying the Water.
From Perry's *Only Sure Guide,* 1818.

An equally quotable preface is found in the *Analytical Spelling Book* by John Franklin Jones, New York, 1823. The compiler says of the reading matter in his book that —

Something was wanted, in American schools to replace the lessons, which have been copied from book to book, since the reign of Queen Anne. It is the intention, in the present work to advance principles suited to the rising generation, in the United States. Beast, reptiles and insects are not represented in this volume, as the equals of rational beings; because such a supposition is repugnant to nature, science, and correct moral sentiment. Most of the fables so long employed in schools, are particularly improper for small children, who should be taught by literal examples, before they can comprehend figures of rhetoric or draw inferences from remote hints. The fancy of converting inferior animals into "*teachers of children*," has been carried to ridiculous extravagance.

Thus he throws Æsop overboard. Here is a lesson to show what Mr. Jones could do in the way of " penning readings " : —

Keep clear of the boy that tells lies, for he is a bad boy.

O how I like to read my book, and be a good child, and mind what my pa and ma tell me !

Let the best child in school have a good ripe red peach, and five blue plums, and ten grapes, and a nice new book.

> Pinks smell sweet.
> Good girls are neat.
> A leech sucks blood.
> Ducks play in mud.

The great feature of the speller is the " Story of Jack Halyard," which fills thirty closely printed pages. Jack lived on a New Jersey farm. He was nine years of age, and had an older brother Charles and two younger sisters Mary and Betsey. His father was " very honest," and his mother —

was a woman of engaging manners, and unblemished character.   Jack's teacher, Mr. Clement, was very fond of him,
and used to call him little General Washington, because he
acted with so much honor and manliness.   Jack scorned
the vile mischief that low bred fellows sometimes practice,
and which they seem to think very cunning.

If he saw a silly fellow skulk behind a bench, or behind
another boy, to do some sly trick, while the teacher was
looking the other way, he would say, when they went out,
that bad scholars took more pains to be dunces than would
be needed to become men of talents.

Jack's little sisters were charming girls, very fond of
learning; and, when he came home, he would find pretty
stories for Mary to read, and teach Betsey in her a b abs.
He always treated his mother and sisters with great attention, and was very polite to other ladies of his acquaintance.

The story goes on to say that "Jack's conduct
began to attract notice in the town where he lived."
Major Wilson, "a gentleman of distinction," whose
house was about four miles distant from Mr. Halyard's, had a ten-year-old son, named Peter, "and
Peter was inclined to be idle and childish."   When
other boys were sliding and skating, Peter would sit
moping indoors.   One day the lads were asking
among themselves where Peter was, and Solomon
Belmot said, "Oh, he is sitting in the corner to keep
the cat from eating the tongs.   That is all he is good
for; the ninny is too lazy even to play."

Major Wilson was mortified, at having such a shameful
lubber of a son.   He thought of Jack Halyard, and concluded the best thing he could do, would be to get so smart
a boy to come and live a while with his son.

Jack's father agreed, and during the five weeks Jack stayed, "Peter was so altered, he hardly appeared to be the same boy." Among other things Jack cured his companion of timidity.   It iş told that —

One day as they were in a pasture together, Peter was scared almost to death, at the sight of a rattle snake.   He ran and screamed, as if the terrible creature was going to swallow him alive; but Jack like a hero, without being at all afraid, got a good stick and killed the snake.   "These animals," said Jack, "are like tattling, mischief making people : they are very poison; but dangerous only when they creep in secret, and bite before they are seen."

Jack talked much and very sensible with Peter, and Major Wilson was so much pleased with the change in his son, that he said Jack Halyard was worth five times his weight in gold, and he made him a present of a likely colt. "My good little friend," said the major to Jack, and he almost shed tears while he said it, "the great happiness of parents is in seeing their children do well.   If Peter should ever make an honorable man, it will be in part owing to what you have done for him.   Take this colt.   I hope, my dear fellow, you may live to ride him to congress."

Jack led him home and felt as rich as King Cre-sus. The colt was all over as black as a mink; but the hired man was a queer fellow, and he named this black colt *Snow-ball*.

The best people in this world are not perfect; and Jack, though so excellent a boy, committed some great errors. The first disgraceful thing he did, was when he was about five years old.   He got to a bottle of rum, very slily, and tasted a little; at first it made his mouth smart, and his nose tingle.   He soon got over this, and thought it would be a pretty notion to take another dram : but he found that this was very poor business.   Several children have killed themselves by drinking ardent spirits in this way.   Jack

was not dead drunk, but tipsey.   He staggered off like a
crazy fellow, nearly half a mile from the house; said some
most ridiculous, vulgar, silly things; and was saucy to an
old man.   He even abused his mother after he had been

**The Smart Boy; leading home his
Black Colt Snowball.**

From Jones's *Analytical Spelling-book*, 1823.

carried sick, to the house, and put on the truckle bed; but
at last he grew stupid and went to sleep.

Mr. Halyard, the next day, called his tippling son, and
asked him what he had been about.   Jack was still weak,
and so much ashamed, that he hardly dared to look his

father in the face. He clasped his arm around his pa's leg, and hung down his head. But though this little boy had done wrong he despised a falsehood. He told the facts as nigh as he could remember, without any quibbling. Jack's father was so glad to find him honest in owning his fault that he did not say a harsh word.

Jack had turns of the colic, especially, if he eat unripe fruit; but he bore these things like a young philosopher, and felt above the silly whining, that is sometimes heard among children. The whooping cough, he passed lightly through, and considered it hardly worth minding; but he found the measles much more serious, and at one time rather forgetting himself was somewhat peevish.

The narrative continues to tell of Jack's cleverness and the increasing honors he won through five chapters. "But there is no lasting happiness here below," it says, and the final pages record that Mr. Halyard had his best horse stolen and that he was to an expense of "above sixty dollars in chacing the thief, and getting back the horse." Soon afterward a flood drowned five of his cattle and a number of his sheep, his crops were much damaged, and he himself was "taken extremely sick with a bilious fever" and died. His dying precepts fittingly close the story.

One would fancy there could not be another youth with the perfections of Jack Halyard; yet that this impression is a mistake is shown by the tale below, which is also taken from Jones's speller.

THE LITTLE SAWYER, FRANK LUCAS.

Mrs. Corbon kept a village school in the state of New-York. She had a noble mind and was a friend to all good

children.   One cold morning in the winter, a small boy
came along, with a saw on his arm, and wanted this lady to
hire him to saw wood.   She said, one of her neighbors
would like to saw the wood and she did not wish to hire
any body. else.   " O dear," said the boy, "what shall I do ?
My father is blind, mother is sick, and I left my sister crying at home, for fear poor ma will die.   I take care of them,
as well as I can, but they have nothing to eat."   Mrs.
Corbon had never seen this lad before; but she perceived
he was a boy of uncommon goodness.   He shivered very
much with the cold; for he was but thinly drest, and his
ear locks were white with frost.   The lady asked him to
come in and warm himself.   Are you not hungry, said
Mrs. Corbon?   Not much ma'am.   I had some potatoe
for dinner yesterday.   Did you not have supper last night?
No ma'am.   Nor breakfast, this morning?   " Not yet :
but no matter : I shall get some by and by.   If I try to do
well, God will protect me : for so my precious mother says.
I believe she is the best woman in the world.   If I did not
think she was, I would not say so."   " You are a brave
lad," said the lady.   " I will be your friend, if you have
not another on earth ; "   and the tears sparkled in her eyes
as she gave him a biscuit with a piece of meat, on a small
plate.   Thank you, ma'am, said Frank; if you please, I
will keep them to carry home.   Don't you think, ma'am,
that any body will hire me to saw wood ?   Yes, my dear
little fellow, she answered, I will give you money to saw
mine.   He thanked her again, and ran to the wood pile to
begin his work.   The lady put on her cloak and went out
among her neighbors.   She told them Frank was one of the
best boys she had ever seen, and hoped they would do something to help the little fellow provide for the family.   So
they came to her house, where he was, and one gave him
a six cent piece, another a shilling, and a third twenty-five
cents, till they made up nearly three dollars.   They pre-

sented him a loaf of bread, part of a cheese, some meat and cake, a jug of milk, and some apples; with a snug basket to put them all in: so that he had as much as he could carry.   He told them he was very much obliged; but he chose to work and pay for what he had if they would

The Little Sawyer.
From Jones's *Analytical Spelling Book.*

let him.   They said he might see to that another time. We are going, said Mrs. Corbon, to send the things to your mother.   Frank hurried back, tugging his load, and the whole family cried for joy.   Bless your dear heart, said his poor blind father; come here and let me get hold of you.

My dear wife, a blessing has come upon us all for the sake of our dutiful child.   He is one of nature's noblemen. The good man raised his hands in prayer, and thanked the Creator of the world for giving him so hopeful a son.

It is thirty years since this affair happened, and the same Frank Lucas is now a judge, and one of the first men in the county where he lives.   His father is at rest.   Twenty summers, the bell-flower has bloomed, on his peaceful grave. His mother has grown very old and feeble.   She still lives with her son.   Judge Lucas is married to a charming lady, and has five children.   They go to school ; and their father tells them they must love God ; honor their parents and teachers, and be kind to all ; and that the way for a poor little boy to become a great and happy man, is, to be honest, industrious and good.

A poem from Picket's *Juvenile Spelling-book*, New York, 1823.

The Lamb.

A tear bedews my Delia's eye,
To think yon playful lamb must die :
From crystal spring and flow'ry mead
Must in his prime of life recede ;
Erewhile in sportive circle, round
She saw him wheel, and frisk and bound ;
From rock to rock pursue his way,
And on the fearful margin play.
She tells with what delight he stood
To trace his features in the flood ;
Then skipp'd aloof with quaint amaze ;
And then drew near again to gaze.
She tells me how with eager speed
He flew to hear my vocal reed ;

And how with critic face profound,
And steadfast ear, devour'd the sound.
His every frolic light as air,
Deserves the gentle Delia's care;
And tears bedew my Delia's eye,
To think yon playful lamb must die.

The Danger of Temptation.

THE silly fish, while playing in the brook,
Hath gorg'd and swallow'd the destructive hook;
In vain he flounces on the quiv'ring hair,
Drawn panting forth to breathe the upper air;
Caught by his folly in the glitt'ring bait,
He meets his ruin and submits to fate.

Moral.

Avoid base bribes : the tempting lure display'd,
If once you seize, you perish self-betray'd.
Be slow to take when strangers haste to give,
Lest of your ruin you the price receive.

A Poetical Fable.

From Picket's *Juvenile Spelling-book*, 1823.

Owl.

Owls eat mice, and live in the woods.

A Fragment from *The New York Spelling-book*, 1823.

Bolles's Spelling-book, New London, 1831, is given an odd individuality by the fact that "each page is embellished by select proverbs and maxims." These bits of wisdom are printed in small type on the borders of the pages, one at the top, one at the bottom, and one on each side. There is a comparatively large amount of other reading matter, and frequent illustrations. The longest story in the book is about —

ALMIRA AND JANE.

Almira was a very thoughtful girl; she took delight in viewing the beauties of nature; and for this purpose, often took a walk near the close of the day.

On her return, one evening she was accosted by Jane, who, though younger than herself, was always pleased with Almira's company, and requested the pleasure of walking with her the next day.

Jane informed her mother of what had passed; and made request, that she and her little brother, might join Almira in her ramble.

Her Mamma was very willing, and said, as she was about to go; Do not forget, my child that it is God, who permits you to enjoy so many pleasures.

By this time Almira had arrived and Jane and George were ready to go with her.

Almira and Jane soon began to converse, and little George listened with attention.

How pleasant it is, said Jane, to see the earth decked so

gaily; the grass so fresh and green, and do see the little lambs yonder!

Al. O yes; emblems of innocence; how sweetly they play; the musick of the birds also affords me much pleasure. Indeed I sometimes rise very early to hear them; but I do not say right, I rise because their sweet notes seem to say; Awake, and give thanks too. The same God that made them, and teaches them to sing, made us, and takes care of us.

Ja. And bestows on us many blessings which they never knew.

Geo. But how can you say so; sister? I think the birds are very happy, and sometimes wish, that, like them, I could skip from bough to bough.

Ja. Why, George, they know very little; they were never taught to read, as we have been.

Al. Nor did they ever hear of heaven; but we, if we love the Lord, and obey him, may hope to be happy here, and happy in the world to come.

Geo. Now I see the folly of my wishes; I think I shall never, again, desire to be a bird; I would much rather learn to read, and become wise.

Ja. Have we not yet arrived at the extent of your walk; Almira?

Al. Yes; on the banks of this little rivulet I admire to sit among the shrubs, or under the shade of some of the willows.

Ja. George, I believe, is delighted by looking into the the brook; what do you see, George?

Geo. Some frogs, and a great many little fishes. But they are so shy, and nimble, that, before I can touch them they dart away.

As they walked along the side of the stream Jane began to be very pensive:

I have been thinking, said she, that the God who made,

and takes care of all these things, must be very great, and very good.

Al. He is so, indeed; he is worthy of all our praise.

Ja. If he makes this earth so pleasant, what must heaven be?

Al. What does the word of God say? Eye hath not seen; neither has it entered into the heart of man, to conceive the glory, that shall be revealed in that world. O may we meet in heaven; we shall then be happy indeed.

The evening drew on, and they returned home; little George being so well pleased, that he related the whole story to his papa.

The several lessons following the above are philosophies on life and nature that in manner of expression are reminiscent of the Psalms in the Bible. I quote one of them: —

They that go down to the sea in ships, that do business in the great waters; these see the work of the Lord, and his wonders in the deep.

For he commandeth, and raiseth the stormy wind, which lifteth up the waves thereof.

They mount up to the heaven; they go down again to the depths; their soul is melted because of trouble.

They reel to and fro, and stagger like a drunken man, and are at their wits' end.

Then they cry unto the Lord and he bringeth them out of their distress.

He maketh the storm a calm, so that the waves are still.

Then are they glad because they be quiet: so he bringeth them to their desired haven.

Here is a sample of the verse contained in the book: —

THE ORPHAN.

My father and mother are dead,
　No friend or relation I have;
And now the cold earth is their bed,
　And daisies grow over their grave.

I cast my eyes into the tomb
　The sight made me bitterly cry;
I said, and is this the dark room,
　Where my father and mother must lie?

I cast my eyes round me again,
　In hopes some protector to see;
Alas! but the search was in vain,
　For none had compassion on me.

I cast my eyes up to the sky,
　I groan'd, though I said not a word;
Yet God was not deaf to my cry;
　The friend of the fatherless heard.

O yes — and he graciously smil'd
　And bid me on him to depend;
He whisper'd — " Fear not, little child,
　For I am thy father and friend."

One lesson of an unusual sort was three pages
of information on various subjects under the title
"Common Things," and I reprint several paragraphs.

The rainbow is formed by the reflection and decomposi-
tion of the sun's rays on the drops of falling water.

Electricity is a subtle fluid which pervades most bodies
and is capable by certain operations, of being accumulated
in certain substances to a greater or less degree.

Ignis Fatuus is a light supposed to be of a phosphorick nature, frequently seen in mines, marshy places, and stagnant water; from its resemblance to a candle in a lantern it has been vulgarly called, Jack with a lantern, or Will with a wisp.   People have sometimes been misled by following these lights.

Man and Horse.   **Mad Bull.**

A Horse drinking.   **Boy in danger.**

Children should be careful not to provoke a bull, or get over into the field where one is.   Alas! for that little boy that is running with all his might: see his hat flying behind him, and the mad bull close at his heels.

Part of a Page.
From *The New York Spelling-book.*

The two short reading lessons below are from *The Young Tyro's Instructer,* "comprising all that is really useful in a spelling-book to instruct a child in his native tongue."   New York, 1834.

A pig can eat a fig.
A cat can eat a rat.
A fly sat on a pie.
A bee sat on a pea.

Boys must learn to spell, read, and write,
And try to learn with all their might;
Then they will be wise, good, and great,
And, in due time, may serve the state.

No. 5.

  Ram and Dam.

Has the dam a lamb?
What is a dam?
What is a lamb?
Ann can catch the
lamb by the ham.

cram	cramp
dram	damp
ham	camp
sham	scamp
slam	lambs

No. 6.

 **Nag and Bags.**

A nag and some bags.
Jack holds the nag.
It is a black nag.
See the rags on Jack's
back.

snag	hag
bag	shag
brag	Jack
rag	tack
rag-ged	tact
cags	act

A Page.
From Parsons's *Analytical Spelling Book*, 1836.

Parsons's *Analytical Spelling Book*, Portland, Maine,
1836, was decidedly more attractive in its makeup

Q

than most books of the period.   It had a good deal
of variety and sparkle, and the author in enumer-
ating its virtues in his preface says that with it
" Parents who have little skill in teaching can learn
their children to read, where there are no schools,
and adults with little assistance can learn by themselves."   He does not begin the lessons with the
alphabet as was usual in books of this sort.   Instead,
he requires the pupils " to learn letters only to make
out definite words."   The lessons start with a picture of a rat, and the author directs the teacher to
" gather all the a, b, c, and a, b, ab scholars round
him, and ask them, ' What is the first picture ? '
' A rat,' say they.   ' Well, here is his name under
him.   You are now to learn to read his name.' "
Then they were drilled to recognize the three letters
that formed the word.

On looking along through the book it is noticeable that the statements and questions in the lessons

A Mule.

are often trivial and irrelevant, and
the happy-go-lucky way in which
several subjects are introduced and
mixed up in the same lesson must
have proved rather confusing to the
youthful mind.   For instance, this
picture of a melancholy-looking mule
is accompanied by the remarks that —

Mules are good to pull.
Mules are mute.
They make no noise.
Use the mule well.

A-buse no man.
Give to all their due.

At the end it is uncertain whether the mule is a man, or the man mentioned is a mule.

Of the next picture we are told "The pail has a wire bail," though it is perfectly plain that the bail is wooden.

A Pail.

Here are several consecutive sentences under a picture of a hen. They seem to have some occult but not easily perceived connection.

Hens lay eggs
Sev-en eggs to a keg
Sev-en hens to a keg
Sev-en eggs to a hen

A Girl.

On page 9 is a picture of a girl with what looks like a flower in her hand ; yet the text reads, " Ann and her fan," and it also asks, " Has Ann an ap-ple ? " The same picture reappears on page 17 ; but meanwhile the girl has changed her name and the text says, " Let Jane tell her tale," and states that " Jane has a cape on her neck."

Then here is a picture from a little farther along in the book with the following sentences beneath it :

A toad in the grass.
Toads can hop far.
See his long hind legs.

Can he swell as large as a goat ?
How many toads would load a cart ?
Grass is mown with a scythe when it is grown.
Pa groans with a pain in his arm.

Is it not perfectly plain that the " toad " in the

A Toad.
From Parsons's *Analytical Spelling Book*.

picture is a frog? What is the sense of asking if he can swell as large as a goat, or how many would fill a cart?—as if toads were in the habit of swelling monstrously and of being loaded into carts ; and what is the matter with Pa? Has he been mowing, or has he been loading toads, or what does cause his pain ?

Turn a few more pages and we find a lesson that sounds as if it were intended for humor. I give several extracts : —

A smith can **steel** an axe by welding a strip of steel on the edge. The Bible says, " Thou shalt not **steal**."
You could be kind if you **would**.
Chairs are made of **wood**.
A dog will **scent** a fox.
James is **sent** away for laughing.
Girls **vail** their faces in the sun.
Brooks run through **vales**.
Hear the horse **neigh**.
One who lives near, is a **neigh**-bor.
Boys **need** dinner ; girls **knead** dough.

The book conveys information about punctuation as follows : —

You see a little round dot, once in a while as you read. It means that you should let your voice fall, as if you were done read-ing, and stop while you could say, one, two, three, four. Thus : —

"Lot is dead.   One two three four.   He died last night. One two three four.   His mother, one his old mother is sick." This little dot is called a pe-ri-od.

Large,   larger,   largest.

The top is large.   The bell is larger.   The ox is largest.

A Comparison.

From Parsons's *Analytical Spelling Book.*

The use of emphasis is explained with similar lucidity.

Suppose you wished to call your brother at a distance, and he should not hear you at first would you not repeat it in this way : —

JOSEPH !!!

JOSEPH !!

Joseph !

growing louder every time ?   That is called raising the key.

Again, suppose you wished to ask your pa, if you may go a fishing with Jacob; and you are afraid he does not hear. You would ask this way : —

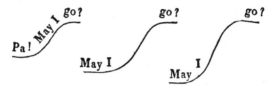

Occasionally at the end of a lesson which has not quite filled out the page the space is utilized for bits of advice and wisdom such as —

See that haggard, bloated, red-faced, hopeless looking drunkard, holding upon the fence! He began by drinking a *little*, and never meant to take too much. If you would not be a drunkard, never taste any thing that can make drunk.

"Swear not at all." It is vulgar — it is degrading — it is profane to swear.

114   KEEP YOUR TEETH SOUND.

anatomy	renovate	┌──────┐
anatomist	renovating	│ **233** │
anatomical	renovated	└──────┘
drug	invigorate	accuse
druggist	invigorated	accusing
apothecary	animate	accused
		accusation

Part of a Page.
From *Spelling and Thinking*, 1841.
At the top of each page was a maxim.

One of the most peculiar of the old spellers was *Exercises in Orthography*, a Providence publication dated 1826. The title-page says that the book is "designed to assist young persons to spell with accuracy and effect," though from the look of the lessons you would think the whole thing was contrived for a joke. The spelling is in fact as bad as ingenuity can make it, and yet the volume is intended seriously and this crazy spelling is supposed to stimulate the pupil's interest. The preface advises that "The scholar should always be provided with a dictionary, and in order to rectify the false orthography the teacher should require him to copy with care each paragraph of this work; it is then presumed very considerable advantage will be found in the use of this compilation." Below are characteristic extracts: —

Nolledge is the best foundashun ov happines. Its kultevashun in yuth promotes vertshu, bi kreating habits ov menttal disseplin; and bi inkulkating a sense ov morral oblegashun.

Menny nashuns liv nakid in kavurns undur ground, purform no labur, and depend for thare subsistens on the spontaneus produkts ov the erth, and on the flesh ov animals, witsh tha destroy bi simpel strattajems.

The arts ov savvidje life inklude the arts ov swimming, hunting, taking ame with missil weppons, and prokuring fire.

The art ov swimming depends furst in keeping the arms and hands undur watur; in protruding only the fase and part ov the hed out ov the water; and then uzing sutsh akshun, as wil derekt the boddy in enny partikulur korse.

Hunting is performed bi most savvidge nashuns on fut, and with menny ov them the prinsepal weppon is the klub. Therefore the swiftest and strongest uzhualy bekum tsheefs.

In taking ame with missel weppons, the presizhun witsh savvidje nashuns have attaned is wondurful.   In throing a stone, tha seldum mis the smalest mark; tha transfiks fish in the watur; nok down burds on the wing; and strike evury enemy with unerring egzaktnes.

Among savvidjes, the uzhual mode ov produsing fire is bi the rapid frikshun ov too peeses ov wood til tha produse flames.   Having no mettels, tha do not pozzes the simpel methud ov kommunikating a spark to tinder, bi the violent kollizhun ov flint and steal.

In 1843 a similarly strange educational scheme was perpetrated under the title *Companion to Spelling-books*.   A single specimen of the more than three hundred lessons in the book will suffice.

> I have seen thy wonderous mite,
> Thro' the shaddows of the night;
> Thou who slumb'rest not nor sleapest,
> Blessed are they Thou kindly keepest!
> Thine the flaming sphear of light,
> Thine the darkness of the night,
> Thine are all the gemms of ev'n
> God of angels!   God of Heav'n!
> God of life, that fade shall never!
> Glory to thy name fore ever!

Such a medley of mistakes would soon confuse even a good speller, and the plan is worse than use-less unless one wants to acquire the orthography of a Josh Billings or an Artemus Ward.

IX

THE first period of American school-book authorship was characterized by erratic efforts and random shots in many directions. It did not become the general custom to put forth books in nicely graded series until well toward the middle of the nineteenth century, and in consequence many isolated spellers, primers, and readers were published and used for a brief period within a limited area. Readers of any sort for beginners were very few previous to 1825. So far as I am aware the first was *The Franklin Primer*, published in 1802, "containing a new and ufeful felection of Moral Leffons adorned with a great variety of elegant cuts calculated to ftrike a lafting impreffion on the Tender Minds of Children." The elegant cuts were a frontispiece portrait of Benjamin Franklin and about a dozen text illustrations of Bible scenes.

The book in size and general appearance had very much the look of a *New England Primer*. Indeed, the introduction says it was intended "as a fubftitute for the old Primer which has of late become almoft obfolete." The most important portions of the volume were "a variety of tables, moral leffons and fentences, a concife hiftory of the World,

appropriate Hymns, and Dr. Watts, and the Af-
fembly of Divines' Catechifms." The history of
the world was entirely Biblical, and began with the

THE FRANKLIN PRIMER.

MOSES killing the Egyptian.

From *The Franklin Primer*, 1802.

creation and ended with Christ's resurrection.   For
an example of the miscellany in the book I quote
a poem entitled : —

Leſſons in Verſe.

WHEN the Sun doth riſe you muſt go up each day,
  And fall on your knees, and to God humbly pray :
Then kneel to your parents, their bleſſing implore,
And when you have money, give ſome to the poor.
Your hands and your face, in the next place waſh fair,
And bruſh your apparel and comb out your hair.

Then wiſh a good morning to all in your view,
And bow to your parents, and bid them adieu ;
Salute every perſon as to ſchool you go ;
When at ſchool, to your maſter due reverence ſhow.
And if you can't read, pray endeavour to ſpell,
For by frequently ſpelling you'll learn to read well.

Shun all idle boys, and the wicked and rude ;
And pray, only play with thoſe boys who are good.
To church you muſt every Sunday repair,
And behave yourſelf decently while you are there.
At the cloſe of the day, ere you go to your reſt,
Kneel again to your parents, and be again bleſt :
And to the Almighty again humbly pray,
That he may preſerve you by night and by day.

The next book of this class was *The Child's Instructor*, Philadelphia, 1808. A peculiar typographical feature is the use of the long *s* in some
parts of the book, and the short *s* in others. Most
printers had discarded the former altogether by this
time. In Chapter I are the alphabet, some columns
of three and four letter words, and a number of short
sentences, of which the first is —

> A bird that can sing, and will
> not sing, must be made to sing.

Chapter II starts thus : —

1. Now George, you know all the letters.
    Now you must learn to spell and read.
    A good boy will sit and mind his books.
2. Knife, fork, spoon, plate, dish, cup, bowl, mug, jug,
pot, pan, tub, chair, ta-ble, bed, box, fire, wood, shov-el,
tongs, bel-lows.
3. What is your name?   My name is George.   How
old are you?   Four years old.   Do you go to school?
Yes, sir.   Can you spell?   Yes, sir, a little.
4. Bread, but-ter, cheese, meat, pud-ding, pye, cake,
beef, pork, veal, soup, salt, pep-per, su-gar, ho-ney, jel-ly,
car-rot.

This alternation of spelling and reading paragraphs
is soon abandoned, and the spelling words are confined to a paragraph at the end of each lesson.
Perhaps the most noticeable thing in the lessons is
the constant reiteration of the idea that it is profitable both spiritually and materially to be good.

All dutiful children who do as they're bid,
Shall be lov'd, and applauded, and never be chid ;
And their friends, and their fame, and their wealth fhall
    increafe,
Till they're crown'd with the bleffings of plenty and peace.

Frank is a good boy; he loves his school, and learns to
read.   He can spell hard words and is head of the class.
Frank shall have a new hat, and new shoes, and go to the
fair.

Good boys and girls go to church.   Did you go to

church? Billy went to church, and so did Betsey. The church is the house of God; and God loves little children when they go to church.

When you go to church you must sit still, and hear what the preacher tells you; he tells you to be good children and love your parents, and then God will bless you.

Do you know who makes it rain? I will tell you: God makes it rain. Do you see that dark cloud rising in the west? That cloud will bring thunder and lightning and rain. You need not be afraid; God makes it thunder; and he will not let it hurt you if you are good.

The following are some of the longer lessons in the latter part of the book. The unmitigated blackness of the lad's character portrayed in the first of these is quite impressive.

Description of a BAD BOY.

A bad Boy is undutiful to his father and mother, difobedient and ftubborn to his mafter, and ill-natured to all his play-fellows. He hates his book, and takes no pleafure in improving himfelf in any thing. He is fleepy and flothful in the morning, too idle to clean himfelf, and too wicked to fay his prayers.

He is always in mifchief, and when he has done a fault, will tell twenty lies in hopes to clear himself. He hates that any body fhould give him good advice, and when they are out of fight, will laugh at them. He fwears and wrangles, and quarrels with his companions, and is always in fome difpute or other.

He will fteal whatfoever comes in his way; and if he is

not catched, thinks it no crime, not confidering that God fees whatfoever he does.   He is frequently out of humour, and fullen and obftinate, fo that he will neither do what he is bid, nor anfwer any queftion that is afked him.

In fhort, he neglects every thing that he fhould learn, and minds nothing but play and mifchief; by which means he becomes as he grows up a confirmed blockhead, incapable of any thing but wickednefs or folly, defpifed by all men of fenfe and virtue, and generally dies a beggar.

He that giveth to the poor, lendeth to the Lord.

There was a poor man who was charitable to excefs; for he gave away all that he had to relieve the neceffities of others; chufing rather to throw himfelf upon Providence, than to deny an alms to any one who afked him, fo long as he had any thing to beftow.

Being at length, by his conftant liberalities, reduced to a very indigent condition, he was forced to betake himfelf to digging for a livelihood.   Yet notwithftanding he gained his own bread by hard labour, he ceafed not to fhew his wonted kindneffes to the poor; giving them whatever he could poffibly fpare from his own neceffities.

One day as he was digging in the field, he found feveral earthen pots of gold, fuppofed to be buried there in the time of the wars.   The good man carried this huge treasure home to his houfe, with all imaginable privacy.

And having diftributed the greateft part of it in charity, he was going with the laft referve to the houfe of a diftreffed widow, to whom he gave a fufficient fum to relieve her wants, being all he had left: When as he was returning home he found a jewel in the high-way, which being fold, yielded him ten thoufand crowns.

This was a noble bank for new liberalities, and a convincing argument, that there was fomething more than mere

chance which thus ſtrangely recruited his purſe; that it
might not lack ſomething to give to the poor.

> Bleſt is the man whoſe bowels move,
> And melt with pity to the poor;
> Whoſe ſoul with ſympathizing love,
> Feels what his fellow ſaints endure.
> His heart contrives for their relief,
> More good than his own hands can do:
> He in the time of general grief,
> Shall find the Lord hath bowels too.

A book very like the one I have been describing, both in title and text, was the *Child's Instructer
and Moral Primer*, published at Portland, Maine,
in 1822. The stories in it have to do mostly
with such children as Timothy Trusty, who "is
very desirous to learn"; Patty Primp, whose
notion is that "to be a lady one must be idle, careless, proud, scorn inferiors, calumniate the absent,
read novels, play at cards, and excel in fine dress";
John Pugg, whose "face and hands you would
think were not washed once in a fortnight"; and
Tom Nummy, who "hates his book as bad as the
rod." Some of the other suggestively named characters are Tim Delicate, Charles Mindful, Caroline
Modesty, Susy Pertinence, Cynthia Spindle, and
Jack Fisty-Cuff. Except for Cynthia, you know
what to expect of each without further details.

To indicate how scarce elementary readers were
in the first quarter of the nineteenth century, I
quote from the preface to Leavitt's *Easy Lessons in
Reading*, Keene, New Hampshire, 1823: —

The compiler has been excited to the present under-
taking by representations that there is no reading book to
be found at the bookstores, suitable for young children, to
be used intermediately, between the Spelling-Book and the

Eager Students.

A title-page vignette in Leavitt's *Easy Lessons*, 1847.

English or American Reader.
The Testament is much
used for this purpose ; and,
on many accounts, it is admirably adapted for a reading book in schools.   But it
is respectfully submitted to
the experience of judicious
teachers, whether the pe-
culiar structure of scripture
language is not calculated
to create a tone?   I am persuaded it would be better to
place a book in the hands of learners, written in a more
familiar style.   Such a work, I flatter myself, will be found
in the following pages.   The selections contain many
salutary precepts and instructive examples, for a life of
piety and morality, of activity and usefulness.

Mr. Leavitt later supplemented his *Easy Lessons*
with a Second Part.   In this the most noteworthy
portion was a series of sentences to illustrate the
sounds of the letters.   The chaotic paragraphs
which follow are fair samples : —

The baboon blabbed and blubbered, dabbled in ribbons,
gabbled in gibberish, played hob-nob with a robin, brow-
beat the tabby, made a hubbub for the rabble, bribed a na-
bob, and barbarously bamboozled a booby.

Our daddy did a deed, at dawn of day, that doubled the
depredations of the dogged ducks and drakes, deceived the
doubting dunce, addled the dandy paddy, and drove the sad-
dled and bridled dog down the downward road.

A giddy, giggling girl gave a noggin of gruel to a big beggar with green glass goggles, going out of a greasy groggery.

Nathan Noonan knows his nose; no man knows I know he knows his nose; his nose knows he knows his nose.

An alliteration with a somewhat different purpose is the one below. It was designed as an exercise to teach the pupils to "avoid the vulgar error of clipping off the final g."

I am thinking of going to singing meeting, this evening, in hope of hearing the bells ringing, and of seeing ranks of smiling, loving, languishing lasses.

Then here is a group of sentences that seem to have suffered an earthquake shock, but they simply show the appropriate use of the rising and falling inflection.

Did you act properly, or improperly?
Did he ride to school, or did he walk?
Did you run away, or did you run home?
That remedy is worse than the disease.

Sentences illustrating Inflection.
From Leavitt's *Easy Lessons*, 1847.

A poem from *The Fourth Class Book*, Brookfield, Massachusetts, 1827.

LITTLE CHARLES

Well, Charles is highly pleased to day,
I gave him leave to go and play

R

Upon the green, with bat and ball ;
And when he heard his playmates call,
Away he sprung across the plain,
To join the little merry train,
But here he comes — why, what means this ?
I wonder what has gone amiss, —
Why, Charles, how came you back so soon ?
I gave you leave to stay till noon.

I know it, sir, and I intended
To play till every game was ended ;
But, to say truth, I could not bear
To hear those little fellows swear —
They cursed so bold and fearlessly
That the cold chills ran over me —
For I was seized with awful dread
That some of them would drop down dead —
And so I turned and came away,
For, Pa, I was afraid to stay !

An attractive little book published in 1830 was
The Clinton Primer.   It was named after De Witt
Clinton, whose portrait appeared on its paper cover.
Illustrations were used freely, and the body of the
book was made up of reading at the top of the pages,
spelling columns in the middle, and arithmetic at
the bottom.   I reprint some rather naïve fragments
from the earlier lessons, and two of the longer lessons
complete.

It is a mule.   I see a mule ; do you ?
He has a flute ; let him play on his flute.

Ripe pears are good for boys and girls, but it is a sin to
eat too many of them.   They often cause sickness.

Who does not love the robin?   He sings a most lovely note.

The raven is not a fine bird nor a very good bird; he has been known to pull up corn.

THE HORSE RACE

Who loves a horse race?   Are not too many fond of it?   Does it not lead to many evils, and to frequent ruin? Never go to a horse race.   Mr. Mix had one child, whom he called Irene; he had also a good farm, and some money. He went to the races with his child, dressed in black crape for the loss of her mother.   Here Mr. Mix drank freely, and bet largely, and lost all he was worth.   At night he went home a beggar; took a dose of brandy, and died before morning, leaving his child a pennyless orphan. Never go to a horse race.

THE COACH AND TWO.

Who is she that is growing up to the good fortune of riding in a coach and two?   She is the girl who rises with the rising day; — whose hands and face are made clean; — whose hair is cleared of snarly locks, and neatly rolled in papers; and whose clothes are clean and whole though never gay.   She who loves

The Coach and Two.
From *The Clinton Primer*, 1830.

her book, her school, the truth, and her parents, and also the path of peace and virtue.   I now see her through the window of the carriage, and I hear her say: —

"What though I ride in a coach and pair,
    And in dress and food like a princess fare;
I'll not be proud like the haughty Moor,
    Nor stop my ear at the cry of the poor."

The next selection is from Worcester's *A Second Book for Reading and Spelling*, Boston, 1830. It is a story wherein merit is so promptly rewarded as to take one's breath away.

MR. WOOD AND CHARLES BELL.
From Worcester's *Second Book*, 1830.

One day, when Mr. Wood took a walk to the end of the town, he saw Charles Bell, who lives with his Aunt Jane, hard at work in his aunt's garden.

"I think you are warm, Charles," said Mr. Wood.

Charles held up his head, and made a bow, and. said — "Yes, sir; my aunt says, corn is so scarce, and bread so dear, that I must work, or else she cannot keep me."

"You seem to be a nice boy," said Mr. Wood; "will you come and live with me? I will give you as much bread as you want, and will not make you work so hard."

But Charles thought his aunt needed him. So Mr. Wood told Charles to call at his house and he would give him a dollar and some good books, and he also offered to send Charles to school. Charles replied that he would refer the matter to his aunt. She was agreeably disposed, and he called on Mr. Wood and got the books. No doubt he got the dollar also, though that is not mentioned. Better still, his benefactor arranged to have him go to school, and " He was so good a boy and learned so fast that Mr. Wood sent him to college."

THOU SHALT NOT STEAL.
From Worcester's *Second Book.*

Here is pictured a youth of another sort. The text says : —

See that little boy creeping softly along on tiptoe towards his mother's tea-table. See him lift the cover of the sugar-pot and as quickly as possible, put one piece in his mouth, and another in his pocket.

His name is William Morton.   His kind mother is sitting at the fire place mending his clothes, with his little baby sister asleep on her lap.   She does not think that William is thus taking what is not his own.

William goes on from day to day, taking apples, and cakes, and sugar, without leave ; and what is worse, he tries hard to conceal it, and even tells lies about it.

Does William know that this is stealing ?   Does he remember that this is breaking the EIGHTH COMMANDMENT of the Lord his God.

THE SLEIGH-RIDE.
From Worcester's *Second Book.*

For a final selection from Worcester's book I give this letter which Lucy Turner, thirteen years old, wrote to her mother, who was spending a month in Boston at the home of Lucy's aunt, Mrs. White. It serves as a dreadful example to all children who, like Lucy, "never take any pains to learn to spell."

Mi deer Mama,

Wen yu cum bak, wee shal awl bee pleesed.   Evry wun seams dul becaus yu air gon.

Farther se*z* hee wonts yu too sta longe enuff too hav ay gude vissit ; butt ie no hee wil bee gladd whenn yure vissit iss ovur.

Jaims gose too skule and ie thinke hee behaivs wel. Saror stais att hom, and wurks withe mee. Wee awl injoy gude helth.

Doo rite mee ay lettur, and tel mee abowt Bosten, and ant Wite's foax, and hou soone wee ma expekt yu.

Yure verry luving childe,

Lucy Turner.

Now, only think how much grieved and ashamed her mother must have been, when she found that Lucy had spelled only her name and one word right.

Two Pages.

From Gallaudet's *The Child's Picture Defining Book*, 1830
Reduced one-half.

Gallaudet's *The Child's Picture Defining and Reading Book*, Hartford, 1830, had a half-page cut on

every left-hand page.   Its author was evidently a
man of much keener and more sympathetic pedagogic perception than most of the makers of school
books and the plan of the book was quite interesting.   The idea was to teach the meaning of words
through the " language of pictures," and each of the
engravings in the first part of the book is accompanied by a list of the most prominent objects in it
and with a few short, simple phrases.   The cuts are
repeated in the latter part of the book, but this time
the text that goes with each is a little story.

Here is an illustration from *The Progressive Reader
or Juvenile Monitor*, Concord, New Hampshire, 1830:

A Bird.

From *The Progressive Reader,*
1830.

We are told that the bird it de-
picts " sang from morning till
evening and was very handsome."   Caroline, the little girl
to whom the bird belonged,
" fed it with seeds and cooling
herbs and sugar, and refreshed
it daily with water from a clear
fountain."   But at length it
died.   " The little girl lamented
her beloved bird, and wept sore."
Then her mother bought another " handsomer than the
former, and as fair a songster."

" But Caroline wept still more," and her mother,
" amazed," asked the reason.   Caroline replied it
was because she had wronged the bird that died by
eating a piece of sugar herself that her mother had
given her for the bird.   The mother saw then why

Caroline had been so distressed. It was "the sacred voice of nature in the heart of her child."

"Ah!" said she, "what must be the feelings of an ungrateful child at the grave of its parents."

The longest narrative in the book was entitled —

The good Samaritan.
From *The Progressive Reader.*

CHARLES BRUCE TELLS HIS ADVENTURES.

When I was about twelve years old, an Indian by the name of Splitlog, came to my father's house in Boston. He was generally esteemed a good Indian, and he loved my father, because he once saved his life, when he was attacked by some sailors in the streets of Boston.

He asked my father to let me go home with him. He told me of excellent sport they had in shooting squirrels and deer where he lived; so I begged my father to let me go, and he at length consented.

Splitlog lived near Northampton, at the foot of a mountain called Mount Holyoke, just on the bank of Connecticut river.

There is a good road from Boston to Northampton now, and the stage travels it every day. But the road was bad when I went with Splitlog, and there were no stages in America then.

So Splitlog and I set out on foot. The second day we arrived at Worcester. It was then a very little town, and there were no such fine houses there as now.

The fourth day we arrived at Splitlog's house, which was a little wigwam at the foot of mount Holyoke.

In this little house we found Splitlog's wife and three children; two boys and a girl. Splitlog's wife roasted some bear's meat, and gave us some bread made of pounded corn, which formed our supper.

We sat on the floor, and took the meat in our fingers, for the Indians had no knives or forks. I then went to bed on some bear skins, and slept well.

Early in the morning, Splitlog called me from my sleep, and told me they were going into the woods a-shooting, and that I must go with them. I was soon ready and set out with Splitlog and his two sons.

It was a fine bright morning in October. The sun was shining on the top of mount Tom and mount Holyoke. We ascended Holyoke, through the woods.

At length we climbed a high rock, from which we could see the beautiful valley far below us, in the centre of which was the little town of Northampton.

"Do you see those houses?" said Splitlog to me. "When my grand-father was a boy, there was not a house where you now see so many. That valley, which now belongs to white men, then belonged to red men. But hark! I hear a squirrel chattering; we must go and find him. Whist!" said Splitlog, "and follow me."

We all followed accordingly, and soon discovered a fine grey squirrel sitting in the top of a walnut tree with a nut in his fore paws.

Splitlog beconed to his youngest son, who drew his bow, and discharged his arrow, which whistled over the back of the squirrel, but did not touch him.

Splitlogs eldest son immediately discharged his arrow, which struck the squirrel in the side, and brought him instantly to the ground.

After this adventure, we proceeded cautiously through the woods. We had not gone far, when Splitlog beckoned to us all to stop.

"Look yonder," said he to me, "on that high rock above us." I did so and saw a young deer, or fawn, standing upon the point of a rock, which hung over the valley.

Splitlog now selected a choice arrow, placed it on the bow, and sent it whizzing through the air. It struck the fawn directly through the heart.

The little animal sprang violently forward over the rock, and fell dead, many feet below, where Splitlog's sons soon found him. We now returned to Splitlog's house carrying the fawn with us.

This hunt was the chief event in Charles Bruce's visit and a few day, later he returned to Boston.

Among the engravings in the book is the one reproduced herewith. The text says: —

To give a better idea of the figure and appearance of the lion, I have procured this picture of a young lion; by which you will see that lions, when a few weeks old, are only as large as small dogs.

A Young Lion.

From *The Progressive Reader.*

The zebra picture is accompanied by the statement that "His appearance is very beautiful, and he is esteemed one of the handsomest of quadrupeds."

"A Handsome Quadruped."
From *The Progressive Reader*.

The French.
From *The Progressive Reader*.

Of the squirrel we are told "Its tail constitutes its greatest singularity, as well as its principal ornament. It is also not less useful than ornamental; for being sufficiently large and bushy to cover the whole body, it serves as an excellent defence against the inclemencies of the weather. It also greatly assists it in clinging and adhering to trees."

The most ambitious poem in the book is the one reprinted in part below : —

STORY OF AMERICA IN VERSE

Columbus was a sailor brave,
The first that crossed th' Atlantic wave.
In fourteen hundred and ninety-two,
He came far o'er the ocean blue,
Where ne'er a ship had sailed before,
And found a wild and savage shore,
Where naked men in forests prowled,
And bears and panthers roamed and howled.

At length, when years had passed away,
Some English came to Virginia ;
'Twas sixteen hundred seven ; be sure
You let this in your mind endure ;
For 'twas the first bold colony
Planted in North America ;
The first that laid the deep foundation,
On which has since been built a nation.
Well, here they raised a far-famed Town
On James' river, called Jamestown.
They struggled hard 'gainst many sorrows,
Sickness and want, and Indian arrows ;
But bold and strong at length they grew,
And were a brave and manly crew.

'Twas eight years after this, — I mean
The year sixteen hundred fifteen, —
Some Dutch, from Holland, settled pat on
An Island which they called Manhattan,
And straight they sat themselves to work,
And built the city of New-York.
Now let the laughing wags and jokers
Say that the Dutch are stupid smokers ;
We only tell, that, dull or witty,
They founded famous New-York city ;
The largest city in the west,
For trade and commerce quite the best.

A curious lesson found in *The Union Primer*,
1832, was this : —

A boy who was idle and wicked, saw an old man with
poor clothes on — he went up to him as he was in the
grave-yard, and said, " Father, you are in a very miserable
condition if there is not another world." " True, son,"

replied the old Christian, " but what is your condition if
there is ?   I have a plenty to keep me warm and dry, but I
fear you have not that which can keep your soul from
Hell."

A Depiction of Wickedness.
Printed above the Ten Commandments in *The Union Primer*, 1832.

The compiler of *The Child's Guide*, a popular and
in many ways admirable text-book, published at
Springfield, Massachusetts, in 1833, urges that the
pupils should read " very distinctly and slowly," and
he says, " When *I* used to go to school I found
these *lines* in my book : —

> Learn to speak *slow ;* all other graces
> Will follow in their proper places."

As an aid to clear comprehension and correct
enunciation the text is well peppered with words in
italics to indicate that such words are " emphatical."
On the next page is the frontispiece.   No wonder
" all the boys looked" when they discovered their

master had been carrying a prickly thing like that in his pocket. It seems the master had happened along that morning while a group of boys were pounding chestnuts out of some green burs they had knocked

" He put his hand into his pocket again, and took out the chestnut burr, and all the boys looked at it."

Frontispiece to *The Child's Guide*, 1833.

off a tree, and he heard them declaring that the chestnuts " ought to grow right out in the open air, like apples; and not have such vile prickly *skins* on them." He asked for one of the burs, and ap-

parently carried it in his pocket all day, for the text
says : —

That afternoon, when it was about time to dismiss the
school, the boys put away their books, and the master read
a few verses in the Bible and then offered a prayer, in which
he asked God to forgive all the sins any of them had committed that day, and to take care of them during the night.
After this he took his *handkerchief* out of his pocket, and
put his hand into his *pocket* again, and took out the chestnut *burr*, and all the boys *looked* at it.

Then the master, through questions and explanations, satisfied the scholars that prickly burs are the
only proper and safe covering for chestnuts.

In a lesson farther on, entitled "The Listener,"
are recounted the tribulations of Charlotte Walden,
who "had a constant desire to hear what everybody
was saying," and who if sent out of the room when
her father and mother did not wish her to hear
their conversation, stopped outside the door "with
her ear close to the key-hole."

One of her *curls* once got entangled in the *key*, and when
her father suddenly opened the door, she fell forward into
the room, and hurt her *nose* so that it *bled*.

When she knew that her mother had *visitors* in the parlor, or that her father had *gentlemen* there with him on *business*, she would quit her lessons or her playthings, and come
softly down stairs and listen at the door ; or would slip into
the garden and crouch down under the open *window*, that
she might hear what they were *saying*.

Once when she was stooping, half double, under the
parlor window, her father, not knowing that she was *there*,

and finding that a fly had got into the glass of beer that he was going to drink, went to throw out the *beer*, and emptied the tumbler on Charlotte's *head*.

But neither these nor other mishaps reformed her until one evening she secreted herself at the top of the cellar stairs to listen to the servants talking in the kitchen. She fell asleep, and about midnight tumbled off the stairs on to a heap of coal. Her screams awakened the household, she was taken to her room, and sickness and repentance and never-did-so-any-more followed as a matter of course.

" Dear uncle, I cry almost all day long."
From *The Child's Guide.*

This shows the habit of the times in presenting right and wrong to the youthful mind. There was always the same sharp contrast; evil suffered prompt and severe punishment, and good was as promptly and decisively rewarded, while reforms were astonishingly sudden and complete. Actual experience

s

must have been sorely disappointing to the child who believed these character-myths. Here is another typical reading-book story from *The Child's Guide*. It is called —

THE IDLE SCHOOL BOY.

I will tell you about the *laziest* boy you ever heard of. He was indolent about *every thing*. When he had spelled a word, he drawled out one syllable after another, as if he were afraid the syllables would *quarrel*, if he did not keep them a great ways *apart*. Once, when he was saying a lesson in Geography, his Master asked him, " What is said of *Hartford?* " He answered, " Hartford is a flourishing comical town."

He meant it was a " flourishing, *commercial* town "; but he was such a dunce, that he *never* knew what he was about.

Another day, when his class were reciting a lesson from the Dictionary, he made a mistake, worse than all the rest. The word, A-ceph-a-lous, was printed with syllables divided as you see; the definition of the word was, " without a head."

The idle boy had often been laughed at for being so very *slow* in saying his lesson; this time he thought he would be very *quick* and *smart*; so he spelled the word before the Master had a chance to put it out. And how do you think he spelled it ?

" A-c-e-p-h, Aceph," said he ; " A louse without a head." The boys laughed at him so much about this, that he was obliged to leave school.

You can easily guess what luck this idle boy had. His father tried to give him a good education, but he would be a dunce; not because he was a *fool*, but because he was too lazy to give his *attention* to any thing.   He had a considerable fortune left him; but he was too lazy to take *care* of it; and now he goes about the streets, with his hands in his pockets, begging his bread.

"Two Wicked Birds."
From Pierpont's *The Young Reader*, 1835.

The above engraving from Pierpont's *The Young Reader*, illustrates a story "about two foolish cocks that were always quarrelling, which is very naughty." These two wicked birds "were hardly out of the shell before they began to peck at each other, and they never looked pretty, because their feathers were pulled off in fighting till they were quite bare." They seem, however, to have plenty of feathers in the picture.   As was to be expected, they came to an ill end, and they got only their just deserts when a fox ate them both.

Lovell's *Young Pupils' Second Book*, New Haven, 1836, followed the plan of *The Child's Guide* in the use of italics, but what it particularly prided itself on

was its pictures.   These it says are of " a superior
order."   They consisted chiefly of " compound
cuts," all of the same general style as the one reproduced herewith.   The preface claims that the compound cuts are certain to " make a deep and *lasting*
impression, aiding the memory by storing it with
useful and accurate knowledge.   After the child has
pored over them, the details which follow will be
read with anxiety and delight."   The text accompanying the cut selected was this : —

The Goat.

His horns are made into

knife and fork handles.

His skin is made into

gloves.

A " Composite Cut."

From Lovell's *The Young Pupils' Second Book*, 1836.

Not many goats are raised in this country.   They *gnaw*
the bark of trees and spoil them, so they have not been
suffered to increase.   In some parts abroad, and most of
all in the east of the world, there are *many* goats.   The
he-goats have long *horns*.   Young goats are called *kids*, and
are full of play, and skip about in a very droll manner.
In a *wild* state, goats climb steep rocks, and can *stand* and
spring where few other an i mals would *dare to go*.   The
goat has a very strong and un pleas ant smell, but his flesh

Going to the Fields.

The pretty little Bird.

From *American Juvenile Primer*, 1838.

is very good to eat.   The *milk* of the goat is also very
nice to drink, and is used as a *cure* for some dis eas es.
The skin of the *kid* is made into soft leather gloves.
Goats' horns are used for *handles* of knives and forks.
The hair is often made into garments.

The following is a lesson which combines natural
history, moral training, and religion : —

The Hen.

Of all feathered an i mals, there is none more useful
than the *common hen*.   Her eggs supply us with *food* during
her life, and her flesh affords us del i cate meat after her
death.   What a *moth er ly* care does she take of her young !
How closely and ten der ly does she *watch* over them, and
cover them with her wings ; and how bravely does she
defend them from e ver y en e my, from which she herself
would *fly away in terror*, if she had not them to protect !
While this sight reminds you of the wisdom and goodness of *her* Cre a tor, let it *also* remind you of the care
which your *own* mother took of you, during your helpless
years, and of the grat i tude and duty which you *owe* to her
for all her kindness.

I quote below bits from various lessons : —

Many apple trees live above a *thousand* years, and it is
said there are some trees which were not destroyed when
the *world was drowned*.

Of all the horses in the world, some of the finest are
said to be bred in *England*.   The English racers often go at
the rate of a *mile* in *two minutes* ; and some of them have
been known to go a mile in one minute.

Does any body *live* on the moon ?

That, my dear, is what we can not certainly know; the moon being at too great a distance for us to discover any living creatures upon it. But, judging from what we *can* discover, and from the general resemblance of the moon to the earth, we have reason to suppose that the moon *may* be in hab it ed by rational, in tel li gent creatures, capable of knowing and praising their Creator.

The Sun.

The sun is above a *million* times larger than the *earth*; and like the earth, turns round about *itself*. It was formerly supposed to be an immense *body* of *fire*; but this opinion is no longer entertained by those who appear to be *best* acquainted with the subject.

They think it can not be a body of fire, because, in that case the nearer we approached to it, the greater degree of warmth we should feel. But the *contrary* is the fact; it is ascertained, that upon very *high* mountains the air is much colder than it is below. Besides, by looking at the sun through a glass made for the purpose, we perceive some *dark spots* upon it, which would not be the case were it a body of fire. We conclude, therefore, that the sun is *not* a body of fire.

What then *is* the sun?

The sun is understood to be an immense ball, or globe, surrounded with an *illumined atmosphere*, which acting upon the air that *en com pass es* the earth and other planets, in a manner we are *un ac quaint ed* with, produces light and heat.

A Topsy-turvy Hat.
From Bentley's *The Pictorial Primer*, 1842.

Mandeville's *Primary Reader*, New York, 1849, endeavors to teach words and their meanings by elaborate repetitions and combinations. The text makes a very queer patchwork. Here is a lesson where the words the child is specially to learn are " par-rot, ti-ger, cam-el." It might have been just as well in deference to the pictures not to have talked so much of cages and carts.

This is a par-rot in a cage against the wall.

That is a ti-ger in a cage upon a cart.

This must be a cam-el.

Doubtful Statements.
From Mandeville's *Primary Reader*, 1849.

The text goes on to say : —

Every tame parrot was once a wild parrot in the woods.
Some men have several parrots in the same cage against the wall, but this man has but one.
Every tiger is not young, but some tigers are old tigers.
Camels are high, long, large and strong.
The camel is not wild and fierce like the tiger in the cage on the cart, but tame and mild.
Some parrots can talk like any boy or girl.
No one should put his hand or his head in the cage of the fierce tiger.
All camels will carry men and women, boys and girls, as well as a large horse, or a strong mule.

Below is a specimen of what the book can do when it undertakes to tell a story : —

Two boys went out in-to the snow, with a lit-tle sled. One was na-med James, the oth-er was na-med Sam-u-el. James said to Sam-u-el, "You dare not go on that pond with your sled." Sam-u-el said, "Yes, I dare, but it is wrong; be-cause fa-ther said we must not do it." Then James laugh-ed and said, "What of that? Fa-ther can-not see us; for he is at work in the shop."

Was not James a wick-ed boy? He was. He for-got that God saw him all the time.

Sam-u-el beg-ged him not to take the sled on the pond, be-cause the ice was thin. But James was ob-stin-ate, and went on the thin ice a great way. Then Sam-u-el went back to the house and read in his Sun-day-school book.

After Sam-u-el had read a lit-tle while, he heard a noise out of doors. It was James's voice. Sam-u-el was fright-en-ed, and ran out, and there saw James in the wa-ter. The ice was bro-ken, and James was up to his neck in the pond. The poor boy was scream-ing for some-bod-y to come and take him out. Sam-u-el took a long pole, and held the end of it, and James caught hold of the oth-er end and crawl-ed out. His moth-er was ver-y sor-ry. She was a-fraid James would be sick; and he was sick a long time. But there was an-oth-er thing which made her more sor-ry still. It was his be-ing so wick-ed.

The selections I have made show certain salient and picturesque features of the old-time readers, but leave many books entirely unmentioned. I have said nothing of the readers edited by Lyman Cobb, who was the first to compile a thoroughly complete and well-graded series. Worcester's books soon followed, and Sanders's came a little later, and by 1850 Town, McGuffy, Russell, Swan, and others were in the field and the series idea was firmly established.

X

ADVANCED READERS

FOR several decades in the early days of the Republic the Catechism, the Psalter, and the Bible continued to be extensively used in the schools, and served for drilling the pupils in the art of reading. But the child could not acquire a taste for reading from such sources, nor obtain from them information concerning history, or the world about him, or the world at large. There was a demand for more freedom in the use of secular material in the school curriculum. The national life was developing rapidly, interests were broadening, and a steady theological diet was no longer satisfying. Besides, the general unity of religious doctrine which characterized the people earlier had given place to diversity, and Calvinism had strenuous opponents. As a result there was a marked increase in the number and variety of the schoolbooks, and in these the nature of the child, his inclinations, tastes, and desires became more and more dominant factors in the choice and arrangement of the subject-matter. Instead of demanding that the child should adjust himself entirely to the course of study, efforts were made to adjust the course of study to the requirements of the child.

The first reader produced on this side of the Atlantic was compiled by the industrious Noah Webster, shortly after the Revolution, as the Third Part of his *Grammatical Institute*.   Hitherto, the spellers and New England Primers were the only text-books containing exercises in reading.   Webster's title-page describes his book as "An American Selection of Leſſons in Reading and Speaking calculated to improve the minds and refine the taſte of youth, to which are prefixed Rules in Elocution and directions for expressing the Principal Paſſions of the Mind."   From the prefatory matter I have taken the several paragraphs which follow : —

Let each ſyllable be pronounced with a clear voice, without whining, drawling, liſping, ſtammering, mumbling in the throat, or ſpeaking through the noſe.

If a perſon is rehearſing the words of an angry man, he ſhould aſſume the ſame furious looks ; his eyes ſhould flaſh with rage, his geſtures ſhould be violent, and the tone of his voice threatening.   If kindneſs is to be expreſſed, the countenance ſhould be calm and placid, and wear a ſmile, the tone ſhould be mild, and the motion of the hand inviting.

Mirth or *laughter* opens the mouth, criſps the noſe, leſſens the aperture of the eyes, and ſhakes the whole frame.

Grief is expreſſed by weeping, ſtamping with the feet, lifting up the eyes to heaven, &c.

Fear opens the eyes and mouth, ſhortens the noſe, draws down the eye-brows, gives the countenance an air of wildneſs ; the face becomes pale, the elbows are drawn back parrallel with the ſides, one foot is drawn back, the heart beats violently, the breath is quick, the voice weak and trembling.

Boafting is loud and bluftering. The eyes ftare, the face is red and bloated, the mouth pouts, the voice is hollow, the arms akimbo, the head nods in a threatening manner, the right fift fometimes clenched and brandifhed.

The bulk of the book is made up of three departments — " Narration," " Lessons in Speaking," and " Dialogues." In one lesson with the caption " Rules for Behavior," we find this advice : —

Never hold any body by the button or the hand, in order to be heard through your story ; for if the people are not willing to hear you, you had much better hold your *tongue* than hold *them*.

Here are the opening paragraphs of a tale entitled

MODESTY, DOUBT, AND TENDER AFFECTION.

CALISTA was young and beautiful, endowed with a great fhare of wit and folid fenfe. Agathocles, whofe age very little exceeded hers, was well made, brave and prudent. He had the good fortune to be introduced to Califta's home, where his looks, wandering indifferently over a numerous circle, foon diftinguifhed and fixed upon her.

But recovering from the fhort ecftacy occafioned by the firft fight, he reproached himfelf, as being guilty of rudenefs to the reft of the company ; a fault which he endeavoured to correct by looking round on other objects. Vain attempt ! They were attracted by a powerful charm, and turned again towards Califta. He blufhed as well as fhe, while a fweet emotion produced a kind of fluttering in his heart, and confufion in his countenance.

Of course, after that, Agathocles became a frequent caller, and in every visit " he difcovered fome new perfection in the fair Califta."

At laft he refolved to open his heart to her; but he did not do it in the affected language of a romantic paffion. " Lovely Califta," faid he ingenuoufly, " it is not mere efteem that binds me to you, but a moft paffionate and tender love. I feel that I cannot live without you : Can you, without violence to your inclinations, confent to make me happy ? I may love you without offence; 'tis a tribute due to your merit : But may I flatter myfelf with the hopes of fome fmall return ? "

A coquette would have affected to be difpleafed at fuch a declaration. But Califta not only liftened to her lover without interrupting him, but anfwered him without ill-nature, and gave him leave to hope. Nor did fhe put his conftancy to a tedious trial : the happinefs for which he fighed was no longer delayed, than was neceffary to prepare for the ceremony.

Another lesson from which I wish to quote is —

SELF-TORMENTING

SERGEANT *Tremble* and his wife, during a time of general health, feel as eafy and fecure as if their children were immortal. If there are no cancers, dyfenteries, fmall-pox, bladders in the throat, and fuch like things to be heard of, they almoft bid defiance to death; but the moment information was given that a child fix miles off, had the throat diftemper, all comfort bade adieu to the houfe; and the mifery then endured from dreadful apprehenfions, left the difeafe fhould enter the family, is unfpeakable.

The old fergeant thought that when the wind blew from that quarter, he could fmell the infection, and therefore

ordered the children to keep in the houfe, and drink worm-
wood and rum, as a prefervation againft contagion.   As for
Mrs. *Tremble*, her mind was in a ftate of ceafelefs agitation
at that time.   A fpecimen of the common fituation of the
family is as follows.

Sufy, your eyes look heavy, you don't feel a fore throat,
do you?   Hufband, I heard *Tommy* cough in the bed room
juft now.   I'm afraid the diftemper is beginning in his
vitals, let us get up and light a candle.   You don't feel any
fore on your tongue or your mouth, do you, my dear little
chicken?   It feems to me Molly did not eat her breakfaft
with fo good a ftomach this morning as fhe ufed to do.   I
fear she has got the diftemper coming on.

To be fhort, the child that had the diftemper died; and
no other child was heard of, in thofe parts, to have it; fo
that tranquility and fecurity were reftored to Mr. *Tremble's*
family, and their children regarded as formerly, proof
against mortality.

THE

LITTLE READER's

ASSISTANT;

CONTAINING

I. A number of Stories, moftly taken from the hiftory of America, and adorned with Cuts.

II. Rudiments of Englifh Grammar.

III. A Federal Catechifm, being a fhort and eafy explanation of the Conftitution of the United States.

IV. General principles of Government and Commerce.

V. The Farmer's Catechizm, containing plain rules of hufbandry.

All adapted to the capacities of children.

Portion of Title-page. 1791.

About 1790 Webster published another reader, a square little book called *The Little Reader's Assistant*. It contained "familiar ftories in plain language for the benefit of children, when they firft begin to read without fpelling." In other words, it was a middle-class reader. A good many years were still to pass before any one would devise a primary reader. The first part of Webster's book is largely

STORY OF COLUMBUS.

From *The Little Reader's Assistant.*

a relation of the early settlers' experiences with the Indians. No details are too grewsome to be omitted, and the effect on the imaginations of "Little Readers" could not have been altogether salutary; for the stories were sure to be recalled whenever a child had to encounter alone the mysterious dusk of evening or the gloom of night. The book has the honor to be the earliest reader to use

illustrations, and several of the weird little pictures
are here reproduced.   The art of engraving as
practised in this country was very crude, and these
are fair examples of the rough-hewn primitiveness
of the book illustrations of the period.   Their un-
couthness was still further emphasized by the paper
on which they were printed, for all the paper of
early American manufacture was inferior, and very
little, even of the best, was of a snowy whiteness.

The first picture in Webster's book illustrated the
" Story of Columbus," and I suppose that is Columbus himself waving his hat from the mast-head.   The
sea has a very lively appearance, and there is some
doubt whether the artist has delineated an expanse of
white-capped waves or a multitude of leaping fish.

A " Christian" Indian getting the Best of a Heathen Indian.
From Webster's *The Little Reader's Assistant.*

The text accompanying the picture of the two
Indians says the individual behind the rock was

Night Attack of Indians on Major Waldron's House, Dover, N.H.

Captain John Smith a Captive in Serious Danger.
From *The Little Reader's Assistant*.

friendly to the English. He was pursued by one
of his enemies and betook himself to this refuge;
" but feeing his purfuer on the other side, waiting to
shoot him as he lifted his head above the rock he

put his hat upon his gun, and raifed it flowly above the rock. The Indians feeing it, fired a ball through it; and before he could load his gun again, the chriftian Indian fhot him through the head."

The cut showing the predicament of Captain John Smith must have been very interesting to the old-time school children, and equally so the spirited portrayal of Putnam and the Wolf. You can see

Putnam and the Wolf.
From *The Little Reader's Assistant.*

the rope attached to Putnam's leg and his comrades up above gripping it, ready to pull him forth. We can fancy very well the damage to that hero's clothes and person as he was hauled out, if the picture gives a truthful impression of the jaggedness of the rocks.

The street scene shows " Charles Churchill the poet. As he was returning home one night at a late hour, he was accofted by a female, whofe air and manner raifed his curiofity to take particular

T

notice of her.   She appeared to be about fifteen
years old, and handfome, but pinching want had
given her beauty a fickly caft, and the horrors of
difpair were feen in the languid fmile which fhe put

The Benevolent Churchill.
From *The Little Reader's Assistant.*

on while fhe fpoke."   Churchill gave her a piece
of money whereat " fhe fell upon her knees in the
ftreet, and raifing her eyes and hands to heaven, fhe
remained in that pofture for fome time, unable to
exprefs the gratitude that filled her heart."   She
told her benefactor a sad tale of distress, and he
learned she had parents dependent on her.   So he
went with her to her home garret and there the rest
of the family were soon on their knees around the
poet, and he "gave them ten guineas."

    The final picture is of a queer-looking beast that
one would hardly recognize if it were not labelled.
The text says : —

THE Buffalo, found in the woods of America, is a large animal with black, fhort horns. He has a large beard under his lower jaw, and a large tuft of hair upon his head, which falls down upon his eyes and gives him a hideous look. He has a large bump of rifing on his back, beginnig at his hips and increafing to his fhoulders. This is covered with hair, fomewhat reddifh, and very long. The reft of the body is covered with black wool; a fkin produces about eight pounds of wool, which is very valuable.

The Buffalo.

From *The Little Reader's Assistant.*

The buffalo has a good fmell, and will perceive a man at a great diftance, unlefs the wind is in the man's favor. His flefh is good, but the bull's is too tuff, fo that none but the cow's is generally eaten. His fkin makes good lether — and the Indians ufe it for fhields.

The last half of the book is devoted to a "Farmer's Catechizm," mostly agricultural instruction, but starting off with some general laudation like —

Q. Why is farming the *beſt* buſineſs a man can do?

A. Becauſe it is the moſt neceſſary, the moſt helthy, the moſt innocent, and moſt agreeable employment of men.

Q. Why is farming the moſt *innocent* employment?

A. Becauſe farmers have fewer temptations to be wicked than other men. They live much by themſelves, ſo that they do not ſee ſo many bad examples as men in cities do. They have but little dealing with others, ſo that they have fewer opportunities to cheat than other claſſes of men. Beſides, the flocks and herds which ſurround the farmer, the frolicks of the harmleſs lambs, the ſongs of the cheerful birds, and the face of nature's works, all preſent to the huſbandman examples of innocence, beauty, ſimplicity and order, which ought to impreſs good ſentiments on the mind and lead the heart to God.

One of the most popular of the early readers was Caleb Bingham's *The American Preceptor*, Boston, 1794. The preface declares that —

In making ſelections for the following work, a preference has been given to the productions of American genius. The compiler, however, has not been wholly confined to America; but has extracted from approved writers of different ages and countries. Convinced of the impropriety of inſtilling falſe notions into the minds of children, he has not given place to romantic fiction. The compiler pledges himſelf, that this book contains neither a word nor a ſentiment which would " raiſe a bluſh on the cheek of modeſty."

Most of the early reading books drew their materials largely from British sources, and American contributions were for a long time mainly from the speeches of the Revolutionary orators. Typical subjects were : Frailty of Life, Benevolence of the Deity, Popery, Rules for Moderating Our Anger, Reflections on Sun Set, Character of a Truly Polite Man, The Child Trained Up for the Gallows. These and the rest of their kind were all " extracted from the works of the most correct and elegant writers." The books were also pretty sure to contain selections from the Bible, and some had parts of sermons. Indeed, nearly all the matter was of a serious, moral, or religious character.

From the *American Preceptor* I quote a portion of

A Dialogue between two School Boys, on Dancing.

Harry. Tom, when are you going to begin your dancing? You will be fo old in a fhort time as to be afhamed to be feen taking your five pofitions.

Thomas. I don't know as I fhall begin at all. Father fays he don't care a fig whether I learn to jump any better than I do now; and, as I am to be a tradefman, he is determined to keep me at the reading and writing fchools.

Har. That muft be very dull and dry for you. And what good will all fuch learning do you, fo long as you make the awkward appearance you do at prefent? I am furprifed at your father's folly. So becaufe you are to be a tradefman, you are not to learn the graces!

Thus they go on, Thomas representing wisdom and Harry folly, and though neither convinces the other, they make it very plain where the reader's sympathies ought to be.

Another very successful book of Bingham's, published about a dozen years later than his Preceptor, was *The Columbian Orator*, a compilation of dialogues and pieces suitable for declamation. Perhaps nothing in the book more generally pleased or was oftener heard from the school platform than

---

LINES SPOKEN AT A SCHOOL–EXHIBI-
TION, BY A LITTLE BOY
SEVEN YEARS OLD.

YOU'D scarce expect one of my age,
  To speak in public, on the stage;
And if I chance to fall below
Demosthenes or Cicero,
Don't view me with a critic's eye,
But pass my imperfections by.
Large streams from little fountains flow;
Tall oaks from little acorns grow:
And though I now am small and young,
Of judgment weak, and feeble tongue;
Yet all great learned men, like me,
Once learn'd to read their A, B, C.
But why may not Columbia's soil
Rear men as great as Britain's isle;
Exceed what Greece and Rome have done,
Or any land beneath the sun?
Mayn't Massachusetts boast as great
As any other sister state?
Or, where's the town, go far and near,
That does not find a rival here?
Or where's the boy, but three feet high,
Who's made improvements more than I?
These thoughts inspire my youthful mind
To be the greatest of mankind;
Great, not like Caesar, stain'd with blood;
But only great, as I am good.

In the extract below we get a glimpse of very primitive educational conditions. The book vouches for what is depicted as still true to life in some vicinities, though not nearly as applicable as formerly. The scene is a public house.

Enter SCHOOL-MASTER, *with a pack on his back.*

Schoolmaster. How fare you, landlord? what have you got that's good to drink?

Landlord. I have gin, West-India, genuine New England, whiskey, and cider brandy.

Schoolm. Make us a stiff mug of sling. Put in a gill and a half of your New England; and sweeten it well with lasses.

Land. It shall be done, Sir, to your liking.

Then the schoolmaster asks if the landlord knows of any vacancy in the local schools, and is informed they are without a master in that very district, and the three school-committeemen were to be at the tavern directly to consult on school matters. The landlord says the last master " was a tyrant of a fellow and very extravagant in his price. He grew so important the latter part of his time, that he had the frontery to demand *ten dollars* a month and his board." He never patronized the landlord's bar, and was always in his chamber of an evening " poring over his musty books." Finally the severity of his discipline roused the neighborhood, and he was hooted out of town.

The three committeemen, accompanied by the parson, at length appeared at the tavern, and the schoolmaster applies for a position. He acknowledges that he has never had more than a year's schooling, and that he knows nothing of geography or grammar, but he can read a newspaper without spelling more than half the words, and has "larn'd to write considerably, and to cypher as fur as Division." Most important of all, he will work for five dollars a month, and the committee hire him. The parson alone protests.

By far the most copiously illustrated of any of the earlier readers was a thin 12mo published in Philadelphia in 1799, called *The Columbian Reading Book, or Historical Preceptor*, "a collection of Authentic Histories, Anecdotes, Characters, &c. &c. calculated to incite in young minds a love of virtue, from its intrinsic beauty, and a hatred of vice from its disgusting deformity." From the 164 short lessons I make several selections.

Spirited Reproof of a Woman.

An Appeal to King Philip.
From *The Columbian Reading Book*, 1799.

PHILIP, rising from an entertainment at which he had sat for some hours, was addressed by a woman, who begged him to hear her cause. He accordingly heard it, and, upon her saying some things not pleasing to him, he gave sentence against her. The woman immediately, but very calmly, replied, " I appeal." " How," says Philip, " from your king? To whom then?" " To Philip when fasting," returned the woman. The manner in which he received this answer would do honour to the most sober prince. He afterwards gave the cause a second hearing, found the injustice of his sentence, and condemned himself to make it good.

Gasconade.

A Gentleman of Gascony who inherited two thousand crowns a year from his father, commenced living at Paris, and being a gay volatile genius, soon squandered his fortune, and was reduced to the lowest ebb of wretchedness. Yet he never lost his spirit and courage; but with the small pittance he had left, he purchased a mule and turned water-carrier. Some time

A Meeting of Old Friends in the Streets of Paris.
From *The Columbian Reading Book*.

afterwards, as he was trafficking his merchandize up and down the streets, he happened to meet two of his old companions, who would have avoided him for fear of giving him pain, at being caught with such an equipage. But he sprang forward and saluted them with his usual freedom; and, when they seemed to pity his ill fortune, briskly interrupted them by saying, " That he had forty thousand crowns worth of water in the Seine, but for want of servants, was obliged to sell it himself."

The Clever Indian.
From *The Columbian Reading Book.*

The retort Courteous.

A white man meeting an Indian asked him, "whose Indian are you?" To which the copper-faced genius replied, "I am God Almighty's Indian: whose Indian are you?"

Philosophy an unfailing refuge.

The Philosopher.
From *The Columbian Reading Book.*

ZENO, a philosopher of Cyprus, turning merchant for his better support, was always unfortunate by losses at sea, insomuch that he was reduced to one small vessel; and having advice that it was also cast away in the ocean, and nothing saved, he received the news with cheerfulness, saying, " O Fortune, thou hast acted wisely, in forcing me to throw off the rich attire of a merchant to put on the mean and despised habit of a scholar, and return me back to the school of philosophy, where there is nothing to lose, and the most satisfactory and durable things to be gained."

Successful Bravery.

Mr. GILLET, a French quarter-master, going home to his friends, had the good fortune to save the life of a young woman, attacked by two ruffians. He fell upon them, sabre in hand, unlocked the jaw of the first villain, who held a dagger to her breast, and at one stroke pared the nails of the other just above the wrist. Money was offered by the grateful parents;

A Rescue.

From *The Columbian Reading Book.*

he refused it; they offered him their daughter, a young girl of 16, in marriage; the veteran, then in his 73rd year, declined, saying, " Do you think that I have rescued her from instant death, to put her to a lingering one, by coupling so lively a body with one worn out with age ? "

Few of the early text-books enjoyed more favor than Staniford's *The Art of Reading*, Boston, 1807. The title-page says it contains "A variety of selected

and original pieces, Narrative, Didactic, Argumenta-
tive, Poetical, Descriptive, Pathetic, Humorous, and
Entertaining, together with Dialogues, Speeches,
Orations, Addresses, and Harangues." The
following is an example of what the book calls
humorous : —

AWKWARDNESS IN COMPANY.

1. WHEN an awkward fellow first comes into a room,
he attempts to bow, and his sword, if he wears one, gets
between his legs, and nearly throws him down, Confused
and ashamed, he stumbles to the upper end of the room,
and seats himself in the very place where he should not.
He there begins playing with his hat, which he presently
drops ; and recovering his hat, he lets fall his cane ; and,
in picking up his cane, down goes his hat again.   Thus
'tis a considerable time before he is adjusted.

2. When his tea or coffee is handed to him, he spreads
his handkerchief upon his knees, scalds his mouth, drops
either the cup or saucer, and spills the tea or coffee in his
lap.   At dinner, he seats himself upon the edge of his chair,
at so great a distance from the table, that he frequently
drops his meat between his plate and his mouth ; he holds
his knife, fork, and spoon, differently from other people ;
eats with his knife to the manifest danger of his mouth ;
and picks his teeth with his fork.

3. If he is to carve he cannot hit the joint ; but, in
laboring to cut through the bone, splashes the sause over
every body's clothes.   He generally daubs himself all over ;
his elbows are in the next person's plate ; and he is up to
the knuckles in soup and grease.   If he drinks, 'tis with his
mouth full, interrupting the whole company with, " To
your good health, Sir," and " My service to you ; " perhaps
coughs in his glass, and besprinkles the whole table.

4. He addresses the company by improper titles; mistakes one name for another; and tells you of Mr. What d'ye call him, or you know who; Mrs. Who'ist there, what's her name, or how d'ye call her; He begins a story; but, not being able to finish it, breaks off in the middle, with, " I've forgot the rest."

I also reprint one of the dialogues. It is intended to illustrate the prejudices of the vulgar against academies. The participants in the conversation are Old Trumpet, Goody Trumpet, and their son, Leander.

OLD TRUMPET, *alone.*

A PLAGUE and Satan confound such ignorance, says I; what, the dog is ruin'd and undone for ever and for 'tarnally. Must I feed and pamper and lodge the puppy? ay, ay, and send him to the Mackademy, and give him larning — and for what? good Lord, for what? O! snakes, toads and dung worms! O! the Mackademy! My son Len will be ruin'd!

Enter GOODY TRUMPET *in haste.*

G. Trum. Well there now, husband, I can't, no nor I wont bear it any longer — for would you think it? our Leander is gone crazy, and's a fool, and melirious, and — and —

Old T. Yes, yes, that's as clear as the sun — that I'll vow to any day. He's a fool, and a dog, and crazy, and — and — what was the word you us'd?

G. T. Pshaw! you're a 'tarnal pesterment. You're too old to larn any thing but how to wear horns —

Old T. No, no, that's a lie — I've larnt that a ready —

there's not a ram in the flock that wears horns more tremariously than I do.

G. T. Ha, ha, ha, tremariously, O distravagant! well, my son's a fool and my husband a jack-ass — but hark you, this chip o' yourn, this Mackademicianer, inserts that our tin quart is brim full, when I shook, and shook, and shook every atom, and morsel, and grain of beer out of it — and there was not a bit nor a jot in't any more than there is in his head, not a bit more.

Old T. Ay, ay, I warrant ye, nothing more brovebler — yes, yes, and he told me about the dentity of pinticles in fire — and as how the proximation to fire made the sentiments of heat. Odd's buds! he's ruin'd, he's undone! Well, well, I'll go to the Protector, (Preceptor) I'll pound him — I'll mawl him — I'll see if he'll make Len a fool again —

G. T. Well, well, take him away, take him home, — I'll larn him. If you'll let him alone — I believe I can make him know a little something. But the conceptor! I'll strip his head for him — I'll make it as bare as an egg — I'll pull his soul case out.

Old T. Why good George! I sent him to the mackademy to get larning. If this is larning, my dog knows more than the Protector and the Mackademy besides.

Enter LEANDER.

Old T. How now, how now, coxcomb! Why, Len, you're a fool! You're crazy, you're melirious, as your poor mother says.

Leander. Sir, you know you have a right to command your own, but I think, Sir, that the abuse of such power is worse than the want of it. Have I, Sir, deserved such treatment!

Old T. Yes, you have reserved the gallows — ay, ay,

Len, you must be chained in a dark room and fed on bread and water — O the Mackademy !

Leander. You may arraign me, Sir, with impunity for faults which I in some instances have been guilty of — but my improvements in the liberal arts and sciences, have been, I believe, equal to most of my standing, and I am confident, Sir, that I have asserted nothing but what is consistent with the philosophy of our times.

Old T. Your dosolophys may go to Beelzebub, and you may go with them, Sir, and be hang'd, Sir — O the Conceptor, and Mackademy may go to Beelzebub and be hang'd and they will ! Come home, Len, you sha'nt go there any more, you'll be ruin'd and undone for ever, and for 'tarnally !

A reader with a special purpose was *The Mental Flower Garden, or an Instructive and Entertaining Companion for the Fair Sex,* New York, 1808. It was full of sugar-coated wisdom and mild sentiment as was befitting in a text-book for " female youth," and no effort was spared to use highly polished and becoming language on all occasions. Its tone was very like that it recommended for " epistolary writing — *easy, genteel* and *obliging,* with a choice of words which bear the most civil meaning, and a generous and good-natured *complaisance.*"

Scott's and Lindley Murray's readers were the only ones by English compilers to be widely circulated in this country. Murray's several readers continued in use until the middle of the nineteenth century. They were stupid-looking, fine-print volumes, full cf profundity and never lapsed into the shallow amateurishness of some of our American school-books.   Yet the information imparted was occasionally rather peculiar, as for instance what is said about

The Cataract of Niagara, in Canada, North America.

This amazing fall of a hundred and fifty feet perpendicular is made by the river St. Lawrence, one of the largest rivers in the world, a river that serves to drain the waters of almost all North America into the Atlantic Ocean.   It will be readily supposed, that such a cataract entirely destroys the navigation of the stream : and yet some Indians in their canoes, it is said have ventured down it in safety.

I reproduce from Scott's book one of four plates illustrating an introductory chapter, " On the speaking of Speeches at schools."   The text advises —

The Speaker.

From Scott's *Lessons in Elocution*, 1814.

Reduced one-half.

If the pupil's knees are not well formed, or incline inwards, he must be taught to keep his legs at as great a distance as possible, and to incline his body so much to that side on which the arm is extended, as to oblige him to rest the opposite leg upon the toe ; and this will in a great measure, hide the defect of his make.

When the pupil has got in the habit of holding his hand and arm properly, he may be taught to move it, that is, to raise the arm in the same position as when gracefully taking off the hat.   (See Plate.)   When the hand approaches to the head, the arm should, with a jerk, be suddenly straightened, at the very moment the emphatical word is pronounced.   This coincidence of the hand and voice, will greatly enforce the pronunciation.

Below is a part of one of the lighter pieces in *The Common Reader*, by T. Strong, A.M., Green-field, Massachusetts, 1818.

The Flower Girl.
From Strong's *The Common Reader*, 1818.
Reduced one-third.

THE FLOWER GIRL.

" Pray buy a nosegay of a poor orphan ! " said a female voice, in a plaintive and melodious tone, as I was passing the corner of the Hay-market.   I turned hastily and beheld a girl about fourteen, whose drapery, though ragged, was clean, and whose form was such as a painter might have chosen for a youthful Venus.

Her neck, without colouring, was white as snow; and her features, though not regularly beautiful, were interesting,

u

and set off by a transparent complexion; her eyes, dark and intelligent, were shaded by loose ringlets of a raven black, and poured their supplicating beams through the silken shade of very long lashes.

On one arm hung a basket full of roses, and the other was stretched out towards me with one of the rose buds. I put my hand into my pocket and drew out some silver — "take this, my pretty girl," said I.

The narrator added some kindly and highly moral remarks for her benefit, and she caught his hand and

burst into a flood of tears. The actions and the look touched my soul; it melted, and a drop of sympathy fell from my cheek.

"Forgive me, Sir," said she, while a blush diffused itself over her lovely face. "You will pardon me when I tell you they were the first kind words I have heard since I lost all that was dear to me on earth."

"Can I leave this poor creature?" said I, pensively. "Shall I quit thee, fair flower, to be blown down by the rude blast of adversity! to droop thy lovely head beneath the blight of early sorrow! No! thou hast once bloomed beneath the cheerful sun of domestic content, and under it thou shalt bloom again."

My heart beat with its sweet purpose, and the words of triumphant virtue burst from my lips. "Come, thou lovely deserted girl! come and add one more to the happy group who call me father! thou shalt be taught with them that virtue which their father tries to practice."

Her eyes flashed with frantic joy; she flung herself on her knees before me. I raised her in my arms; I hushed her eloquent gratitude, and led her to a home of happiness and piety; and the poor orphan of the Hay-market is now the partner of my son!

The scene of this story is one of the busiest parts of London; but the illustration which accompanies it shows a New England country road, with three curious little loads of hay standing in a wayside field to suggest a hay-mart.

The Catamountain.
From *The Improved Reader*, 1827.

Here is a lesson which purports to have been written by a Missourian. It is from Pierpont's *The National Reader*, Boston, 1827.

The Worm.

Who has not heard of the rattle-snake or copperhead! An unexpected sight of either of these reptiles will make even the lords of creation recoil: but there is a species of worm found in various parts of this state, which conveys a poison of a nature so deadly, that, compared with it, even the venom of the rattlesnake is harmless. To guard our readers against this foe of human kind, is the object of this communication.

This worm varies much in size. It is frequently an inch through, but, as it is rarely seen, except when coiled, its length can hardly be conjectured. It is of a dull leaden colour, and generally lives near a spring or small stream of water, and bites the unfortunate people, who are in the *habit of going there to drink*. The brute creation it never molests. They avoid it with the same instinct that teaches the animals of Peru to shun the deadly coya.

Several of these reptiles have long infested our settlements, to the misery and destruction of many of our fellow-citizens. I have, therefore, had frequent opportunities of being the melancholy spectator of the effects produced by the subtle poison which the worm infuses.

The symptoms of its *bite* are terrible. The eyes of the patient become red and fiery, his tongue swells to an immoderate size, and obstructs his utterance; and delirium of the most horrid character, quickly follows. Sometimes, in his madness, he attempts the destruction of his nearest friends.

If the sufferer has a family, his weeping wife and helpless infants are not unfrequently the objects of his frantic fury. In a word, he exhibits all the detestable passions that rankle in the bosom of a savage; and such is the *spell* in which his senses are locked, that, no sooner has the unhappy patient recovered from the paroxysm of insanity, occasioned by the bite, than he seeks out the *destroyer*, for the sole purpose of being *bitten again*.

I have seen a good old father, his locks as white as snow, his steps slow and trembling, beg in vain his only *son* to quit the lurking place of the worm. My heart bled when he turned away; for I knew the fond hope, that his son would be the "staff of his declining years," had supported him through many a sorrow.

Youths of Missouri, would you know the name of this reptile? It is called the *Worm of the Still*.

The next selection is from *The General Class-Book*, Greenfield, Massachusetts, 1828.

Dialogue between Mrs. Lackwit, Mrs. Goodsense, etc.

MRS. LACKWIT. Scat you little beast! See that kitten. She has been patting my ball of yarn, and rolling it all over the floor, till it is half unwound. There, take that box in the ear, and learn better manners.

CAROLINE. Poor kitten! I am afraid, mother, you have hurt her.

MRS. L. Hurt her? I meant to, and I wish I had killed her.

Now that robin sets up his tune, which I suppose we must hear till sunset. The old rooster too must come and crow like thunder at the very door, so that I, cannot hear myself speak; and to crown all, somebody has let the calves into the yard, and there they are galloping and racing over the table-cloths, which I had laid out to bleach. O, what a world we live in.

Caroline, cannot you be still? Do mind your needle. Surely we have noise enough without your singing or playing.

CAR. Dear mother, I am afraid you are not well. Does your head ake?

MRS. L. No; but my ears ake; and my heart akes.

MRS. GOODSENSE. My dear Mrs. Lackwit, as your children have been confined six hours in school to-day, would it not be well to let them go and play a little while in the yard?

MRS. L. No; the girls would be tanned, and become black as negroes, and the boys would be more noisy than ever. Mrs. Goodsense, how can you live with your eight children? I have only four, and it often seems as if I should be distracted.

Then Mrs. Goodsense explains and advises, and finally, Mrs. Lackwit concludes she will follow her neighbor's example.

One book of a very unusual sort was Comstock's *Rhythmical Reader*, Philadelphia, 1832. While the latter half is not unlike other books of its class, the earlier pages are an appalling mass of cabalistic signs. It is an endeavor by a system of notation to treat discourse like music, and to teach how to read with perfect ease and rhythm.

PART OF THE EPISCOPAL BURIAL SERVICE.

FROM THE BOOK OF COMMON PRAYER.

Rather slow.

3 | I am the | res ur- | rection | and the | life, |

| saith the | Lord ; | | he that be- | lieveth in | me, |

| though he were | dead, | yet shall he | live ; |

Specimen Lines.

From Comstock's *The Rhythmical Reader*, 1832.

Another unusual reader of about the same date was *The Christian Reader*, a stout volume, entirely made up of tracts, except for a half-dozen hymns inserted at the end.

Still another peculiar reader was *The Farmer's School-Book*, Albany, 1837, "published to take the place of such useless, unintelligible reading as Murray's *English Reader*, and other readers in common use, which never give the children one useful idea for the practical business of life." The book conveys a good deal of information, but I am afraid the author was disappointed in his expectation that "Chymistry, The Nature of Manures, Raising Calves, Making and Preserving Cheese," and similar topics which filled out the list of chapters would

" seize the feelings and get the attention of every child that is learning to read."

A Picture.

From Emerson's *The Second-class Reader*, 1833, illustrating a popular poem which began :

You are old, Father William, the young man cried,
  The few locks which are left you are gray ;
You are hale, Father William, a hearty old man ;
  Now tell me the reason, I pray.

In the days of my youth, Father William replied,
  I remembered that youth would fly fast,
And abused not my health and my vigor at first,
  That I never might need them at last.

A volume of more than ordinary interest was *The Monitorial Reader*, Concord, New Hampshire, 1839, and from it I make a number of excerpts.

That Red Stuff.

Father, said a little boy, in the lisping accents of youth, what is that red stuff you have just been drinking, and which makes you wink so? What do you call it? Hush, my son, it is *medicine*. This inquiry was put by a sweet looking child, as I was entering the door of a grocery to purchase a few articles for my family.

The tradesman had just drained his glass, and leaning on a cask, in which was burned the word *Brandy*, was wiping his mouth on the sleeve of his coat; while the little one stood watching his motions with a sweet affectionate look of the son, blended with the curiosity and simplicity of childhood. "Excuse me," said I, "but oh, tell your inno-cent reprover, that *it biteth like a serpent and stingeth like an adder*. Deceive him not."

The man looked abashed and with a private admonition, I left him.

The lesson closes with appropriate comments, but what the drinker did is not stated.

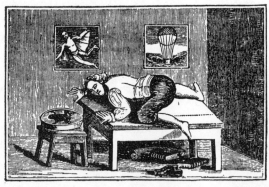

Sir Nicholas Gimcrack who "spread himself out on a large table, and placing before him a bason of water with a frog in it, he struck with his arms and legs as he observed the animal do." Thus he learned "to swim on dry land; but he never ventured himself in the water."

From *The Intelligent Reader*, 1834.

A Retired Sailor " instructing his sister's grand-children."
From Adams's *The Monitorial Reader*, 1839.

Borrowing.

" My dear," said Mrs. Green to her husband one morning, " the meal we borrowed from Mr. Black a few days
ago, is almost out, and we must bake to-morrow."

" Well," said her husband, " send and borrow a bushel
at Mr. White's; he sent to mill yesterday."

" And when it comes, shall we return the peck we borrowed more than a month ago from the widow Grey ? "

" No," said the husband gruffly, " she can send for it
when she wants it.   John do you go down to Mr. Brown's
and ask him to lend me his axe to chop some wood this
forenoon ; ours is quite dull, and I saw him grinding his
last night.   And James, do you go to Mr. Clark's, and

ask him to lend me a hammer — and you may as well borrow a few nails, while you are about it."

A little boy now enters and says, " Father sent me to ask if you had done with his hoe, which you borrowed a week ago last Wednesday; he wants to use it."

" Wants his hoe, child? What can he want with it? I have not half done with it. Tell him to send it back, though, as soon as he can spare it."

They sit down to breakfast. " O la!" exclaims Mrs. Green, " there is not a particle of butter in the house — James, run over to Mrs. Notable's, she always has excellent butter in her dairy, and ask her to lend me a plateful."

After a few minutes James returns; " Mrs. Notable says she has sent you the butter, but begs you to remember, that she has already lent you *nineteen* platefuls, which are scored on the dairy door."

" Nineteen platefuls," exclaimed the astonished Mrs. Green, holding up both her hands; " it is no such thing — I never had half that quantity; and if I had, what is a little plateful of butter? I should never think of keeping an account of such a trifling affair — I declare, I have a great mind never to borrow any thing of that mean creature again, as long as I live."

The narrative goes on to relate other borrowing episodes in the Green family, and closes with the statement that —

After all, the lowest, the most degraded class of borrowers, are NEWSPAPER BORROWERS; fellows who have not soul enough to subscribe for a newspaper, yet long to know its contents; who watch with lynx-eyed vigilance for the arrival of the mail, and when their more generous neighbor receives his paper, send their boys with messages like the following.

" Mr. Borrowall wishes you would be kind enough to lend him your paper for *one minute*. There is something particular in it, that he wants to see; he'll send it back before you want to read it."

The Pot of Baked Beans.

O! how my heart sighs for my own native land,
  Where potatoes and squashes and cucumbers grow;
Where cheer and good welcome are always at hand,
  And custards and pumpkin pies smoke in a row;
    Where pudding the visage of hunger serenes,
    And what is far dearer, the pot of *bak'd beans*.

Let Maryland boast of her dainties profuse,
  And large water-melons, and cantelopes fine;
Her turtle and oysters, and terrapin stews,
  And soft crab high zested with brandy and wine;
    Ah! neither my heart from my native land weans;
    Where smokes on the table the pot of *bak'd beans*.

The pot of *bak'd beans!* with what pleasure I saw it,
  Well season'd, well pork'd by some rosy fac'd dame;
And when from the glowing hot oven she'd draw it,
  Well crisp'd and well brown'd to the table it came;
    O, give me my country, the land of my teens, —
    Of the dark Indian pudding, and pot of *bak'd beans*.

The pot of *bak'd beans!* Ah, the muse is too frail,
  Its taste to descant on, its virtues to tell;
But look at the sons of New-England so hale,
  And her daughters so rosy — 'twill teach thee full well;
    Like me it will teach thee to sigh for the means
    Of health, and of rapture! — the pot of *bak'd beans*.

The most interesting feature of Lovell's *The Young Speaker*, New Haven, 1844, was the numerous pictures. The book, as a whole, was planned for a school reader, but it was the purpose of the pictures to "inculcate the art of graceful and eloquent gesture." The first of the two engravings reproduced

presents the side view of a boy making his bow before an audience. With a gentle but assured step, he approaches to near the front of the platform, a little on the right of the centre, then pausing for a moment, he casts his eyes with a diffident respect, over the audience; slides out his *left* foot on the toe, in a straight line; then supporting the body on that foot, he draws in the right foot until its *heel* comes

Making the Preliminary Bow to the Audience.
From Lovell's *The Young Speaker*, 1844.

into the *middle* or hollow of the *left* foot; he then presses his legs together, and dropping his eyes modestly to the floor, brings his body into a slight and graceful curve, the *arms* hanging perfectly *free*. In this posture the body is kept for an instant; he then rises slowly to an erect attitude, and is ready to commence speaking.

The second cut indicates how to express " painful observation, surprise, alarmed compassion, and the like."

An Expressive Attitude.
From Lovell's *The Young Speaker*.

XI

ARITHMETIC

MOST teachers, even in the days of the first settlers, gave some instruction in mathematics, but it was a long time before such instruction was made obligatory. In Massachusetts only reading and writing were required in the elementary schools until the enactment of a law in 1789, which said there must also be arithmetic, the English language, orthography, and decent behavior. Of these added requirements the first was generally felt to be of the most practical importance, and a reputation as an "arithmeticker" was to any teacher a valuable asset. Nothing was more likely to assist a man in getting a school than the ability to do any sum in arithmetic. To be "great in figures" was to be learned.

Books by native writers in all departments had begun to supersede those imported from England, and in place of Hodder's and Dilworth's Arithmetics, the famous treatise by Nicholas Pike of Newburyport, published in that town in 1788, gained wide acceptance — an acceptance aided, no doubt, by the flattering testimonials it received from George Washington and other dignitaries. It was a pretentious 8vo of 512 pages with a range almost encyclopædic, and it served to give tone to all the arithmetic study

of the early district-school period.   Rules were omnipresent in it.   There was indeed a rule for nearly
every page, and many of them were calculated to
tax the understanding of a pupil severely to grasp
their meaning.   Some of the problems, too, required for their mastery a great deal of genuine
mathematical capacity.

A majority of the district-school pupils, including practically all the girls, ciphered only through
the four fundamentals of addition, subtraction, multiplication, and division, with a short excursion into
vulgar fractions.   They won distinction among their
mates if they penetrated into the mysteries of the
Rule of Three; and to cipher through " Old Pike "
was to be accounted a prodigy.

The manuscript of this first American arithmetic
was ready in 1785, and after the manner of early
school-book authors, both in this country and in
England, " Nicholas Pike, Esq.," submitted it in
that form to various worthies to get their opinions
as to its merits.   They responded with polite com-
mendations, which, as was usual, were printed in the
book.   For many years after the volume was issued,
it held the foremost place among text-books of its
class.   A preface in 1793 to an abridged edition, especially prepared for use in the public schools, speaks
of the larger book as " That celebrated work, which
is now uſed as a claſſical book in all the Newengland
Univerſities."

Here are a few items from the table of contents
that will give some idea of the ground Pike attempted
to cover : —

Extraction of the Biquadrate Root
Penſions in Arrears at Simple Intereſt
Barter
Alligation Medial
Of Pendulums
A Perpetual Almanac
To find the Time of the Moon's Southing
Table of the Dominical Letters according to the Cycle
of the Sun
To find the Year of Indiction
Table to find Eaſter from the year 1753 to 4199
Plain Oblique Angular Trigonometry
To meaſure a Rhombus
To gauge a maſh Tub
The Proportions and Tonnage of Noah's Ark.

Congress established "Federal money" on the
decimal plan in 1786; but twenty years elapsed before its use became at all general, and Pike treats
it as something of a curiosity. English money was
our standard. In that denomination accounts were
kept, and until after the first decade of the nineteenth
century, it continued to have prominent place in our
arithmetics. Coins of many kinds were current during the early years of the republic, and the school
children had to learn the comparative value of these
moneys. Besides Federal money, there were four
varying currencies issued by the individual states.
Then there were English and Irish coins, and the
Continental Johannes, Pistoles, Moidores, Doub-
loons, etc. The labor involved in the computation
of ordinary business transactions at this period was
appalling.

I have mentioned the Rule of Three. It was recognized as an arithmetical landmark and I give Pike's definition : —

The Rule of Three teacheth, by having three numbers given, to find a fourth, that fhall have the fame proportion to the third, as the fecond to the firft.

This is sufficiently clear ; but some of the book's explanations are quite unintelligible to the present generation, as for instance : —

When tare, and tret and cloff are allowed.

Deduct the tare and tret, and divide the futtle by 168, and the quotient will be the cloff, which fubtract from the futtle, and the remainder will be the neat.

One fails to make any sense out of such a jumble until he reads the definitions appended to it.

Tare is an allowance, made to the buyer, for the weight of the box, barrel, or bag which contains the goods bought.

Tret is an allowance of 4 ℔ in every 104 ℔ for wafte, duft, &c.

Cloff is an allowance of 2℔ upon every 3 cwt.

Suttle is, when part of the allowance is deducted.

Neat weight is what remains after all allowances are made.

Another rule that has an equally unfamiliar sound to modern ears is this : —

To find the Gregorian Epact.

Subtract 11 from the Julian Epact : If the fubtraction cannot be made, add 30 to the Julian Epact ; then fubtract, and the remainder will be the Gregorian Epact; if nothing remain, the Epact is 29.

In the tables of weights and measures are Wine Measure and Ale or Beer Measure in good and regular standing among the rest. These were generally included in all the early school arithmetics. Cloth Measure, as Pike gives it, consists chiefly of Nails, and Ells Flemish, Ells English, and Ells French; Long Measure starts with "3 Barley corns make 1 inch;" and in Dry Measure we find "2 Quarts make 1 Pottle, 2 Bufhels make 1 Strike, 2 Strikes make 1 Coom, 2 Cooms make 1 Quarter, 4 Quarters make 1 Chaldron, 5 Quarters make 1 Wey, 2 Weys make 1 Laft." The following paragraph shows the interesting manner in which the author expressed himself when he had a problem to propound : —

An ignorant fop wanting to purchafe an elegant houfe, a facetious gentleman told him he had one which he would fell him on thefe moderate terms, viz. that he fhould give him a penny for the firft door, 2d. for the fecond, 4d. for the third, and fo on, doubling at every door, which were 36 in all : It is a bargain, cried the fimpleton, and here is a guinea to bind it; Pray, what would the houfe have coft him ? Anf. £286331153 1s. 3d.

A small book much used in the old schools was *An Introduction to Arithmetic*, by Erastus Root, Norwich, Connecticut, 1796. Queerly enough, it omits fractions, "not becaufe I think them ufelefs," the author explains in his preface, "but becaufe they are not abfolutely neceffary." He gives unusual space

x

as compared with other arithmetics of the time to the recently adopted decimal " Federal Money," of which he says : —

It is expected that before many years fhall elapfe, this method of reckoning will become general throughout the United States.   Let us, I beg of you, Fellow-Citizens, no longer meanly follow the Britifh intricate mode of reckoning. — Let them have their own way — and us, ours. — Their mode is fuited to the genius of the government — for it feems to be the policy of tyrants, to keep their accounts in as intricate, and perplexing a method as poffible ; that the fmaller number of their fubjects may be able to eftimate their enormous impofitions and exactions.   But Republican money ought to be fimple and adapted to the meaneft capacity.   This mode of reckoning may feem a little odd at firft, but when the coins of the United States come into circulation, it will foon become familiar.

Copperplate Engraving on the Title-page of Sarjeant's *Arithmetic*, 1788.

Below are two of the shorter problems in the book : —

What is the difference between fix dozen dozen and half a dozen dozen? Anf. 792.

What is the difference between twice twenty-five and twice five, and twenty? Anf. 20.

From a similar book, *The Youth's Assistant:* " Being a plain, Eafy, and Comprehenfive Guide to Practical Arithmetic," published in the same town as Root's and at about the same time, I quote this problem illustrative of old-time travel from tavern to tavern: —

I demand the diftance from the Town-houfe in Norwich, to Bull's in Hartford; fuppofing it to be nine miles from faid Town-houfe to Aldin's in Lebanon, from Aldin's to White's Andover fourteen, from White's to Marfh's Eaft Hartford twelve, from Marfh's Eaft Hartford to Benjamin's ditto three, from Benjamin's to Bull's two?

Anfwer, 40 miles.

A book that rivalled " Old Pike " in popularity was the Arithmetic by Daniel Adams published in 1801. It had large pages, and on these was blank space after each problem for the student to record the process of solution. The preface advises that the operation should be " first wrought upon a slate or waste paper," and afterward transcribed.

Another popular early arithmetic was Nathan Daboll's *Schoolmaster's Assistant*, and I quote from it the several problems which follow: —

Divide $4\frac{1}{2}$ gallons of brandy equally among 144 soldiers.
Ans. 1 *gill* a-piece.

How much shalloon that is $\frac{3}{5}$ yard wide, will line $5\frac{1}{2}$ yards of camblet which is $1\frac{1}{4}$ yard wide? *Ans.* $16\frac{1}{24}$ *yds.*

If a pistareen be worth 14⅖ pence, what are 100 pistareens worth ?·   *Ans.* £6.

A privateer of 65 men took a prize which being equally divided among them, amounted to 119 l. per man; what is the value of the prize ?   *Ans.* £7735·

Seven gentlemen met at an inn, and were so well pleased with their host, and with each other, that they agreed to tarry so long as they together with their host, could sit every day in a different position at dinner; how long must they have staid at said inn to have fulfilled their agreement ?

Ans. 110$\frac{170}{365}$ *years.*

A, B and C, playing at cards, staked 324 crowns; but disputing about tricks, each man took as many as he could; A got a certain number; B as many as A and 15 more; C got a fifth part of both their sums added together: how much did each get?   *Ans. A* 127½, *B* 142½, *C* 54.

> If to my age there added be,
> One-half, one-third, and three times three,
> Six score and ten the sum will be;
> What is my age, pray shew it me ?

Ans. 66.

Problems from Walsh's *Mercantile Arithmetic*, Northampton, Massachusetts, 1807 : —

If 8 boarders drink a barrel of cider in 12 days, how long would it laſt if 4 more came among them ?

Anſ. 8 days.

Three boys, John, James and William, buy a lottery ticket for 3 dols. of which John pays 90 cts. James 1 dol. and William the remainder. This ticket is entitled to a prize of 2000 dollars, ſubject to a deduction of 12½ per cent. how much is each to receive ? Anſ. John 525 dols. James 583 dols. 33⅓ cts. William 641 dols. 66⅔ cts.

What length of cord will fit to tie to a cow's tail, the other end fixed in the ground, to let her have liberty of eating an acre of grafs, and no more, fuppofing the cow and tail to be five yards and a half?   Anf. 6,136 perches.

A certain perfon married his daughter on new year's day and gave her hufband one fhilling towards her portion, promifing to double it on the firft day of every month for one year; what was her portion?   Anf. £. 204 15f.

How much will 10 ferons of cochineal come to weighing neat 724 okes 73 rotolas, at 80 piaftres per oke?
Anf. 57978,40 piaftres.
How much will 189 bazar mauds 31 feer 8 chittacks of fugar come to, at 6 rupees per maud?
Anf. 1138 rupees, 11 annas, 6 pice.

The last two examples deal with foreign weights, measures, and money terms under the head of Exchange. The several selections below are from Thompson's *The American Tutor's Guide*, Albany, 1808 : —

A man overtaking a maid driving a flock of geese, said to her, how do you do, sweetheart?   Where are you going with these 100 geese?   No Sir, said she, I have not 100; but if I had as many, half as many, and seven geese and a half, I should have 100 : How many had she?   *Ans.* 37.
A person was 17 years of age 29 years since, and suppose he will be drowned 23 years hence : Pray in what year of his age will this happen?   *Ans. In his* 69*th* year.

The illustration on the next page is one of eight little cuts that helped to elucidate problems in square root.   No other arithmetic up to this time had employed any cuts save very formal diagrams.

In the midst of a meadow,
  Well stored with grass ,
I've taken just two acres,
  To tether my ass :
Then how long must the cord be,
  That feeding all round ;
He mayn't graze less or more, than
  Two acres of ground.

Ans.   55½ *yards.*

An Illustrated Problem.

From Thompson's *The American Tutor's Guide*, 1808.

Here is an example from *The Science of Numbers made Easy*, by Leonard Loomis, Hartford, 1816. The hero of it not only was well supplied with money, but had his cash very picturesquely distributed about his person.

Harry told Thomas, that he had got 580,50 cts. (Bank Bills) in his hat, and he had got twice as much in his pocket book; besides 15,23 cts. silver money in his purse, and four cents that had slipped out of his pocket into his boot; pray tell me if you can, how much money he had ?

Ans. 1756,77 cts.

From *The Scholar's Arithmetic*, by Jacob Willetts, Poughkeepsie, New York, 1817 : —

When hens are 9 shillings a dozen, what will be the price of 6 dozen of eggs, at 2 cents for 3 eggs ?

Ans. 48 cts.

If the posterity of Noah, which consisted of six persons at the flood, increased so as to double their number in 20 years, how many inhabitants were in the world two years before the death of Shem, who lived 502 years after the flood ? *Ans.* 201,326,586.

When first the marriage knot was ty'd
  Between my wife and me,
My age was to that of my bride,
  As three times three to three.
But now when ten, and half ten years
  We man and wife have been,
Her age to mine exactly bears,
  As eight is to sixteen;
Now tell, I pray, from what I've said,
  What were our ages when we wed?
  Ans. { Thy age, when marry'd must have been
         { Just forty-five : thy wife's fifteen.

A workman was hired for 40 days upon this condition, that he should receive 20 cts. for every day he wrought, and should forfeit 10 cts. for every day he was idle; at settlement he received 5 dollars : How many days did he work and how many days was he idle? *Ans.* wrought 30 days, idle 10.

The most remarkable thing about the above example in the extreme moderateness of the man's charge. It seems rather severe to require a forfeit from a man who is working at twenty cents a day.

A large volume " containing Vulgar, Decimal, and Logarithmical Arithmetick," by Beriah Stevens, was published at "Saratoga Springs" in 1822 with a special claim to attention, by reason of a process it introduced for proving the correctness of one's figuring, and which it called " casting out the nines." I reprint the directions for proving subtraction.

Cast the nines out of the minuend, and note down the excess above the nines on a cross; then cast the nines out of the subtrahend and note the excess as before; lastly cast the nines out of the' remainder, and add the excess last found, and the excess of the subtrahend together, and if the sum of both be equal to the excess found in the minuend the work is allowed to be right.

An efficient force in raising the standard of mathematical instruction was the publication of Warren Colburn's *Intellectual Arithmetic* in 1821.   Previously all arithmetic had been scarcely intelligible ciphering; but Colburn gives a multitude of simple problems to be done mentally.   These cultivated quick comprehension and accuracy, and made it easy to apply what was acquired to the affairs of everyday life.   The best teachers lost no time in putting the book into use, and it determined the character of all subsequent text-books.   From the very first, its sale was prodigious, and during the next half century more than two million copies were circulated.

Among the books patterned more or less closely after Colburn's was a little volume called the *Franklin Arithmetic*, Springfield, Massachusetts, 1832.   This had a moral purpose, and proposed to improve on the other works then in vogue by the use of " questions, the solution of which will convey to the mind some important truth.   It seems rather out of place for a teacher to sit down with a pupil to calculate the gain or loss on the sale of gin, or lottery tickets. In one of our excellent and popular books on mathematical science, there are two or three questions which the scholar cannot solve without knowing

how many cards there are in a pack." To show
how the book is made interesting and enlightening,
I quote rather freely : —

How many letters in the word. JOHN ?
How many in the word SMITH ?
How many letters in both names, JOHN and SMITH ?
How many hands have a boy and a clock ?

In eighteen hundred and thirty-one, 119 persons died of
drunkenness in New York, and 137 in Philadelphia ; how
many in both ?

Hudson's Bay was discovered 10 years before the settlement at Plymouth, and Bagdad was taken by the Turks
18 years after ; how long a time passed between ?

Take E from the word HOPE, and how many letters
would be left ? and what would it be then ?

A man had seven children ; two of them were killed by
the fall of a tree ; how many had he left ?

A boy played three days in a week ; how many did he
work ?

Four rivers ran through the garden of Eden, and one
through Babylon ; how many more ran through Eden than
Babylon ?

Judas, one of the twelve apostles, hung himself ; how
many were there left ?

John Baptist was beheaded after Christ 32 years, and
the book of Revelation was written in 87 ; how long after
John was beheaded ?

Adam was 930 years old when he died, and 130 when
Seth was born ; how old was Seth when Adam died ?

Miss Fanny Woodbury was born in 1791, and died in
1814 ; Miss Hannah Adams lived to to be 53 years older ;
how old was Hannah Adams ?

"Adonibezek said, 3 score and 10 kings, having their
thumbs and their great toes cut off, gather their meat

under my table " (Judges i. 7.); how many thumbs and toes did Adonibezek cut off?

At Surat is a hospital for sick animals, in which there is a tortoise that has been there 75 years; what is 3 eights of the number?

The Baltimore rail-road cars run 12 miles an hour; what is $\frac{4}{7}$ of it?

A human body, if baked until all moisture is evaporated, is reduced in weight as 1 to 10; a body that weighs 100 pounds living, will weigh how much when dry?

The book closes with an appendix of biographical paragraphs containing facts relating to persons referred to in the problems. The paragraphs are of this sort : —

HOMER lived in Greece about 3 thousand years ago; he was a school teacher and a poet. He wrote two poems, one called the Iliad, which is an exhibition of bodily strength; the other called the Odyssey, which is an exhibition of the strength of the mind.

WILLIAM SHAKESPEARE is distinguished as a writer of dialogues. He lived in England; when a boy, he fell in company with bad boys, who stole some deer, and were punished; he was obliged to leave home; he went to London, and brought himself into notice by taking so good care of the horses of those that came to the theatre.

ALEXANDER THE GREAT was a great warrior; he conquered the world, and wept because there were no more worlds to conquer. He then gave himself up to dissipation, and died in a fit of debauch.

MISS FANNY WOODBURY died in Beverly, Mass. She was an eminently pious young lady. Her life is printed, and is a very interesting book for young ladies to read.

Miss Hannah Adams was a native of Massachusetts. She had a feeble constitution, and never went to school much; she studied and read by herself, and acquired much knowledge.

5. One stage has four horses. How many horses have two stages?

6. Then 2 times 4, or *twice* 4 are how many?

7. Here are three boats, and each boat contains three men. How many men in all?

8. 3 times 3 are how many?

Part of a Page.

From Barnard's *A Treatise on Arithmetic*, 1830.

The earliest arithmetic I have seen that used pictures as an aid to beginners was Barnard's, published at Hartford in 1830. The book claimed to be "rendered entertaining to the pupil by a great variety of amusing problems." Some of these took the form of a continued story, as:—

1. John made 3 marks on one leaf of his book, and six on another. How many marks did he make?

2. His teacher punished him, for soiling the book, by giving him 4 blows on one hand, and 5 on the other. How many blows did he strike him?

3. 7 boys laughed at him on one side of the house, when he was punished, and 2 on the other. How many boys laughed?

See this flock of black-birds: they have lighted upon the bars of a gate, and are all singing together. Find how many there are on each separate bar.

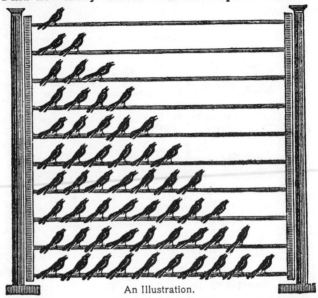

An Illustration.

From Lesson First of Emerson's *The North American Arithmetic*, Part First, 1838.

The pictures were confined to the early lessons in the first pages, and the book as a whole was designed for the older pupils. We had no primary arithmetics until 1838, when Emerson's *The North American Arithmetic, Part First*, appeared with illustrations scattered all through it. This was a genuine beginner's book of the modern type. The preface deprecated the fact that "the practice of postponing arithmetic till children arrive at the age of nine or ten years still prevails in many of our schools," and the bright little volume no doubt fulfilled the author's hope that it " would make the study both profitable and pleasant for young learners."

5 boys came up to recite, but 2 of them were sent back for having no lessons.   How many recited?

There were 7 farmers, 3 of whom drank rum and whisky, and became miserable; the rest drank water. and were healthy and happy. How many drank water?

Two Examples in Subtraction.
From Emerson's *The North American Arithmetic*, Part First.

The final quotation in this chapter is one of many jingles in Underhill's *New Table-Book*, 1846.

Two pennies had John
His sister had 1,
They gave them to me,
And then I had 3,
Thus you may see
That 2 and 1 make 3.

XII

I N colonial days geography was spoken of as "a diversion for a winter's evening," and acquaintance with it was considered an accomplishment rather than a necessity. Some rudimentary instruction in the science was occasionally given at the more advanced schools, but the topic was not taken up in the elementary schools until after the Revolution. A knowledge of it was first made a condition for entering Harvard in 1815, and a dozen years more elapsed before Massachusetts named it among the required studies in the public schools. To begin with, it was not introduced as a separate study, but the books were used as readers. The same was true of the early school histories. However, geography presently won a place of its own and kept it in spite of the protests that the scholars' attention was thereby being taken away from " cyphering."

The pioneer of American authors of school geographies was Jedidiah Morse. On the title page of most editions of his books his name was appended with " D. D. Minifter of the Congregation in Charleftown, Maffachufetts." He was born in 1761, graduated from Yale in 1783, and the year following published at New Haven his first geography. Later he put forth several other geographies, large and small, became a compiler of gazetteers, wrote various important historical and religious works, was one of the founders of Andover Theological Seminary, and for more than thirty years

Jedidiah Morse.

served as pastor of the First Church in Charlestown.   He won fame not only in his own country, but was recognized abroad as a man of distinguished attainments, and a number of his books were translated into French and German.   His *Geography*

Made Easy, a small leather-bound 12mo of about four hundred pages, was for many years by far the most popular text-book dealing with this subject. My copy, dated 1800, is dedicated

TO THE

Young Masters and Misses

Throughout the UNITED STATES

Two maps of double-page size are the only illustrations — one a map of the world, the other of North America.

GEOGRAPHY MADE EASY.

A Heading.
From an edition of 1800.

The earlier pages treat of the " Doctrine of The Sphere, Of Astronomical Geography, Of Globes and their Use," etc. But soon we come to the *History of the Discovery of America*, and then to a *General Description of America*." In the latter chapter is much that is interesting and picturesque.

It includes, as do all the early geographies, a good many imaginative travellers' tales picked up from newspapers and other chance sources without any pains being taken to verify them or to inquire as to the reliability of their authors. In fact, it sometimes seems as if the more fabulous the story the better its chance to be recorded in the school text-books. We get very entertaining glimpses of the limitations of geographical knowledge at the time in the following extracts from Morse.

The *Andes*, in South America, ſtretch along the Pacific Ocean from the Iſthmus of Darien to the Straits of Magellan. The height of Chimborazo, the most elevated point in this vaſt chain of mountains is 20,280 feet, above 5000 feet higher than any other mountain in the known world.

North America has no remarkably high mountains. The moſt conſiderable are thoſe known under the general name of the *Allegany Mountains*. Theſe ſtretch along in many broken ridges under different names from Hudſon's River to Georgia. The *Andes* and the *Allegany Mountains* are probably the ſame range interrupted by the Gulf of Mexico.

Who were the firſt people of America? And whence did they come? The Abbe Clavigero gives his opinion in the following concluſions : —

"The Americans deſcended from different nations, or from different families diſperſed after the confuſion of tongues. No perſon will doubt the truth of this, who has any knowledge of the multitude and great diverſity of the American languages. In Mexico alone *thirty-five* have already been diſcovered."

But how did the inhabitants and animals originally paſſ to America?

Y

The quadrupeds and reptiles of the new world paffed there by land. This fact is manifeft from the improbability and inconfiftency of all other opinions.

This neceffarily fuppofes an ancient union between the equinoxial countries of America and thofe of Africa, and a connexion of the northern countries of America with Europe on the E. and Afia on the W. The beafts of cold climes paffed over the northern ifthmufes, which probably connected Europe, America, and Afia; and the animals and reptiles peculiar to hot countries paffed over the ifthmus that probably connected S. America with Africa. Various reafons induce us to believe that there was formerly a tract of land which united the moft eaftern part of Brazil to the moft weftern part of Africa; and that all the fpace of land may have been funk by violent earthquakes, leaving only fome traces of it in that chain of iflands of which Cape de Verd, Afcenfion, and St. Matthew's Ifland make a part. In like manner, it is probable, the northweftern part of America was united to the northeaftern part of Afia, and the northeaftern parts of America to the northweftern parts of Europe, by Greenland, Iceland, etc.

QUADRUPEDE ANIMALS within the United States: *Mammoth.* This name has been given to an unknown animal, whofe bones are found in the northern parts of both the old and new world. From the form of their teeth, they are fuppofed to have been carniverous. Like the elephant they were armed with tufks of ivory; but they obvioufly differed from the elephant in fize; their bones prove them to have been 5 or 6 times as large.

A late governor of Virginia, having afked fome delegates of the Delawares what they knew refpecting this animal; the chief fpeaker informed him that it was a tradition handed down from their fathers, " That in ancient times a herd of them came to the Big-bone licks, and began an univerfal deftruction of the bears, deer, elks, buffaloes, and

other animals which had been created for the ufe of the
Indians; that the Great Man, above, looking down, and
feeing this, was fo enraged that he feized his lightning,
defcended to the earth, feated himfelf upon a neighboring
mountain, on a rock, on which his feat and the print of
his feet are ftill to be feen, and hurled his bolts among them
till the whole were flaughtered, except the big bull, who,
prefenting his forehead to the fhafts, fhook them off as
they fell; but at length, miffing one, it wounded him in
the fide; whereupon, fpringing round, he bounded over the
Ohio, the Wabafh, the Illinois, and finally over the great
lakes, where he is living at this day."

Sapajon, Sagoin. There are various fpecies of animals
faid to inhabit the country on the lower part of the Miffif-
fippi, called Sapajons and Sagoins. The former are capable of fupporting themfelves by their tails; the latter are
not. They have a general refemblance to monkeys, but
are not fufficiently known to be particularly defcribed.

The sapajon and sagoin are not as mythical as
might be fancied from what the book says of them.
They both belong to the monkey tribe, but dwell
in South America instead of on the lower Mississippi.   Another curious item is this : —

Grey Squirrels fometimes migrate in confiderable numbers. If in their courfe they meet with a river, each of
them takes a fhingle, piece of bark, or the like, and carries it to the water; thus equipped they embark, and erect
their tails to the gentle breeze, which foon wafts them over
in fafety; but a fudden flaw of wind fometimes produces
a deftructive fhipwreck.

Fifty " quadrupede " animals are described in all,
and then we have a section devoted to " Birds."

Next "Amphibious Reptiles" are considered, after
that "Serpents," and finally "Fifhes." Here are
sample paragraphs : —

The *Wakon Bird*, which probably is of the fame fpecies
with the Bird of Paradife, receives its name from the ideas
the Indians have of its fuperior excellence; the Wakon
Bird being in their language the bird of the Great Spirit.
Its tail is compofed of four or five feathers, which are
three times as long as its body, and which are beautifully
fhaded with green and purple. It carries this fine length
of plumage in the fame manner as the peacock does his,
but it is not known whether, like him, it ever raifes it to
an erect pofition.

The *Whitfaw* is of the cuckow kind, being a folitary
bird, and fcarcely ever feen. In the fummer months it is
heard in the groves, where it makes a noife like the filing
of a faw.

Of the *Frog* kind are many fpecies. Pond frog, green
fountain frog, tree frog, bull frog. Befides thefe are the
dufky brown, fpotted frog of Carolina; their voice re-
fembles the grunting of fwine. The bell frog, fo called,
becaufe their voice is fancied to be exactly like that of a
loud cow bell. A beautiful green frog whofe noife is like
the barking of little dogs, or the yelping of puppies. A
lefs green frog, whofe notes refemble thofe of young
chickens. Little gray fpeckled frog, who make a noife
like the ftriking of two pebbles together under the furface
of the water. There is yet an extremely diminutive fpecies of frogs, called by fome, Savanna crickets, whofe notes
are not unlike the chattering of young birds or crickets.
They are found in great multitudes after plentiful rains.

The *Alligator* is a very large, ugly, terrible creature, of
prodigious ftrength, activity, and fwiftnefs in the water.
They are from 12 to 23 feet in length; their bodies are as

large as that of a horfe. The head of a full-grown alligator is about three feet long, and the mouth opens nearly
the fame length. The upper jaw only, moves, and this
they raife fo as to form a right angle with the lower one.
They open their mouths while they lie bafking in the fun,
on the banks of rivers and creeks, and when filled with
flies, mufketoes and other infects, they fuddenly let fall their
upper jaw with furprifing noife, and thus fecure their prey.

The *Rattle Snake* may be ranked among the largeft ferpents in America. If purfued and overtaken, they in-
ftantly throw themfelves into the fpiral coil; their whole
body fwells through rage, their eyes are red as burning
coals, and their brandifhing forked tongues, of the colour
of the hotteft flame, menaces a horrid death.

The *Joint Snake*, if we may credit Carver's account of
it, is a great curiofity. Its fkin is as hard as parchment,
and as fmooth as glafs. It is beautifully ftreaked with
black and white. It is fo ftiff, and has fo few joints, and
thofe fo unyielding, that it can hardly bend itfelf into the
form of a hoop. When it is ftruck, it breaks like a pipe-
ftem; and you may, with a whip, break it from the tail to
the bowels into pieces not an inch long, and not produce
the leaft tincture of blood.

Other snakes mentioned are the " Water Viper,
with a fharp thorn tail, Hog nofe Snake, Coach
Whip Snake, which the Indians imagine is able to
cut a man in two with a jerk of its tail, Ribbon
Snake, Glafs Snake, and Two-headed Snake."

In the list of fishes are noted the " Skip jack,
Minow, Shiner, Dab, Hard Head and Mummy-
chog." Of the Lamprey it is affirmed that

After the fpawning feafon is over, and the young fry
have gone down to the fea, the old fifhes attach themfelves

to the roots and limbs of trees, which have fallen or run into the water, and there perifh. A mortification begins at the tail, and proceeds upwards to the vital part. Fifh of this kind have been found at Plymouth, in New Hampfhire, in different ftages of putrification.

When the general characteristics of the United States have been dealt with, New England is taken up, and we are informed that in this portion of the republic —

Learning is more generally diffufed than in any other part of the globe; arifing from the excellent eftablifhment of fchools in almoft every townfhip and fmaller diftrict.

A very valuable fource of information to the people is the Newfpapers, of which not lefs than thirty thoufand are printed every week, in New England.

Apples are common, and cider conftitutes the principal drink of the inhabitants.

Each state is described in detail, including such topics as " Religion, Military Strength, Literature, Curiofities, Conftitution, and Hiftory." Bridges are constantly referred to — even those over the smaller rivers. We learn, for instance, that across the Piscataqua in New Hampshire a few miles above Portsmouth " has been erected the moft refpectable bridge in the United States, 2600 feet in length," at a cost of nearly seventy thousand dollars. In Massachusetts ten bridges are listed that " merit notice," and, it is added, " Thefe bridges are all fupported by a toll."

Harvard University, the book says, " confifts of four elegant edifices," and we are told that " In Wil-

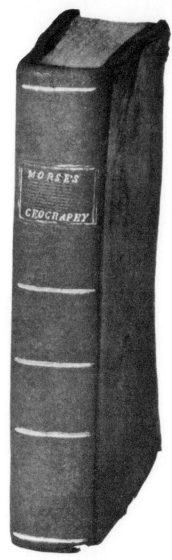

The First American Geography.
Size of book, 12mo.

liamstown is another literary inftitution ftarted in
1790, partly by lottery and partly by the liberal
donation of gentlemen of the town." Boston had
seven schools supported wholly at the public expense, "and in them the children of *every* clafs of
citizens freely affociate." Three of these were " Englifh grammar fchools in which the children of *both*
fexes, from feven to fourteen years of age are inftructed
in fpelling, accenting, and reading the Englifh language with propriety ; alfo in Englifh grammar and
compofition, together with the rudiments of geography." In three schools "the fame children are
taught writing and arithmetic. The fchools are attended alternately, and each of them is furnifhed
with an Ufher or Affiftant. The mafters of thefe
fchools have each a falary of 666 2-3 dollars per
annum payable quarterly." Lastly there was the
" Latin grammar fchool" to which "none are
admitted till ten years of age."

The inhabitants of Boston at this time numbered
24,937. As usual in speaking of important places
a list is given of the " public buildings." There
were " 18 houfes for public worfhip, the ftate houfe,
court houfe, gaol, Faneuil Hall, a theatre, an alms
houfe, and powder magazine." The principal manufactures of the town were "rum, beer, paper hang-
ings, loaf fugar, cordage, fail cloth, fpermaceti and
tallow candles, and glafs."

The final states to be considered in the New England section are " Rhode Ifland and Providence
Plantations," and Connecticut. Perhaps the most
interesting bit in this portion is the statement that

to Hartford, at the head of ship navigation on the
Connecticut River, was brought in boats the produce
of the country for two hundred miles above.   Railroads were as yet undreamed of, and right through
the book navigable streams and canals are treated
as of far more importance than they would be at
present.

Morse in his first edition devoted a paragraph to
the " Connecticut Inhabitants."   Whether he abandoned it because it gave offence, I do not know.   It
says : —

The people of this ſtate are generally induſtrious ſagacious
huſbandmen ; generous and hoſpitable to ſtrangers, and good
neighbours.   But they are characteriſed for being intem-
perately fond of law ſuits and little petty arbitrations.   The
ladies are modeſt, handſome, and agreeable, fond of imitat-
ing new and extravagant faſhions, neat and chearful, and
poſſeſſed of a large ſhare of delicacy, tenderneſs and ſenſi-
bility.   The above character may with juſtice be given to
the ladies of the four New-England States.

Now we come to " *The* SECOND GRAND DIVISION
of the UNITED STATES."   It comprised New York,
New Jersey, Pennsylvania, Delaware, and " Territory
N. W. of the Ohio."   Special attention is paid to
the climate of this tract, which the book says has

but one ſteady trait, and that is, it is uniformly variable.
The changes of weather are great, and frequently ſudden.
On the whole, it appears that the climate is a compound
of moſt of the climates of the world.   It has the moiſture
of Ireland in ſpring ; the heat of Africa in ſummer ; the
temperature of Italy in June ; the ſky of Egypt in autumn ;

the fnow and cold of Norway in winter; the tempefts (in a certain degree) of the Weft Indies, in every feafon; and the variable winds and weather of Great Britain in every month in the year.

From this account of the climate, it is eafy to afcertain what degrees of health, and what difeafes prevail. As the inhabitants have the climate, fo they have the accute difeafes of all the countries that have been mentioned.

Concerning New York City, the book says:—

A want of good water has been a great inconvenience to the citizens; there being but few wells in the city. Moft of the people are fupplied every day with frefh water conveyed to their doors in cafks, from a pump at the head of Queen-ftreet, which receives it from a fpring almoft a mile from the centre of the city. This well is about 20 feet deep, and 4 feet diameter. The average quantity drawn daily from this remarkable well, is 110 hogfheads of 130 gallons each. In fome hot fummer days, 216 hogfheads have been drawn from it, and what is very fingular, there is never more or lefs than about three feet of water in the well. The water is fold commonly at three pence a hogfhead at the pump. The Manhattan Company was incorporated in 1798, for the purpofe of conveying good water into the city, and their works are now nearly completed.

New York then had a population of sixty thousand, which included about three thousand slaves.

In describing the "Territory N. W. of the Ohio" a list is given of its forts "eftablifhed for the protection of the frontiers," and we are told that

both the high and low lands produce vaft quantities of natural grapes, of which the fettlers univerfally make a fufficiency, for their own confumption, of rich red wine. It is afferted that age will render this wine preferable to moft of the European wines. Cotton is the natural production of this country, and it grows in great perfection.

Below are fragments of information about the Southern States, " *The* THIRD *and much the largeſt* GRAND DIVISION *of the* UNITED STATES."

The city of WASHINGTON stands at the junction of the rivers Patomak and the Eaftern Branch. The fituation of this metropolis is upon the great poft road, equi-diftant from the northern and fouthern extremities of the Union. The public offices were removed to this city in the fummer of 1800, and here in future Congrefs will hold their feffions.

In the flat country near the fea-coaft of North Carolina, the inhabitants, during the fummer and autumn, are fubject to intermittent fevers, which often prove fatal. The countenances of the inhabitants during thefe feafons, have generally a pale yellowifh caft, occafioned by the prevalence of bilious fymptoms.

A few years fince, Tenneffee abounded with large herds of wild cattle, improperly called Buffaloes ; but the improvident or ill-difpofed among the firft fettlers, have deftroyed multitudes of them, out of mere wantonnefs. They are ftill to be found on fome of the fouth branches of Cumberland river. Elk or moofe are feen in many places, chiefly among the mountains. The deer are become comparatively fcarce ; fo that no perfon makes a bufinefs of hunting them for their fkins only. Enough of bears and wolves yet remain.

In Maryland, Virginia, and North-Carolina the inhabitants are exceffively fond of the diverfion of horfe racing. Every fpring and fall they have ftated races for three or four days, which collect the fporting gentlemen from every part of the country from 100 to 200 miles. Every poor peaf-

ant has an horfe or two and all the family in ruins, with
fcarcely any covering or provifions; while the nag, with
two or three Negroes rubbing him, is pampered with luxu-
ries to the extreme of high living.

This last item is from the edition of 1784. I
make one more quotation from that edition under
the heading, " Spanifh Dominions in N. America,"
— that is, Florida and Mexico, — and then resume
consideration of the later book.

In California, there falls in the morning a great quantity
of dew, which, fettling on the rofe-leaves becomes hard like
manna, having all the fweetnefs of refined fugar, without
its whitenefs.

The greateft curiofity in the city of Mexico, is their
floating gardens.   When the Mexicans, about the year
1325, were fubdued by the Colhuan and Tepanecan nations, and confined to the fmall iflands of the lake, having
no land to cultivate, they were taught by neceffity to form
movable gardens, which floated on the lake.   Their con-
ftruction is very fimple.   They take willows and the roots
of marfh plants, and other materials which are light, and
twift them together, and fo firmly unite them as to form a
fort of platform, which is capable of fupporting the earth
of the garden.   Upon this foundation they lay bufhes and
over them fpread the mud which they draw up from the
bottom of the lake.   Their figure is quadrangular; their
length and breadth various, but generally about 8 rods long
and 3 wide; and their elevation from the furface of the
water is lefs than a foot.   Thefe were the firft fields that
the Mexicans owned, after the foundation of Mexico;
there they firft cultivated the maize, great pepper and other
plants neceffary for their fupport.   From the induftry of
the people thefe fields foon became numerous.   At prefent

they cultivate flowers and every fort of garden herbs upon
them.   In the largeft gardens there is commonly a little
tree and a little hut, to fhelter the cultivator, and defend
him from the rain or the fun.   When the owner of a garden wifhes to change his fituation, to get out of a bad
neighborhood, or to come near to his family, he gets into
his little boat, and by his own ftrength alone, if the garden
is fmall, or with the affiftance of others if it be large, con-
ducts it wherever he pleafes.

Among the islands off the coast of South America
that are described is " Juan Fernandes 300 miles
weft of Chili," famous for its connection with Defoe's
Robinson Crusoe.   The book tells how Alexander
Selkirk dwelt there and how he was finally rescued,
concluding with : —

During his abode on this ifland he had killed 500 goats,
which he caught by running them down; and he marked
as many more on the ear, which he let go.   Some of thefe
were caught 30 years after, their venerable afpect and ma-
jeftic beards difcovering ftrong fymptoms of antiquity.

Selkirk upon his return to England, was advifed to pub-
lifh an account of his life and adventures.   He is faid to
have put his papers into the hands of Daniel Defoe, to
prepare them for publication.   But that writer, by the help
of thofe papers, and a lively fancy tranfformed Alexander
Selkirk into Robinfon Crufoe, and returned Selkirk his
papers again; fo that the latter derived no advantage from
them.

Part I of the geography closes with " New Dif-
coveries," which it declares " have been numerous
and important."   Here is one : —

The Northern Archipelago.] This confists of feveral groups of iflands fituated between the eaftern coaft of Kamtfchatka and the weftern coaft of America.

The moft perfect equality reigns among thefe iflanders. They feed their children when very young, with the coarf- eft flefh, and for the moft part raw. If an infant cries, the mother immediately carries it to the fea fide, and, whether it be fummer or winter, holds it naked in the water until it is quiet. This cuftom is fo far from doing the chil- dren any harm that it hardens them againft the cold, and they go barefooted through the winter without the leaft in- convenience. The leaft affliction prompts them to fuicide; the apprehenfion of even an uncertain evil, often leads them to defpair; and they put an end to their days with great apparent infenfibility.

A little farther on we find this about the people of the Friendly Islands : —

Their great men are fond of a fingular kind of luxury, which is, to have women fit befide them all night, and beat on different parts of their body until they go to fleep; after which, they relax a little of their labour, unlefs they appear likely to wake; in which cafe they redouble their exertions, until they are again faft afleep.

Part II is devoted to the eastern hemisphere. I quote two paragraphs about Lapland : —

The employment of the women confifts in making nets for the fifhery, in drying fifh and meat, in milking the rein- deer, in making cheefe, and in tanning hides; but it is underftood to be the bufinefs of the men to look after the kitchen, in which, it is faid, the women never interfere.

When a Laplander intends to marry a female, he, or his

friends, court her father with brandy; when with fome difficulty he gains admittance to his fair one, he offers her a beaver's tongue, or fome other eatable, which fhe rejects before company, but accepts of in private.

The father evidently enjoyed his part of the courting and was loath to end his free supply of liquor. "This prolongs the courtfhip fometimes for three years," says the book.

I expected when I turned to the pages devoted to Asia that I would find rats named as an article of Chinese diet, but the rat myth seems to have been of later growth. None of the geographies refer to it until Peter Parley in 1830 shows a picture of a pedler " selling rats and puppies for pies." In spite of this lack Morse's information about the Chinese is by no means uninteresting, as will be seen by the cullings which follow : —

The Chinefe have particular ideas of beauty. They pluck up the hairs of the lower part of their faces by the roots with tweezers, leaving a few ftraggling ones by way of beard. Their complexion towards the north, is fair, towards the fouth, fwarthy; and the fatter a man is they think him the handfomer.

Language.] The Chinefe language contains only 330 words, all of one fyllable : but then each word is pro-nounced with fuch various modulations, and each with a different meaning, that it becomes more copious than could be eafily imagined, and enables them to exprefs themfelves very well, on the common occafions of life.

The Chinefe pretend, as a nation, to an antiquity beyond all meafure of credibility; and their annals have been car-ried beyond the period to which the fcripture chronology

affigns the creation of the world. Poan Kou is faid by
them to have been the firft man; and the interval of time
betwixt him and the death of the celebrated Confucius,
which was in the year before Chrift, 479, has been reck-
oned from 276,000 to 96,961,740 years.

The descriptions of Africa in Morse's book lack
definiteness, except as regards Egypt and the north
coast. The rest of the continent, "from the Tropic
of Cancer to the Cape of Good Hope," is handled
in a single lump. Of the inland countries Abys-
sinia receives most attention, and we are told that —

The religion of the Abyffinians is a mixture of Chrif-
tianity, Judaifm and Paganifm; the two latter of which
are by far the moft predominant. There are here more
churches than in any other country, and though it is very
mountainous, and confequently the view much obftructed,
it is very feldom you fee lefs than 5 or 6 churches. Every
great man when he dies, thinks he has atoned for all his
wickednefs, if he leaves a fund to build a church, or has
one built in his life-time.

The churches are full of pictures flovenly painted on
parchment, and nailed upon the walls. There is no choice
in their faints, they are both of the Old and New Teftament,
and thofe that might be difpenfed with from both. There
is St. Pontius Pilate and his wife; there is St. Baalam and
his afs; Sampfon and his jaw bone, and fo of the reft.

It makes the beginning of the nineteenth century
seem very barbaric when we read a few pages farther
on that —

In the Guinea or weftern coaft, the Englifh exchange
their woolen and linen manufactures, their hard ware and

fpirituous liquors, for the perfons of the natives.   Among the Negroes, a man's wealth confifts in the number of his family, whom he fells like fo many cattle, and often at an inferior price.

One page near the close of the volume estimates the number of inhabitants in the world and forecasts the probable population of the United States a century later.   It supposes that the number will double every twenty years, and that therefore in 1900 we should be a nation of 160 millions.

In this forecast and in some other respects our author fails to hit the mark, but whatever the book's shortcomings, it was not dull, and it did admirable service in introducing an important study into the old-time schools.

XIII

THE old-time geographies until nearly the middle of the last century were never larger than 12mos and some of them were diminutive 32mos. Up to 1820 they were as a rule bound in full leather, but occasionally the wood or binder's board of the sides was covered with dull blue or marbled paper. Buff-tinted papers with the title and more or less other printing on them were substituted on nearly all the later books. Illustrations also began to be used, at first sparingly, but soon very generously; and instead of being designed for the older pupils the books were made with special reference to the needs of the younger children.

For a score of years after geographies began to be introduced into the schools they depended largely on the use of a globe to make clear the divisions of the earth. It was not long, however, before nearly every book was accompanied by an atlas, and this continued customary to about 1850. Not many of these atlases have survived. They were flimsily made, with paper covers, and the wear and tear of daily use made an end of them. The usual size was either about six by nine inches or nine by eleven

inches.   Comparatively little color was used on the
maps, and even at their newest the atlases must have
looked dull and uninteresting.   To modern eyes the
oddest features of the maps are the vacant or mis-
taken outlines of the northern coasts of this continent, and the general blankness of all its western
portion, with Mexico making a great sweep up into
the present domains of our republic.   Some of the
African maps, too, are given a strange appearance
by the portrayal of an immense line of mountains
— the " Jibbel Kumra or M^{ts} of the Moon " — extending in a continuous and perfectly straight chain
from east to west entirely across the broadest part
of the continent.

J edidiah Morse was the pioneer among American
authors of school geographies, as I have explained
in the previous chapter.   The earliest rival to con-
test the field with Morse's books was a small volume
of questions and answers compiled by Nathaniel
Dwight and published at Hartford in 1795.   Our
own continent is confined to the final third of
Dwight's Geography, while Europe, Asia, and Africa
have the first two-thirds.   How very remote and
unfamiliar many portions of the globe still were can
be judged from the fact that most of the capital
cities in Africa and some even in Asia and Europe
are located by giving their distance and direction
from London.   Thus, " Peterſburgh the capital of
Ruſſia is   1140   miles   north-eaſt from   London.
Pekin the capital of China ſtands eight thouſand
and ſixty-two   miles   ſouth-eaſterly of   London."
Monomotapa, the capital of a country of the same

name " on the fea-shore in the fouthern part of Africa, is built with wood, covered with plafter and ftands about 5,200 miles fouth-eafterly from London." Other curious bits from the geography follow : —

Q. What are the Ruffian funeral ceremonies ?

A. They are fingular : The prieft prays, and fprinkles the corpfe for eight or ten days; it is then buried with a paffport to heaven, figned by the bifhop and another clergyman, which is put between the fingers of the deceafed, and then the people return to the houfe whence they went, and drown their forrow in intoxication. This they commonly do for about forty days, during which time the prieft fays prayers over the grave.

Q. Are there any lakes in Scotland ?

A. There are many; but two are very remarkable : One near Lochnefs is on the top of a hill almoft two miles high. This lake is fmall, but it has never been founded, nor does it ever freeze. About feventeen miles diftant is another lake which is frozen all the year.

Q. What are the perfons and characters of the Scots ?

A. They are generally lean, raw-boned, and have high cheek-bones, which is a characteriftical feature.

Q. What are the diverfions of the Scots ?

A. They are all of the vigorous, athletic kind; such as dancing, *goff* and *curling*. The goff is a fpecies of ballplaying performed with a bat and a ball, the extremity of the bat being loaded with lead, and the party which ftrikes the ball with feweft ftrokes into a hole prepared for the purpofe wins the game.

Q. What are the cuftoms and diverfions of the Irifh ?

A. There are a few cuftoms exifting in Ireland peculiar to this country. Thefe are their funeral howlings and prefenting their corpfes in the ftreets to excite the charity of

ftrangers, their convivial meetings on Sunday, and dancing
to bag-pipes, which are ufually attended with quarreling.

Q. What curiofities are there in France?

A. A fountain near Grenoble emits a flame which will
burn paper, ftraw, etc., but will not burn gun-powder.
Within about eight leagues of the fame place is an inac-
ceffible mountain in the form of a pyramid reverfed.

Q. What are the animal productions of Poland?

A. Buffaloes, horfes, wolves, boars, gluttons, lynxes and
deer. Befides these there is elk, which is faid to be deftroyed in the winter by flies who get into his ears and live
upon his brain.

Q. What curiofities are there in Portugal?

A. There are lakes into which a stone being caft caufes
a rumbling like the noife of an earthquake.

Q. What do you obferve of the inhabitants of Guinea?

A. They are chiefly pagans and idolaters. In Eyo,
where the people are governed by a king who is not abfo-
lute, when they are tired of him, a deputation waits on him
and informs him that it is fatiguing for him to bear the
burden of government any longer, advifing him to take a
little reft. He thanks them and retires to his apartment
as if to fleep, and directs his women to ftrangle him; and
after he expires they deftroy all things which belonged to
him or to themfelves, and then kill one another. His fon
fucceeds to the government, and on the fame terms.

Q. Give a concife defcription of the Giages and Annians.

A. The first inhabit a part of the Congo coaft; the
latter live in the Macaco. The people are cannibals. They
kill and eat their firft-born children; and their friends who
die are eaten by their relations. The king of Macaco
refides in Monfol, where there is a market in which human
flefh is fold, although other meat exifts in plenty. They
efteem it a luxury, and it is faid an hundred prifoners or
flaves are daily killed for the king's table.

Q. What are the characteriſtics of the Hottentots?
A. They are the moſt abject of the human race. They beſmear their bodies with ſoot and greaſe, live upon carrion, old leather, ſhoes, and everything of the moſt loathſome kind; dreſs themſelves in ſheep's ſkins, untanned, turning the wool to their fleſh in the winter, and the other ſide in the ſummer. Their dreſs ſerves them for a bed at night, for a covering by day, and for a winding-ſheet when they die.

Q. What is the temper of the New England people?
A. They are frank and open, bold and enterpriſing. The women are educated to houſe-wifery, excellent companions, and houſe-keepers; ſpending their leiſure time in reading books of uſeful information.

Q. What are their diverſions?
A. Dancing is a favorite one of both ſexes. Sleigh-riding in winter, and ſkating, playing ball, gunning and fiſhing are the principal; gambling and horſe-jockeying are practiſed by none but worthleſs people who are deſpiſed by all perſons of reſpectability, and conſidered as nuiſances in ſociety.

Q. Are there any ſlaves in Maſſachuſetts?
A. NONE.

One geography that had a marked individuality of its own was a thick little volume, mostly in verse, entitled *The Monitor's Instructor*, published at Wilmington, Delaware, in 1804. Speaking of himself in the third person in the introduction the author says, " Unpractised in poetry in a great degree, he has ventured thereupon supposing it to be, in general, rather more taking, with youth, than prose; and though not the most flowery cast, it will, he hopes, answer the end."

> Now let the muse some incense bring,
> As we the works of nature sing,

is the way he begins, and below are extracts culled
here and there from succeeding pages : —

> America (our native) streams,
> Shall first awhile become our themes,
> Both lakes and rivers, great and small,
> Which in th' Atlantic Ocean fall.

After naming the more important coast rivers, the
book remarks : —

> Now o'er these streams thus having glanc'd,
> And hastily, thus far advanc'd,
> Not having left the sounding shore,
> Next their main sources shall explore ;
> And on the wing which poets feign,
> Soar to each mount, skim o'er the plain,
> To find the little purling rill,
> And which the largest rivers fill.

> *   *   *   *   *   *

> One river, of enormous size,
> To west of Mississippi lies. . . .
> The river this call'd Missouri,
> And tow'rd south-east its courses lie,
> This river, from what I can see,
> Can't less than the Ohio be.

Skipping to where the book is describing leading
towns, we find these lines : —

> An island is well known to fame,
> Manhattan is this island's name. . . .

On sou'west end New York doth stand,
Investing all that point of land. . . .
Not fully regular it's plann'd,
Yet very elegant and grand. . . . .
The streets present 'diversity,
And suited to conveniency,
The Broadway has still more of taste
Than any street in all the place. . . .
A street three-score and ten feet wide,
And gently rising from the tide,
Its edifices bold and grand,
Present themselves on either hand;
The most magnificent of all,
Known by the name of Fed'ral Hall,
For pleasantness, it is agreed,
And health, few places this exceed.
In summer come, on every side,
The cooling breezes from the tide.
For winter mildness few excel
This city, of same parallel.

In the prose portion of the book are several curious " paradoxes." Here is one of them : —

Three men went on a journey, in which, though their heads travelled 12 yards farther than their feet, all returned alive, with their heads on.

The *Solution* explains that " If any person should travel round the globe, the space travelled by his head will exceed that his feet travelled " by about the number of yards mentioned.

The next geography from which I make selection is by Benjamin Davies. It was published in 1813.

The first two paragraphs quoted come under the heading "New Holland." This was the accepted name of Australia until the middle of the nineteenth century. The Dutch discovered the continent in 1616, but its size and shape were only vaguely known until Captain Cook explored most of the coast in 1770.

SOME suppose that this extensive region, when more thoroughly investigated, will be found to consist of two, three or more vast islands, intersected by narrow seas.

INHABITANTS. The black bushy beards of the men and the bone or reed which they thrust through the cartilage of the nose gives them a disgusting appearance ; which is not improved by the practice of rubbing fish oil into their skins as a protection from the air and moskitos ; so that in hot weather the stench is intolerable. The women are marked by the loss of the two first joints of the little finger of the left hand ; as they are supposed to be in the way when they coil their fishing lines.

MANNERS AND CUSTOMS IN THE UNITED STATES. Travellers have observed a want of urbanity, particularly in Philadelphia ; and in all the capital cities, an eager pursuit of wealth, by adventurous speculations in commerce, by land-jobbing, banks, insurance offices, and lotteries. The multiplication of inns, taverns and dram shops, is an obvious national evil that calls loudly for legislative interference ; for in no country are they more numerous or more universally baneful. Schools are spread everywhere through the well-settled parts of the country, yet the domestic regulation of children and youth is not duly regarded.

LANGUAGE. The English language is the general one of the union, and is cultivated with great assiduity in all the principal cities and towns. All the classical authors in the English language have been reprinted in America, many of them have passed through several editions, some with great elegance and correctness.

BOSTON is built in a very irregular manner, on a peninsula, at the bottom of Massachusetts bay.

SOUTHERN MANNERS AND CUSTOMS.   The inquisitive traveller as he progresses southward no longer beholds so great a proportion of hardy, industrious, and healthy yeomanry, living on terms of equality and independence; their domestic economy neat and comfortable; their farms well stocked; and their cattle sleek and thriving.   On the contrary he discovers the farmhouses more thinly scattered, some of them miserable hovels; the retreats of small proprietors, who are too indolent or too proud to labour; here and there a stack of corn-fodder, and the cattle looking as miserable as their owners.   A few miles distant perhaps he finds a large mansion house, the property of the lord of two or three thousand acres of land, surrounded by 50 or 100 negro-huts, constructed in the slightest manner; and about these cabins swarms of black slaves.   But it is just to observe that many of the gentry are distinguishable for their polished manners and education, as well as for their great hospitality to strangers.

Cummings's Geography, 1814, apologizes in its preface for adding another "to the number of geographies, already so great as to obstruct, rather than promote improvement."   This preface is very long, and is chiefly made up of directions "designed to assist teachers, who have had but imperfect, or no geographical instruction."   It advises them to "let the pupils always set with their faces towards the north."   Then with their maps before them they will be in proper position to get the points of the compass straight in their minds.

Early in the lessons we are informed that the "Alleganies are in some places, immense masses of rocks, piled one above another in frightful precipices, till they reach the height of more than 10,000 feet above a level with the ocean." In reality not a peak reaches 7000 feet.

During the previous decade Lewis and Clark had made their journey across the continent, and we now find mention of the "Stony Mountains." It was a number of years before the name Rocky was substituted for Stony. On the maps they were sometimes labelled the Chippewan Mountains, and Workman's Geography, in 1805, says the ranges "that lie weſt of the river St. Pierre are called the Shining Mountains, from an infinite number of chryſtal ſtones of an amazing ſize with which they are covered, and which, when the ſun ſhines full upon them, ſparkle ſo as to be ſeen at a very great diſtance."

In the descriptions of the states, we learn from Cummings that the western part of Pennsylvania abounds with excellent coal, but we get no hint of its having any commercial importance. Indeed, coal mining as an industry did not begin until 1820. Before that time coal was in the same category as were petroleum and natural gas, which the book calls "curiosities."

Concerning the Andes in South America, we are told, "These amazing mountains, in comparison with which the Alps are but little hills, have fissures in some places a mile wide, and deep in proportion; and there are others that run under the ground, and resemble in extent a province."

When we come to Europe, we are made to realize the intense cold of the Lapland winters by the statement that, " In attempting to drink the lips are frequently frozen to the cup." It is affirmed, too, that if there is a crust on the snow, " The Laplander travels with his reindeer in a sledge two or three hundred miles a day." Another queer bit is this about the roads in Flanders, an old-time province, which included all the coast region of Belgium and extended into France and Holland. " They are generally a broad causeway, and run several miles in a straight line till they terminate in a view of some magnificent building." These views no doubt gave pleasure, but I think I should have preferred to have the roads continue.

Presently we find the following paragraph : —

In the ocean there are many dangerous whirlpools. That called the *Maelstroom*, upon the coast of Norway, is considered as the most dreadful and voracious in the world. A minute description of the internal parts is not to be expected, since none, who were there, ever returned to bring back information. The body of the waters, that form this whirlpool, is extended in a circle about thirteen miles in circumference. In the midst of this stands a rock against which the tide in its ebb is dashed with inconceivable fury. At this time it instantly swallows up everything that comes within the sphere of its violence. No skill in the mariner, nor strength of rowing, can work an escape ; the vessel's motion, though slow in the beginning, becomes every moment more rapid, it goes around in circles still narrower and narrower, till at last it is dashed against the rocks and instantly disappears. Nor is it seen again

for six hours; till, the tide flowing, it is thrown forth with
the same violence with which it was drawn in.   The noise
of this dreadful vortex still farther contributes to increase
its terror, which, with the dashing of the waters, makes
one of the most tremendous objects in nature."

In another geography of the period we learn that
even " the bellowing struggles of the whale have not
always redeemed him from the danger," and that
" the bottom is full of craggy spires."   The real
maelstrom is caused by the current of the Great
West Fiord rushing between two of the Loffoden
Isles.   Ordinarily it can be traversed without appre-
hension, but when the wind blows directly against
the current, the sea around for several miles is violently agitated and extremely dangerous.

Adams's Geography, 1818, is divided into three
parts — Part I, " Geographical Orthography," consisting of ten pages of names of states, rivers, towns,
etc., to be used as spelling lessons; Part II, " A
Grammar of Geography," fifty pages, being an epitome of main facts " to be committed to memory";
Part III, " A Description of the Earth," making
up the body of the book, " to be read in classes."
The first four excerpts are from Part II, the rest
from Part III.

A MOUNTAIN is a vast protuberance of the earth.

Europe is distinguished for its learning, politeness, government, and laws; for the industry of its inhabitants, and
the temperature of its climate.

The *White Mountains* are the highest not only in New
Hampshire, but in the United States.

Switzerland is a small romantic country, lying upon the

Alps, and is the highest spot in Europe. St. Gothard is the highest mountain.

Navigation on the *Mississippi* is attended with many difficulties and dangers, from the sudden crooks and bends in the river, the falling in of its banks, and more especially from the SAWYERS, so called, which are trees whose roots have by some means become fastened to the bottom of the

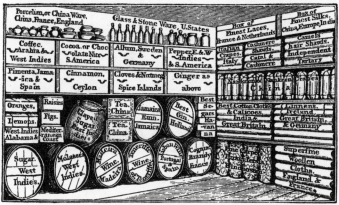

Country Store, exhibiting the Productions of Various Countries.

Frontispiece.

From Willard's *Geography for Beginners*, 1826.

Reduced one-third.

river, in such a manner, that, from the continual pressure of the current, they receive a regular vibratory motion from the resemblance of which to a saw-mill, they have derived their name. Their motion is sometimes very quick, and if they strike a boat, it is immediately upset or dashed to pieces. Vessels are from five to thirty days on their passage up to *New Orleans*, 87 miles; although with a favorable wind, they will sometimes descend in 12 hours.

From New Orleans to *Natchez*, 310 miles, the voyage requires from 60 to 80 days. Ships rarely ascend above that place. It is navigable for boats, carrying about 40 tons, and rowed by 18 or 20 men to the falls of *St. Anthony*.

Cataract of Niagara.
From Worcester's *Elements of Geography*, 1828.

The number of post-offices in the United States in 1811, was 2,043. The mail was carried 46,380 miles in stages, and 61,171 miles in sulkies and on horseback.

Several mineral springs break forth in different parts of the United States. The most celebrated are those of Saratoga and Ballstown in the state of New York. The latter place is much frequented by gay and fashionable people, as well as by invalids.

Beer is the common drink of the inhabitants of *New York State*. The forests abound with bears, wolves, deer, and elks.

Many of the towns and plantations in *Maine* are destitute of any settled minister. Missionaries sent among them have been affectionately received.

Water is brought to *Philadelphia* in a subterraneous canal, from the Schuylkill, and is then raised by steam 30 or 40 feet to a reservoir on the top of a circular edifice, from which it is distributed by bored logs to the different parts of the city.

Pittsburg is supplied with foreign goods chiefly by land from Philadelphia and Baltimore. The price of waggon carriage this distance is from 5 to 6 dollars a hundred pounds weight. The number of inhabitants, in 1810, was 4,768.

A decade later, when Pittsburg had a population of seven thousand, the geographies speak of it as "one of the greatest manufacturing towns in the Union."

I quote further from Adams, beginning with what he has to say of "the floating mills for grinding corn, which are frequently seen on the Ohio River."

Natural Bridge of Virginia.
From Worcester's *Elements of Geography*, 1828.

The mill is supported by two large canoes, with the wheel between them; this is moored wherever they can find the strongest current, nearest to the shore, by the force of which alone the mill is put in operation. It is floated up and down the river whenever a customer calls.

The exports from *Ohio*, consisting of flour, corn, hemp, flax, beef, pork, smoked hams of venison, whiskey, peach brandy, and lumber are mostly sent down the Mississippi to New Orleans. Those boats which descend with the produce rarely return, but on arriving at New Orleans, are taken to pieces and sold for lumber.

Cincinnati is a pleasant, flourishing town. It contains about 3,000 inhabitants. In this town is fort Washington, which commences the chain of forts extending to the westward.

Detroit, the capital of Michigan Territory, is a place of considerable trade, which consists chiefly in a barter of coarse European goods with the natives for furs. The town is surrounded by a strong blockade, through which there are 4 gates. The streets are generally crowded with Indians in the day time; but at night they are all shut out of the town, except such as get admittance into private houses, and the gates are closed.

Whale Fishing.
From Worcester's *Elements of Geography*, 1829.

St. Louis, the capital of the Territory of Louisiana, contains about 200 houses and is well fortified.

The people of *Norway* are justly famed for honesty and industry, and retain their strength so long, that a Norwegian is not supposed incapable of labour, till he is upwards of 100 years old. The inhabitants in some of the interior parts it is said live till weary of life.

Treck-Shuit.
From Worcester's *Elements of Geography*, 1829.

In all the northern parts of *Russia* the winter cold is very terrible. Birds in the act of flying have sometimes been known to drop down dead from the atmosphere in consequence of it; drivers of carriages are frequently frozen to death upon their seats without being able to change their position. At Petersburg, only two months in the year are entirely free from snow.

The CONDOR is undoubted the largest bird that pervades the air. When it alights on the ground, or rises from it, the noise it makes with its wings is such as to

2 A

terrify and almost to deafen any one who happens to be
near the place.

Among the animals peculiar to South America, the
most extraordinary is the SLOTH, or as it was called by
the way of derision, the swift Petre. It is about the size
of an ordinary monkey, but of a most wretched appearance. It never stirs unless impelled by hunger; it is said
to be several minutes in moving one of its legs. Every
effort is attended with a most dismal cry. When this
animal finds no wild fruits on the ground, he looks out
with a great deal of pain for a tree well loaded, which he
ascends moving and crying, and stopping by turns. At
length, having mounted, he plucks off all the fruit and
throws it on the ground, to save himself such another
troublesome journey; and rather than be fatigued in coming down the tree, gathers himself in a bunch, and with
a shriek drops to the ground.

Bridges in Chili.
From Woodridge's *Rudiments of Geography*, 1829.

A similar description of the sloth in Dwight's
Geography includes the statement that " It is so
many days travelling from one tree to another, that
it frequently grows lean during the journey."

Peter Parley's Method of telling about Geography,
1829, was a thin, square little book with leather back
and flexible pasteboard sides.   For years it had an

PETER PARLEY
Going to tell about Geography.

Take care there! take care boys! if you run against my toe,
I'll not tell you another story!

Frontispiece to *Peter Parley's Geography,* 1830.

immense circulation.   The style is simple and collo-
quial; there are numerous pictures and a variety of
maps and diagrams.   Perhaps the portion best re-

membered by those who studied the book is a rhymed
review of the earlier lessons, beginning —

> The world is round, and like a ball
> Seems swinging in the air,
> A sky extends around it all,
> And stars are shining there.

Pains are taken to inculcate good morals and religion, and we find in treating of Asia considerable

English.

A Chinese selling Rats and Puppies
for pies.

From *Peter Parley's Geography*, 1829.

Bible history with appropriate comments. "This
history," the author says, "is exceedingly interesting, and is all true. A great part of the history of
almost all other nations is false; but the Bible tells
us nothing but what is worthy of belief."

The Malte-Brun Geography, 1831, was also written by "Peter Parley," but the materials for the
book were drawn chiefly from the large work by
the noted French geographer, whose name gives

the book its title.   Selections that show something
of the character of the book
and of the times follow: —

Occasional bands of white
hunters and trappers range the
Missouri Territory for furs.
Some of them extend their
expeditions to the foot of the
Rocky mountains, and some
to the shores of the Pacific.
The herds of buffaloes that are
seen in this territory sometimes
amount to 10,000 each.   When
the herd is moving, the ground
trembles, and the grumbling and
bellowing of the multitude is
heard for miles.

Norwegian.

From *Peter Parley's Geography*.

It is probable that, ere long, roads will be cut across

White Bear.

From Olney's *A Practical System of Modern Geography*, 1831.

the Rocky mountains; that lines of stages will convey
travellers from the shores of the Atlantic to the Pacific;

that the borders of the latter ocean will be occupied by towns and villages; and that the immense valleys of the

The Maelstroom.
From Olney's *A Practical System of Modern Geography.*

Missouri, the Arkansas and the Columbia, now given up to the dominion of savages and wild beasts, will present all the busy and varied scenes of a crowded population.

Winter in Canada.
From *The Malte-Brun School Geography,* 1831.

Paris sets the fashions for Europe, and in some measure for America. An immense trade is here carried on in articles of dress. Every week the female fashions are changed, and every month there is a new cut for male attire.

From Woodbridge's *Universal Geography*, 1833, a large thick volume for advanced scholars, I make this extract : —

In 1790 the extent of post-roads in the United States was only 1875 miles; in 1827, it was 105,336. The great roads are usually turnpikes constructed by the state or incorporated bodies and supported by tolls. New England, and the greater part of the Middle States, are intersected in every direction by roads, which are usually well constructed and in good repair.

In the sandy, alluvial country of the Atlantic coast from New York to Florida, the roads are heavy, and not easily improved. The scattered state of population has prevented much attention to roads, in the states south of Maryland : and frequent impediments are presented by the want of bridges and causeways, over the streams and marshes.

In the Western States, during the wet season, many roads are scarcely passable for wheel carriages. The travelling in these states is chiefly by steam boats, on their noble rivers. The small streams are so variable that most of them can be forded during the dry seasons, and bridges are rarely built. The banks are high and steep, and the difficulty of passage is often very great. During high water, many of the streams become impassable, and the traveller encounters serious dangers.

The most important post-road in the United States is that which traverses the states on the Atlantic, a distance of 1,800 miles, passing through all the principal towns from Robbinstown in Maine to Florida.

A plan has recently been invented for constructing roads with iron bars, or railways, on which the wheels of carriages run so easily that they may be drawn from 15 to 30 miles an hour, by means of locomotive steam engines.

Peter Parley, in one of his geographies published in 1837, says of the railroads : —

Progress of Improvement.
From *The Malte-Brun School Geography*, 1842.

They are found so useful, that, for carrying passengers from one place to another, they have, on many routes, taken the place of stage-coaches.   When the cars first began to run, it was amusing to see the astonishment of the horses and cattle, as the engines came snorting, smoking and puffing over the road.   You have heard of the rail road from Boston to Worcester.   Near the latter place is an Insane Hospital, which commands a view of the road.   When the first car came into Worcester, a crazy man was looking out of the window.   " Upon my word," said he, " that's a strange-looking beast and travels desperate fast for such a short-legged crittur."

Scene in Illinois.
From *The Malte-Brun School Geography*, 1842.

Peter Parley's National Geography, 1845, was the earliest, I believe, to take the large, flat quarto

Pilgrims landing at Plymouth.
From Goodrich's *A National Geography*, 1845.

shape. This form enabled it to include good-sized maps and do away with the necessity for a separate

atlas; and in a few years the 12mos had been entirely abandoned. The chapters of the *National Geography* were enlivened with poetical introductions, and there were occasional other verses. The following selection, the last I have to make from the geographies of our forefathers, is this jingle description of "a general custom of moving, in the city of New York, on the first of May."

> Bustle, bustle!   Clear the way!
> He moves, they move, we move, to-day; —
> Pulling, hauling, fathers calling,
> Mothers brawling, children squalling,
> Coaxing, teasing, whimpering, prattling;
> Pots and pans and kettles rattling;
> Tumbling bedsteads, flying bedspreads,
> Broken chairs, and hollow wares,
> Strew the streets — 'Tis *moving* day!

Battle of Lexington.

From Mitchell's *A System of Modern Geography*, 1850.

GRAMMARS, HISTORIES, AND MINOR TEXT-BOOKS

THE two most successful makers of text-books in the period immediately following the Revolution were Noah Webster and Caleb Bingham. The former's spelling-book outstripped the latter's *Child's Companion*, but none of Bingham's books were failures, and his *American Preceptor* and the *Columbian Orator* were more widely used than Webster's readers or any others.

Caleb Bingham was born in what was then the new town of Salisbury in the northwestern corner of Connecticut in 1757. Many Indians still dwelt in the vicinity, and they were of such doubtful character that the people had always to be on their guard against a treacherous assault. Sundays the pioneers went to church armed; and the log structure used for a meeting-house had portholes, and a sentinel was stationed at the door. These frontier conditions gave little chance for education, but tradition says Caleb studied with the minister and thus prepared for college. He entered Dartmouth in 1779, and as soon as he graduated began to teach.

He came to Boston in 1784, and established a school for girls, but presently gave this up and taught in the public schools of the city. Still later he became a bookseller and publisher. He was an old-fashioned man, and almost to the time of his

death, in 1817, went about attired in a cocked hat
and small clothes, white vest and stock, and black
silk stockings. In summer he wore shoes with silver buckles, and in winter white-topped boots.

Next to his reading-books, Bingham's most famous
publication was " *The Young Lady's Accidence :* or a
fhort and eafy Introduction to Englifh Grammar.
Defigned principally for the ufe of young Learners,
more efpecially thofe of the FAIR SEX, though
proper for either." The title-page also contained
this couplet : —

> Delightful tafk ! to rear the tender thought,
> To teach the young idea how to fhoot. —

The date of the first edition was 1799. The book
treats the subject with admirable simplicity and clear-
ness, the type is good, and the little volume is a very
pleasing contrast to the dull, crowded pages of nearly
all the other grammars of the time. A hundred
thousand copies are said to have been sold. It was
the first English grammar used in the Boston schools,
and was one of the earliest grammars ever prepared
by an American author, its only predecessor of importance being Part II of Webster's *Grammatical
Institute.* Both these books gave place to the grammar by Lindley Murray, which in its numerous
abridgments was used for several decades almost
to the exclusion of every other work dealing with
the subject. Murray was born in Pennsylvania in
1745, and as a young man acquired considerable
reputation and wealth as a lawyer in New York City.
But in 1784 he went to England to reside, and it

was there he wrote his grammar, published in 1795, and his several other school-books brought out within the next few years.   Mr. Murray is described as modest in manner, humane and generous, and, in spite of bad health, unfailingly cheerful.   His books were all works of solid merit, though not very palatable to children.   The grammar looks dreary to the last degree now, and it must have had something of the same aspect even in the heyday of its popularity. There is a tradition that a friend of the author's once said to him, "Of all contrivances invented for puzzling the brains of the young your grammar is the worst," and this anecdote is quite believable.   Murray, however, introduced system into the treatment of the subject, and is known not unjustly as " the father of English Grammar."

PRONOUNS.

A man has stolen a bundle, and *he* is running away
with *it*.

Here *he* and *it* are pronouns, because they stand for nouns, and save the trouble of repeating them. If it were not for the pronouns, we should have to say, a man has stolen a bundle, and the man is running away with the bundle; but the pronouns save the necessity of repeating the words *man* and *bundle*.

From *Murray's Grammar*, adapted to the present mode of Instruction by Enoch Pond, 1835.

The study had been adopted in nearly all the schools by 1810, yet few teachers explained its intricacies or did more than make it a drill. The pupils understood little of what the books were intended to impart, and their interest was always at the ebb. It is related of a Pennsylvania school, about 1795, that some scholars, after a short experience with the new study, finding they could make nothing of it, got parental sympathy in their troubles and each came to the master with the report that: " Daddy says I needn't larn grammar. It's no use."

INTERJECTIONS.

Oh ! my poor brother.
From Enoch Pond's *Murray's Grammar.*

That particular master was a grammatical enthusiast and would not let them off. He tried to give the science practical application, and for the purpose of correcting the boys' language while they were at play, he whittled a small piece of thin board into the shape of a paddle. Whenever a boy used a wrong expression, he had to step aside and take the paddle, and he could not play again until he detected some other lad in a grammatical mistake.

PASSIVE VERBS.

My knife has been *opened*.   My scissors have been *ground*.
From Enoch Pond's *Murray's Grammar.*

Then the badge of interdiction was transferred. As a result of this system the scholars became very critical and made marked improvement in their speech.

The most attractive edition of *Murray's Grammar* was " one adapted to the present mode of instruction," by Enoch Pond, Worcester, 1835, a thin little volume with many small engravings illustrating the parts of speech.

Another illustrated text-book dealing with this subject was *The Little Grammarian.* It was of English origin, but was republished in New York in 1829. The text made clear " the leading rules of syntax in a series of instructive and amusing tales." The pictures consisted of twelve half-page steel en-

ADVERBS.

The ship sails SMOOTHLY.

The cars go SWIFTLY.
From Enoch Pond's *Murray's Grammar.*

gravings made to accompany the stories. The author says of his system that he is trying to make agreeable " a subject naturally dry and tedious in the same way that the skilful apothecary gilds his pill and colors the otherwise nauseous draught." Each chapter takes a part of speech, and the narrative in that chapter has that part of speech printed in italics as often as it occurs. These emphatic words occur so often they make the text pages look very queer. Just how effective this method is can be judged from the specimen which follows : —

THE ROBBER AND LITTLE ANN.

Some few years back, *a* poor man, living on one of *the* moors in *the* North of England, whilst busily employed in cutting turf, was cruelly beaten by *an* impious man, because he would not give him his watch and *the* little money he had in his pocket.

The Assault.

From *The Little Grammarian*, 1829.

His little girl (about three years old) had been to visit him, and was asleep on *a* bed of heath at *the* time her father was attacked; but his cries awoke her just in time to catch *a* sight of *the* barbarous thief, as he turned away from *the* mangled and almost lifeless body of her parent. Poor little Ann cried most bitterly as she assisted her poor father in his efforts to reach home, which, after more than *an* hour's toil, he accomplished.

A year or two later little Ann saw *the* assailant at *an* inn and ran into her father's hut in great affright, and called

out, as she swooned away, " I have seen *the* man " ; more
she could not say for tears and faintness. Her mother said
to her husband, " Did you not hear her say *the* man ? If

A Coach WITH *four horses going* FROM *Boston* TO
Providence, WITH *passengers* ON *the outside.*
Prepositions.
From *The Little Grammarian,* 1829.

she had said *a* man, I should have thought some silly fellow
had been playing tricks with *the* child. Surely, John, she
has not seen *the* man who lamed and robbed you ? "

A *beautiful*   A *more beautiful*   The *most beautiful*
BIRD.   BIRD.   BIRD.
The Comparison of Adjectives.
From *The Little Grammarian.*

John hastened to *the* inn, and arrived in time to secure
the man who had assaulted him. *The* man was taken to
prison ; and in *a* few months was sent from England for
life, to repent himself in toil in *a* distant land for *the* crimes

2 B

he had wrought in his own. Now, had Little Ann used *a* instead of *the* in her alarm; *the* thief would have escaped before she had been able to tell her parents what she really meant: hence learn the great difference between *a* or *an* and *the*.

VERBS.

Active.   Passive.   Neuter.
From *The Little Grammarian.*

A Boston edition of *The Little Grammarian* was also published, but a good deal of matter was added, and, instead of illustrating the stories, the pictures were confined to showing the meaning of the parts of speech.

A very fully illustrated book dealing with a sub-

Girl learning her lesson.

Description of picture. Old-fashioned furniture. Girl's attention not diverted by her pets. She seems to have nearly learned her lesson and to be just ready to start for her school.

From Frost's *Easy Exercises in Composition*, 1839.

ject allied to grammar was Frost's *Easy Exercises in Composition*. There were two or three pictures to a page right through the first half of the book, each with a few lines of suggestion under them. By this combination of pictures and short hints the pupils were expected to speedily and easily acquire "the art of expressing their ideas in writing."

Children promised a summer holiday.

Description. Pleasure of anticipating a holiday. Inducement to study hard, and behave well.

From Frost's *Easy Exercises in Composition*.

History was not taken up in the schools until the nineteenth century was well begun. One of the earliest histories of the United States, prepared for school use, was "by a citizen of Mass.," who states in his preface that, "while our schools abound with a variety of reading-books for children and youth, there has never yet appeared a compendious History of the United States fitted for our common schools."

This was 1821. The book was a small volume in full leather without maps or illustrations.

The next year the Rev. C. A. Goodrich published his history, which for a long time surpassed all rivals

Capt. John Smith defending himself from the Indians.

From Goodrich's *A History of the United States*, 1832.

in popularity. Within a dozen years one hundred and fifty thousand copies had been sold. It appeared in various editions, some entirely lacking pictures and none with more than a few insignificant cuts until 1832. Then it was produced in a thick 12mo with forty-eight engravings and a map. Good paper was used and the pictures were excellent for the time, and very well printed.

In 1832, also, Noah Webster put forth a school *History of the United States*, to which was "prefixed a brief Account of our [English] Ancestors, from the dispersion at Babel, to their Migration to America." The book ends with the adoption of the Constitution, because, as Mr. Webster explains, "An impartial history cannot be published during the lives of the principal persons concerned in the transactions related, without being exposed to the charge of undue flattery or censure; and unless

Destruction of Tea in Boston Harbor.
From Goodrich's *A History of the United States.*

history is impartial, it misleads the student, and frustrates its proper object." The individuality of the book is farther emphasized by a chapter of "Advice to the Young"—economical, moral and religious — which the author hopes will "serve, in a degree, to restrain some of the common vices of our country."

Other early school histories of the United States which attained more or less circulation were Hale's, Taylor's, Olney's, and Peter Parley's, the last running up into hundreds of editions. The study of history was not confined wholly to the story of our own nation. Several universal histories were published. Butler's, the earliest to be brought out, included, according to the title-page, "History, Sacred and Profane, from the Creation of the World, to the year 1818, of the Christian Era." It was very Biblical, the author's "first object through the whole work being to show the influence and impor-

Punishment of a man from Billerica, who purchased a gun from a British soldier in Boston, March, 1775.

From Taylor's *A Universal History of the United States,* 1830.

tance of religion — to contrast particularly the religion of Christ and his Apostles, with the religion of

Capture of the Frolick, October 18, 1812.

From Taylor's *A Universal History of the United States.*

the Popes and Mahomet; and to show that Martin Luther was the angel of the gospel for the age in which he lived, and will continue to be the angel of the gospel until the millennial day." The book is illustrated with a number of full-page copper-plate engravings. The one reproduced purports to be a representation of Moscow in flames. The flames are genuine enough, but the city, with its clapboarded houses and slender church spires, bears a suspicious resemblance to the American towns of the period.

Of the other early Universal Histories I will only speak of that by Rev. Royal Robbins, published at Hartford in 1835. It tells the scriptural story

Landing of Columbus.
From Frost's *A History of the United States*, 1837.

of the Creation, "about 5829 years ago," and then mentions, "as a matter of curiosity," a few theories of philosophers and others which do not agree with the Bible narrative. I quote two of these theories and add a few paragraphs from subsequent pages of the book about Adam and Eve.

The negroes of the Congo affirm that the world was made by the hands of angels, excepting their own country, which the Supreme Being constructed himself; that he took great pains with the inhabitants, and made them very black and beautiful; and when he had finished the first man, he was well pleased with him, and smoothed him over the face; and hence his nose, and the noses of all his descendants became flat.

"Conflagration of Moscow."
From Butler's *Sketches of Universal History*, 1818.

Darwin, an infidel, in accounting for the origin of the
world, supposes that the mass of chaos suddenly exploded,
like a barrel of gunpowder, and in that act exploded the

sun, which in its flight, by a similar convulsion, exploded
the earth, which in like manner exploded the moon, and
thus, by a chain of explosions, the whole solar system was
produced and set in regular motion.

Adam and Eve, the names of the first human pair,
were placed by the Diety, in the garden of Eden.   It is
evident that Eden was east of Canaan; but the most extravagant opinions have been entertained on this subject,
and not only the four quarters of the globe, but even the

Demosthenes declaiming upon the Sea-shore.

From Whelpley's *Compend. of History*, 1825.

air and the moon, have been conjectured to include this
delightful abode.

The innocence and felicity of the first pair were of
very short duration.   They violated, with daring impiety,
the sole command of their Maker.   The precise time of
this transaction cannot be determined; but it was probably only a few days after their creation.

The story goes on until we come to the flood, which we are assured must have happened because, " In agreement with the universal voice of tradition, the surface of the earth, in various respects, indicates the occurrence of such a catastrophe. Its broken state, the disposition of its strata, and the remains of marine productions on the tops of the highest mountains, are no doubtful evidence on this subject."

In the second quarter of the nineteenth century, not only did books multiply, but also the subjects included in the school curriculum. I have noted all the studies ordinarily taken up, but occasionally

1 Labyrinthidon.   2 Dinotherium.   3 Birds.

Frontispiece to Godding's *First Lessons in Geology*, 1846.

others were introduced, such as botany, geology,
natural philosophy, physiology, etc. Economics
was even included in the curriculum of some schools.
The most individual of early text-books dealing
with this topic was *The Young American* by S. G.
Goodrich, a simple and entertaining dissertation on
" government and law ; showing their history, nature,
and necessity." It had the usual merits of " Peter
Parley's " books, and without reaching any very

Taking a thief to prison.

From Goodrich's *The Young American*, 1842.

superior or lasting excellence was easy of comprehension and reasonably authoritative. The interest
was much increased by numerous pictures. Another
book, dealing with the more profound things of life,
and yet nevertheless much in vogue in the old district schools, was *The Improvement of the Mind* by
Isaac Watts. It was a lengthy disquisition on the
acquiring of knowledge and character. The book
was generally spoken of as " Watts on the Mind,"

and the title was so printed on the back of the volume. To the younger scholars the title was a puzzle. They could understand having "watts" on the hand, or even "watts" on the nose; but to have "watts" on the mind did not seem possible.

Neither this book nor the others concerned with advanced and special studies impressed themselves on the pupils as did the more elementary studies which have been particularly my theme. With few exceptions all the books showed narrowness and crudity, but time brought a steady improvement. By 1850 the formative period in the manufacture of school-books was over; yet while the later books are much better than the old, they have not the picturesque interest and antiquarian charm that belong to beginnings, and they do not come within the scope of this record of Old-time Schools and School-books.

Printed in the United States of America.

CATALOG OF DOVER BOOKS

Philosophy, Religion

GUIDE TO PHILOSOPHY, C. E. M. Joad. A modern classic which examines many crucial problems which man has pondered through the ages: Does free will exist? Is there plan in the universe? How do we know and validate our knowledge? Such opposed solutions as subjective idealism and realism, chance and teleology, vitalism and logical positivism, are evaluated and the contributions of the great philosophers from the Greeks to moderns like Russell, Whitehead, and others, are considered in the context of each problem. "The finest introduction," BOSTON TRANSCRIPT. Index. Classified bibliography. 592pp. 5⅜ x 8.
T297 Paperbound **$2.00**

HISTORY OF ANCIENT PHILOSOPHY, W. Windelband. One of the clearest, most accurate comprehensive surveys of Greek and Roman philosophy. Discusses ancient philosophy in general, intellectual life in Greece in the 7th and 6th centuries B.C., Thales, Anaximander, Anaximenes, Heraclitus, the Eleatics, Empedocles, Anaxagoras, Leucippus, the Pythagoreans, the Sophists, Socrates, Democritus (20 pages), Plato (50 pages), Aristotle (70 pages), the Peripatetics, Stoics, Epicureans, Sceptics, Neo-platonists, Christian Apologists, etc. 2nd German edition translated by H. E. Cushman. xv + 393pp. 5⅜ x 8. T357 Paperbound **$1.75**

ILLUSTRATIONS OF THE HISTORY OF MEDIEVAL THOUGHT AND LEARNING, R. L. Poole. Basic analysis of the thought and lives of the leading philosophers and ecclesiastics from the 8th to the 14th century—Abailard, Ockham, Wycliffe, Marsiglio of Padua, and many other great thinkers who carried the torch of Western culture and learning through the "Dark Ages": political, religious, and metaphysical views. Long a standard work for scholars and one of the best introductions to medieval thought for beginners. Index. 10 Appendices. xiii + 327pp. 5⅜ x 8. T674 Paperbound **$1.85**

PHILOSOPHY AND CIVILIZATION IN THE MIDDLE AGES, M. de Wulf. This semi-popular survey covers aspects of medieval intellectual life such as religion, philosophy, science, the arts, etc. It also covers feudalism vs. Catholicism, rise of the universities, mendicant orders, monastic centers, and similar topics. Unabridged. Bibliography. Index. viii + 320pp. 5⅜ x 8.
T284 Paperbound **$1.75**

AN INTRODUCTION TO SCHOLASTIC PHILOSOPHY, Prof. M. de Wulf. Formerly entitled SCHOLASTICISM OLD AND NEW, this volume examines the central scholastic tradition from St. Anselm, Albertus Magnus, Thomas Aquinas, up to Suarez in the 17th century. The relation of scholasticism to ancient and medieval philosophy and science in general is clear and easily followed. The second part of the book considers the modern revival of scholasticism, the Louvain position, relations with Kantianism and Positivism. Unabridged. xvi + 271pp. 5⅜ x 8.
T296 Clothbound **$3.50**
T283 Paperbound **$1.75**

A HISTORY OF MODERN PHILOSOPHY, H. Höffding. An exceptionally clear and detailed coverage of western philosophy from the Renaissance to the end of the 19th century. Major and minor men such as Pomponazzi, Bodin, Boehme, Telesius, Bruno, Copernicus, da Vinci, Kepler, Galileo, Bacon, Descartes, Hobbes, Spinoza, Leibniz, Wolff, Locke, Newton, Berkeley, Hume, Erasmus, Montesquieu, Voltaire, Diderot, Rousseau, Lessing, Kant, Herder, Fichte, Schelling, Hegel, Schopenhauer, Comte, Mill, Darwin, Spencer, Hartmann, Lange, and many others, are discussed in terms of theory of knowledge, logic, cosmology, and psychology. Index. 2 volumes, total of 1159pp. 5⅜ x 8. T117 Vol. 1, Paperbound **$2.00**
T118 Vol. 2, Paperbound **$2.00**

ARISTOTLE, A. E. Taylor. A brilliant, searching non-technical account of Aristotle and his thought written by a foremost Platonist. It covers the life and works of Aristotle; classification of the sciences; logic; first philosophy; matter and form; causes; motion and eternity; God; physics; metaphysics; and similar topics. Bibliography. New Index compiled for this edition. 128pp. 5⅜ x 8. T280 Paperbound **$1.00**

THE SYSTEM OF THOMAS AQUINAS, M. de Wulf. Leading Neo-Thomist, one of founders of University of Louvain, gives concise exposition to central doctrines of Aquinas, as a means toward determining his value to modern philosophy. religion. Formerly "Medieval Philosophy Illustrated from the System of Thomas Aquinas." Trans. by E. Messenger. Introduction. 151pp. 5⅜ x 8. T568 Paperbound **$1.25**

THE PHILOSOPHICAL WORKS OF DESCARTES. The definitive English edition of all the major philosophical works and letters of René Descartes. All of his revolutionary insights, from his famous "Cogito ergo sum" to his detailed account of contemporary science and his astonishingly fruitful concept that all phenomena of the universe (except mind) could be reduced to clear laws by the use of mathematics. An excellent source for the thought of men like Hobbes, Arnauld, Gassendi, etc., who were Descarte's contemporaries. Translated by E. S. Haldane and G. Ross. Introductory notes. Index. Total of 842pp. 5⅜ x 8.
T71 Vol. 1, Paperbound **$2.00**
T72 Vol. 2, Paperbound **$2.00**

CATALOG OF DOVER BOOKS

THE CHIEF WORKS OF SPINOZA. An unabridged reprint of the famous Bohn edition containing all of Spinoza's most important works: Vol. I: The Theologico-Political Treatise and the Political Treatise. Vol. II: On The Improvement Of Understanding, The Ethics, Selected Letters. Profound and enduring ideas on God, the universe, pantheism, society, religion, the state, democracy, the mind, emotions, freedom and the nature of man, which influenced Goethe, Hegel, Schelling, Coleridge, Whitehead, and many others. Introduction. 2 volumes. 826pp. 5⅜ x 8.
T249 Vol. I, Paperbound **$1.50**
T250 Vol. II, Paperbound **$1.50**

LEIBNIZ, H. W. Carr. Most stimulating middle-level coverage of basic philosophical thought of Leibniz. Easily understood discussion, analysis of major works: "Theodicy," "Principles of Nature and Grace," Monadology"; Leibniz's influence; intellectual growth; correspondence; disputes with Bayle, Malebranche, Newton; importance of his thought today, with reinterpretation in modern terminology. "Power and mastery," London Times. Bibliography. Index. 226pp. 5⅜ x 8.
T624 Paperbound **$1.35**

AN ESSAY CONCERNING HUMAN UNDERSTANDING, John Locke. Edited by A. C. Fraser. Unabridged reprinting of definitive edition; only complete edition of "Essay" in print. Marginal analyses of almost every paragraph; hundreds of footnotes; authoritative 140-page biographical, critical, historical prolegomena. Indexes. 1170pp. 5⅜ x 8.
T530 Vol. 1 (Books 1, 2) Paperbound **$2.25**
T531 Vol. 2 (Books 3, 4) Paperbound **$2.25**
2 volume set **$4.50**

THE PHILOSOPHY OF HISTORY, G. W. F. Hegel. One of the great classics of western thought which reveals Hegel's basic principle: that history is not chance but a rational process, the realization of the Spirit of Freedom. Ranges from the oriental cultures of subjective thought to the classical subjective cultures, to the modern absolute synthesis where spiritual and secular may be reconciled. Translation and introduction by J. Sibree. Introduction by C. Hegel. Special introduction for this edition by Prof. Carl Friedrich. xxxix + 447pp. 5⅜ x 8.
T112 Paperbound **$1.85**

THE PHILOSOPHY OF HEGEL, W. T. Stace. The first detailed analysis of Hegel's thought in English, this is especially valuable since so many of Hegel's works are out of print. Dr. Stace examines Hegel's debt to Greek idealists and the 18th century and then proceeds to a careful description and analysis of Hegel's first principles, categories, reason, dialectic method, his logic, philosophy of nature and spirit, etc. Index. Special 14 x 20 chart of Hegelian system. x + 526pp. 5⅜ x 8.
T254 Paperbound **$2.00**

THE WILL TO BELIEVE and HUMAN IMMORTALITY, W. James. Two complete books bound as one. THE WILL TO BELIEVE discusses the interrelations of belief, will, and intellect in man; chance vs. determinism, free will vs. determinism, free will vs. fate, pluralism vs. monism; the philosophies of Hegel and Spencer, and more. HUMAN IMMORTALITY examines the question of survival after death and develops an unusual and powerful argument for immortality. Two prefaces. Index. Total of 429pp. 5⅜ x 8.
T291 Paperbound **$1.65**

THE WORLD AND THE INDIVIDUAL, Josiah Royce. Only major effort by an American philosopher to interpret nature of things in systematic, comprehensive manner. Royce's formulation of an absolute voluntarism remains one of the original and profound solutions to the problems involved. Part one, 4 Historical Conceptions of Being, inquires into first principles, true meaning and place of individuality. Part two, Nature, Man, and the Moral Order, is application of first principles to problems concerning religion, evil, moral order. Introduction by J. E. Smith, Yale Univ. Index. 1070pp. 5⅜ x 8.
T561 Vol. 1 Paperbound **$2.25**
T562 Vol. 2 Paperbound **$2.25**
the set **$4.50**

THE PHILOSOPHICAL WRITINGS OF PEIRCE, edited by J. Buchler. This book (formerly THE PHILOSOPHY OF PEIRCE) is a carefully integrated exposition of Peirce's complete system composed of selections from his own work. Symbolic logic, scientific method, theory of signs, pragmatism, epistemology, chance, cosmology, ethics, and many other topics are treated by one of the greatest philosophers of modern times. This is the only inexpensive compilation of his key ideas. xvi + 386pp. 5⅜ x 8.
T217 Paperbound **$1.95**

EXPERIENCE AND NATURE, John Dewey. An enlarged, revised edition of the Paul Carus lectures which Dewey delivered in 1925. It covers Dewey's basic formulation of the problem of knowledge, with a full discussion of other systems, and a detailing of his own concepts of the relationship of external world, mind, and knowledge. Starts with a thorough examination of the philosophical method; examines the interrelationship of experience and nature; analyzes experience on basis of empirical naturalism, the formulation of law, role of language and social factors in knowledge; etc. Dewey's treatment of central problems in philosophy is profound but extremely easy to follow. ix + 448pp. 5⅜ x 8.
T471 Paperbound **$1.85**

Social Sciences

SOCIAL THOUGHT FROM LORE TO SCIENCE, H. E. Barnes and H. Becker. An immense survey of sociological thought and ways of viewing, studying, planning, and reforming society from earliest times to the present. Includes thought on society of preliterate peoples, ancient non-Western cultures, and every great movement in Europe, America, and modern Japan. Analyzes hundreds of great thinkers: Plato, Augustine, Bodin, Vico, Montesquieu, Herder, Comte, Marx, etc. Weighs the contributions of utopians, sophists, fascists and communists; economists, jurists, philosophers, ecclesiastics, and every 19th and 20th century school of scientific sociology, anthropology, and social psychology throughout the world. Combines topical, chronological, and regional approaches, treating the evolution of social thought as a process rather than as a series of mere topics. "Impressive accuracy, competence, and discrimination . . . easily the best single survey," Nation. Thoroughly revised, with new material up to 1960. 2 indexes. Over 2200 bibliographical notes. Three volume set. Total of 1586pp. 5⅜ x 8.
T901 Vol I   Paperbound **$2.35**
T902 Vol II   Paperbound **$2.35**
T903 Vol III Paperbound **$2.35**
The set **$7.05**

FOLKWAYS, William Graham Sumner. A classic of sociology, a searching and thorough examination of patterns of behaviour from primitive, ancient Greek and Judaic, Medieval Christian, African, Oriental, Melanesian, Australian, Islamic, to modern Western societies. Thousands of illustrations of social, sexual, and religious customs, mores, laws, and institutions. Hundreds of categories: Labor, Wealth, Abortion, Primitive Justice, Life Policy, Slavery, Cannibalism, Uncleanness and the Evil Eye, etc. Will extend the horizon of every reader by showing the relativism of his own culture. Prefatory note by A. G. Keller. Introduction by William Lyon Phelps. Bibliography. Index. xiii + 692pp. 5⅜ x 8.   T508 Paperbound **$2.49**

PRIMITIVE RELIGION, P. Radin. A thorough treatment by a noted anthropologist of the nature and origin of man's belief in the supernatural and the influences that have shaped religious expression in primitive societies. Ranging from the Arunta, Ashanti, Aztec, Bushman, Crow, Fijian, etc., of Africa, Australia, Pacific Islands, the Arctic, North and South America, Prof. Radin integrates modern psychology, comparative religion, and economic thought with first-hand accounts gathered by himself and other scholars of primitive initiations, training of the shaman, and other fascinating topics. "Excellent," NATURE (London). Unabridged reissue of 1st edition. New author's preface. Bibliographic notes. Index. x + 322pp. 5⅜ x 8.
T393 Paperbound **$1.85**

PRIMITIVE MAN AS PHILOSOPHER, P. Radin. A standard anthropological work covering primitive thought on such topics as the purpose of life, marital relations, freedom of thought, symbolism, death, resignation, the nature of reality, personality, gods, and many others. Drawn from factual material gathered from the Winnebago, Oglala Sioux, Maori, Baganda, Batak, Zuni, among others, it does not distort ideas by removing them from context but interprets strictly within the original framework. Extensive selections of original primitive documents. Bibliography. Index. xviii + 402pp. 5⅜ x 8.   T392 Paperbound **$2.00**

THE POLISH PEASANT IN EUROPE AND AMERICA, William I. Thomas, Florian Znaniecki. A seminal sociological study of peasant primary groups (family and community) and the disruptions produced by a new industrial system and immigration to America. The peasant's family, class system, religious and aesthetic attitudes, and economic life are minutely examined and analyzed in hundreds of pages of primary documentation, particularly letters between family members. The disorientation caused by new environments is scrutinized in detail (a 312 page autobiography of an immigrant is especially valuable and revealing) in an attempt to find common experiences and reactions. The famous "Methodological Note" sets forth the principles which guided the authors. When out of print this set has sold for as much as $50. 2nd revised edition. 2 vols. Vol. 1: xv + 1115pp. Vol. 2: 1135pp. Index. 6 x 9.
T478 Clothbound 2 vol. set **$12.50**

History, Political Science, Americana

THE POLITICAL THOUGHT OF PLATO AND ARISTOTLE, E. Barker. One of the clearest and most accurate expositions of the corpus of Greek political thought. This standard source contains exhaustive analyses of the "Republic" and other Platonic dialogues and Aristotle's "Politics" and "Ethics," and discusses the origin of these ideas in Greece, contributions of other Greek theorists, and modifications of Greek ideas by thinkers from Aquinas to Hegel. "Must" reading for anyone interested in the history of Western thought. Index. Chronological Table of Events. 2 Appendixes. xxiv + 560pp. 5⅜ x 8.   T521 Paperbound **$1.85**

FARES, PLEASE! by J. A. Miller. Authoritative, comprehensive, and entertaining history of local public transit from its inception to its most recent developments: trolleys, horsecars, streetcars, buses, elevateds, subways, along with monorails, "road-railers," and a host of other extraordinary vehicles. Here are all the flamboyant personalities involved, the vehement arguments, the unusual information, and all the nostalgia. "Interesting facts brought into especially vivid life," N. Y. Times. New preface. 152 illustrations, 4 new. Bibliography. xix + 204pp. 5⅜ x 8.   T671 Paperbound **$1.50**

GARDNER'S PHOTOGRAPHIC SKETCH BOOK OF THE CIVIL WAR, Alexander Gardner. The first published collection of Civil War photographs, by one of the two or three most famous photographers of the era, outstandingly reproduced from the original positives. Scenes of crucial battles: Appomattox, Manassas, Mechanicsville, Bull Run, Yorktown, Fredericksburg, etc. Gettysburg immediately after retirement of forces. Battle ruins at Richmond, Petersburg, Gaines'Mill. Prisons, arsenals, a slave pen, fortifications, headquarters, pontoon bridges, soldiers, a field hospital. A unique glimpse into the realities of one of the bloodiest wars in history, with an introductory text to each picture by Gardner himself. Until this edition, there were only five known copies in libraries, and fewer in private hands, one of which sold at auction in 1952 for $425. Introduction by E. F. Bleiler. 100 full page 7 x 10 photographs (original size). 224pp. 8½ x 10¾.   T476 Clothbound **$6.00**

Art, History of Art,
Graphic Arts, Handcrafts

ART STUDENTS' ANATOMY, E. J. Farris. Outstanding art anatomy that uses chiefly living objects for its illustrations. 71 photos of undraped man, woman, and child are accompanied by carefully labeled matching sketches to illustrate the skeletal system, articulations and movements, bony landmarks, the muscular system, skin, fasciae, fat, etc. 9 x-ray photos show movement of joints. Undraped models are shown in such actions as serving in tennis, drawing a bow in archery, playing football, dancing, preparing to spring and to dive. Also discussed and illustrated are proportions, age and sex differences, the anatomy of the smile, etc. 8 plates by the great early 18th century anatomic illustrator Siegfried Albinus are also included. Glossary. 158 figures, 7 in color. x + 159pp. 5⅝ x 8⅜.   T744 Paperbound **$1.45**

AN ATLAS OF ANATOMY FOR ARTISTS, F Schider. A new 3rd edition of this standard text enlarged by 52 new illustrations of hands, anatomical studies by Cloquet, and expressive life studies of the body by Barcsay. 189 clear detailed plates offer you precise information of impeccable accuracy. 29 plates show all aspects of the skeleton, with closeups of special areas, while 54 full-page plates, mostly in two colors, give human musculature as seen from four different points of view, with cutaways for important portions of the body. 14 full-page plates provide photographs of hand forms, eyelids, female breasts, and indicate the location of muscles upon models. 59 additional plates show how great artists of the past utilized human anatomy. They reproduce sketches and finished work by such artists as Michelangelo, Leonardo da Vinci, Goya, and 15 others. This is a lifetime reference work which will be one of the most important books in any artist's library. "The standard reference tool," AMERICAN LIBRARY ASSOCIATION. "Excellent," AMERICAN ARTIST. Third enlarged edition. 189 plates, 647 illustrations. xxvi + 192pp. 7⅞ x 10⅝.   T241 Clothbound **$6.00**

AN ATLAS OF ANIMAL ANATOMY FOR ARTISTS, W. Ellenberger, H. Baum, H. Dittrich. The largest, richest animal anatomy for artists available in English. 99 detailed anatomical plates of such animals as the horse, dog, cat, lion, deer, seal, kangaroo, flying squirrel, cow, bull, goat, monkey, hare, and bat. Surface features are clearly indicated, while progressive beneath-the-skin pictures show musculature, tendons, and bone structure. Rest and action are exhibited in terms of musculature and skeletal structure and detailed cross-sections are given for heads and important features. The animals chosen are representative of specific families so that a study of these anatomies will provide knowledge of hundreds of related species. "Highly recommended as one of the very few books on the subject worthy of being used as an authoritative guide," DESIGN. "Gives a fundamental knowledge," AMERICAN ARTIST. Second revised, enlarged edition with new plates from Cuvier, Stubbs, etc. 288 illustrations. 153pp. 11⅜ x 9.   T82 Clothbound **$6.00**

THE HUMAN FIGURE IN MOTION, Eadweard Muybridge. The largest selection in print of Muybridge's famous high-speed action photos of the human figure in motion. 4789 photographs illustrate 162 different actions: men, women, children—mostly undraped—are shown walking, running, carrying various objects, sitting, lying down, climbing, throwing, arising, and performing over 150 other actions. Some actions are shown in as many as 150 photographs each. All in all there are more than 500 action strips in this enormous volume, series shots taken at shutter speeds of as high as 1/6000th of a second! These are not posed shots, but true stopped motion. They show bone and muscle in situations that the human eye is not fast enough to capture. Earlier, smaller editions of these prints have brought $40 and more on the out-of-print market. "A must for artists," ART IN FOCUS. "An unparalleled dictionary of action for all artists," AMERICAN ARTIST. 390 full-page plates, with 4789 photographs. Printed on heavy glossy stock. Reinforced binding with headbands. 7⅞ x 10⅝.
                                                               T204 Clothbound **$10.00**

CATALOG OF DOVER BOOKS

BYZANTINE ART AND ARCHAEOLOGY, O. M. Dalton. Still the most thorough work in English—both in breadth and in depth—on the astounding multiplicity of Byzantine art forms throughout Europe, North Africa, and Western Asia from the 4th to the 15th century. Analyzes hundreds of individual pieces from over 160 public and private museums, libraries, and collections all over the world. Full treatment of Byzantine sculpture, painting, mosaic, jewelry, textiles, etc., including historical development, symbolism, and aesthetics. Chapters on iconography and ornament. Indispensable for study of Christian symbolism and medieval art. 457 illustrations, many full-page. Bibliography of over 2500 references. 4 Indexes. xx + 727pp. 6⅛ x 9¼. **T776 Clothbound $7.50**

METALWORK AND ENAMELLING, H. Maryon. This is probably the best book ever written on the subject. Prepared by Herbert Maryon, F.S.A., of the British Museum, it tells everything necessary for home manufacture of jewelry, rings, ear pendants, bowls, and dozens of other objects. Clearly written chapters provide precise information on such topics as materials, tools, soldering, filigree, setting stones, raising patterns, spinning metal, repoussé work, hinges and joints, metal inlaying, damascening, overlaying, niello, Japanese alloys, enamelling, cloisonné, painted enamels, casting, polishing coloring, assaying, and dozens of other techniques. This is the next best thing to apprenticeship to a master metalworker. 363 photographs and figures. 374pp. 5½ x 8½. **T183 Clothbound $8.00**

SILK SCREEN TECHNIQUES, J. I. Biegeleisen, Max A. Cohn. A complete-to-the-last-detail copiously illustrated home course in this fast growing modern art form. Full directions for building silk screen out of inexpensive materials; explanations of five basic methods of stencil preparation—paper, blockout, tusche, film, photographic—and effects possible: light and shade, washes, dry brush, oil paint type impastos, gouaches, pastels. Detailed coverage of multicolor printing, illustrated by proofs showing the stages of a 4 color print. Special section on common difficulties. 149 illustrations, 8 in color. Sources of supply. xiv + 187pp. 6⅛ x 9¼. **T433 Paperbound $1.55**

A HANDBOOK OF WEAVES, G. H. Oelsner. Now back in print! Probably the most complete book of weaves ever printed, fully explained, differentiated, and illustrated. Includes plain weaves, irregular, double-stitched, and filling satins; derivative, basket, and rib weaves; steep, undulating, broken, offset, corkscrew, interlocking, herringbone, and fancy twills; honeycomb, lace, and crepe weaves; tricot, matelassé, and montagnac weaves; and much more. Translated and revised by S. S. Dale, with supplement on the analysis of weaves and fabrics. 1875 illustrations. vii + 402pp. 6 x 9¼. **T209 Clothbound $5.00**

THE STANDARD BOOK OF QUILT MAKING AND COLLECTING, Marguerite Ickis. A complete easy-to-follow guide with all the information you need to make beautiful, useful quilts. How to plan, design, cut, sew, appliqué, avoid sewing problems, use rag bag, make borders, tuft, every other aspect. Over 100 traditional quilts shown, including over 40 full-size patterns. No better book on the market. Index. 483 illus. 1 color plate. 287pp. 6¾ x 9½. **T582 Paperbound $2.00**

DESIGN FOR ARTISTS AND CRAFTSMEN, L. Wolchonok. The most thorough course ever prepared on the creation of art motifs and designs. It teaches you to create your own designs out of things around you — from geometric patterns, plants, birds, animals, humans, landscapes, and man-made objects. It leads you step by step through the creation of more than 1300 designs, and shows you how to create design that is fresh, well-founded, and original. Mr. Wolchonok, whose text is used by scores of art schools, shows you how the same idea can be developed into ·many different forms, ranging from near representationalism to the most advanced forms of abstraction. The material in this book is entirely new, and combines full awareness of traditional design with the work of such men as Miro, Léger, Picasso, Moore, and others. 113 detailed exercises, with instruction hints, diagrams, and details to enable you to apply Wolchonok's methods to your own work. "A great contribution to the field of design and crafts," N. Y. SOCIETY OF CRAFTSMEN. More than 1300 illustrations. xv + 207pp. 7⅞ x 10¾. **T274 Clothbound $4.95**

BASIC BOOKBINDING, A. W. Lewis. Enables the beginner and the expert to apply the latest and most simplified techniques to rebinding old favorites and binding new paperback books. Complete lists of all necessary materials and guides to the selection of proper tools, paper, glue, boards, cloth, leather, or sheepskin covering fabrics, lettering inks and pigments, etc. You are shown how to collate a book, sew it, back it, trim it, make boards and attach them in easy step-by-step stages. Author's preface. 261 illustrations with appendix. Index. xi + 144pp. 5⅜ x 8. **T169 Paperbound $1.35**

THE UNIVERSAL PENMAN, George Bickham. This beautiful book, which first appeared in 1743, is the largest collection of calligraphic specimens, flourishes, alphabets, and calligraphic illustrations ever published. 212 full-page plates are drawn from the work of such 18th century masters of English roundhand as Dove, Champion, Bland, and 20 others. They contain 22 complete alphabets, over 2,000 flourishes, and 122 illustrations, each drawn with a stylistic grace impossible to describe. This book is invaluable to anyone interested in the beauties of calligraphy, or to any artist, hobbyist, or craftsman who wishes to use the very best ornamental handwriting and flourishes for decorative purposes. Commercial artists, advertising artists, have found it unexcelled as a source of material suggesting quality. "An essential part of any art library, and a book of permanent value," AMERICAN ARTIST. 212 plates. 224pp. 9 x 13¾. **T20 Clothbound $10.00**

STIEGEL GLASS, F. W. Hunter. Acclaimed and treasured by librarians, collectors, dealers and manufacturers, this volume is a clear and entertaining account of the life, early experiments, and final achievements in early American glassware of "Baron" Stiegel. An 18th century German adventurer and industrialist, Stiegel founded an empire and produced much of the most highly esteemed early American glassware. His career and varied glassware is set forth in great detail by Mr. Hunter and a new introduction by Helen McKearin provides details revealed by later research. "This pioneer work is reprinted in an edition even more beautiful than the original," ANTIQUES DEALER. "Well worth reading," MARYLAND HISTORICAL MAGAZINE. Introduction. 171 illustrations; 12 in full color. xxii + 338pp. 7⅞ x 10¾.
T128 Clothbound **$10.00**

PINE FURNITURE OF EARLY NEW ENGLAND, R. H. Kettell. A rich understanding of one of America's most original folk arts that collectors of antiques, interior decorators, craftsmen, woodworkers, and everyone interested in American history and art will find fascinating and immensely useful. 413 illustrations of more than 300 chairs, benches, racks, beds, cupboards, mirrors, shelves, tables, and other furniture will show all the simple beauty and character of early New England furniture. 55 detailed drawings carefully analyze outstanding pieces. "With its rich store of illustrations, this book emphasizes the individuality and varied design of early American pine furniture. It should be welcomed," ANTIQUES. 413 illustrations and 55 working drawings. 475. 8 x 10¾.
T145 Clothbound **$10.00**

VITRUVIUS: TEN BOOKS ON ARCHITECTURE. Book by 1st century Roman architect, engineer, is oldest, most influential work on architecture in existence; for hundreds of years his specific instructions were followed all over the world, by such men as Bramante, Michelangelo, Palladio, etc., and are reflected in major buildings. He describes classic principles of symmetry, harmony; design of treasury, prison, etc.; methods of durability; much more. He wrote in a fascinating manner, and often digressed to give interesting sidelights, making this volume appealing reading even to the non-professional. Standard English translation, by Prof. M. H. Morgan, Harvard U. Index. 6 illus. 334pp. 5⅜ x 8.
T645 Paperbound **$2.00**

THE BROWN DECADES, Lewis Mumford. In this now classic study of the arts in America, Lewis Mumford resurrects the "buried renaissance" of the post-Civil War period. He demonstrates that it contained the seeds of a new integrity and power and documents his study with detailed accounts of the founding of modern architecture in the work of Sullivan, Richardson, Root, Roebling; landscape development of Marsh, Olmstead, and Eliot; the graphic arts of Homer, Eakins, and Ryder. 2nd revised enlarged edition. Bibliography. 12 illustrations. Index. xiv + 266pp. 5⅜ x 8.
T200 Paperbound **$1.65**

STICKS AND STONES, Lewis Mumford. A survey of the forces that have conditioned American architecture and altered its forms. The author discusses the medieval tradition in early New England villages; the Renaissance influence which developed with the rise of the merchant class; the classical influence of Jefferson's time; the "Mechanicsvilles" of Poe's generation; the Brown Decades; the philosophy of the Imperial facade; and finally the modern machine age. "A truly remarkable book," SAT. REV. OF LITERATURE. 2nd revised edition. 21 illustrations. xvii + 228pp. 5⅜ x 8.
T202 Paperbound **$1.60**

THE AUTOBIOGRAPHY OF AN IDEA, Louis Sullivan. The pioneer architect whom Frank Lloyd Wright called "the master" reveals an acute sensitivity to social forces and values in this passionately honest account. He records the crystallization of his opinions and theories, the growth of his organic theory of architecture that still influences American designers and architects, contemporary ideas, etc. This volume contains the first appearance of 34 full-page plates of his finest architecture. Unabridged reissue of 1924 edition. New introduction by R. M. Line. Index. xiv + 335pp. 5⅜ x 8.
T281 Paperbound **$1.85**

THE DRAWINGS OF HEINRICH KLEY. The first uncut republication of both of Kley's devastating sketchbooks, which first appeared in pre-World War I Germany. One of the greatest cartoonists and social satirists of modern times, his exuberant and iconoclastic fantasy and his extraordinary technique place him in the great tradition of Bosch, Breughel, and Goya, while his subject matter has all the immediacy and tension of our century. 200 drawings. viii + 128pp. 7¾ x 10¾.
T24 Paperbound **$1.85**

Miscellaneous

THE COMPLETE KANO JIU-JITSU (JUDO), H. I. Hancock and K. Higashi. Most comprehensive guide to judo, referred to as outstanding work by Encyclopaedia Britannica. Complete authentic Japanese system of 160 holds and throws, including the most spectacular, fully illustrated with 487 photos. Full text explains leverage, weight centers, pressure points, special tricks, etc.; shows how to protect yourself from almost any manner of attack though your attacker may have the initial advantage of strength and surprise. This authentic Kano system should not be confused with the many American imitations. xii + 500pp. 5⅜ x 8.
T639 Paperbound **$2.00**

CATALOG OF DOVER BOOKS

THE MEMOIRS OF JACQUES CASANOVA. Splendid self-revelation by history's most engaging scoundrel—utterly dishonest with women and money, yet highly intelligent and observant. Here are all the famous duels, scandals, amours, banishments, thefts, treacheries, and imprisonments all over Europe: a life lived to the fullest and recounted with gusto in one of the greatest autobiographies of all time. What is more, these Memoirs are also one of the most trustworthy and valuable documents we have on the society and culture of the extravagant 18th century. Here are Voltaire, Louis XV, Catherine the Great, cardinals, castrati, pimps, and pawnbrokers—an entire glittering civilization unfolding before you with an unparalleled sense of actuality. Translated by Arthur Machen. Edited by F. A. Blossom. Introduction by Arthur Symons. Illustrated by Rockwell Kent. Total of xlviii + 2216pp. 5⅜ x 8.

> T338 Vol I Paperbound **$2.00**
> T339 Vol II Paperbound **$2.00**
> T340 Vol III Paperbound **$2.00**
> The set **$6.00**

BARNUM'S OWN STORY, P. T. Barnum. The astonishingly frank and gratifyingly well-written autobiography of the master showman and pioneer publicity man reveals the truth about his early career, his famous hoaxes (such as the Fejee Mermaid and the Woolly Horse), his amazing commercial ventures, his fling in politics, his feuds and friendships, his failures and surprising comebacks. A vast panorama of 19th century America's mores, amusements, and vitality. 66 new illustrations in this edition. xii + 500pp. 5⅜ x 8.

> T764 Paperbound **$1.65**

THE STORY OF THE TITANIC AS TOLD BY ITS SURVIVORS, ed. by Jack Winocour. Most significant accounts of most overpowering naval disaster of modern times: all 4 authors were survivors. Includes 2 full-length, unabridged books: "The Loss of the S.S. Titanic," by Laurence Beesley, "The Truth about the Titanic," by Col. Archibald Gracie; 6 pertinent chapters from "Titanic and Other Ships," autobiography of only officer to survive, Second Officer Charles Lightoller; and a short, dramatic account by the Titanic's wireless operator, Harold Bride. 26 illus. 368pp. 5⅜ x 8.

> T610 Paperbound **$1.50**

THE PHYSIOLOGY OF TASTE, Jean Anthelme Brillat-Savarin. Humorous, satirical, witty, and personal classic on joys of food and drink by 18th century French politician, litterateur. Treats the science of gastronomy, erotic value of truffles, Parisian restaurants, drinking contests; gives recipes for tunny omelette, pheasant, Swiss fondue, etc. Only modern translation of original French edition. Introduction. 41 illus. 346pp. 5⅝ x 8⅜.

> T591 Paperbound **$1.50**

THE ART OF THE STORY-TELLER, M. L. Shedlock. This classic in the field of effective story-telling is regarded by librarians, story-tellers, and educators as the finest and most lucid book on the subject. The author considers the nature of the story, the difficulties of communicating stories to children, the artifices used in story-telling, how to obtain and maintain the effect of the story, and, of extreme importance, the elements to seek and those to avoid in selecting material. A 99 page selection of Miss Shedlock's most effective stories and an extensive bibliography of further material by Eulalie Steinmetz enhance the book's usefulness. xxi + 320pp. 5⅜ x 8.

> T635 Paperbound **$1.50**

CREATIVE POWER: THE EDUCATION OF YOUTH IN THE CREATIVE ARTS, Hughes Mearns. In first printing considered revolutionary in its dynamic, progressive approach to teaching the creative arts; now accepted as one of the most effective and valuable approaches yet formulated. Based on the belief that every child has something to contribute, it provides in a stimulating manner invaluable and inspired teaching insights, to stimulate children's latent powers of creative expression in drama, poetry, music, writing, etc. Mearns's methods were developed in his famous experimental classes in creative education at the Lincoln School of Teachers College, Columbia Univ. Named one of the 20 foremost books on education in recent times by National Education Association. New enlarged revised 2nd edition. Introduction. 272pp. 5⅜ x 8.

> T490 Paperbound **$1.50**

FREE AND INEXPENSIVE EDUCATIONAL AIDS, T. J. Pepe, Superintendent of Schools, Southbury, Connecticut. An up-to-date listing of over 1500 booklets, films, charts, etc. 5% costs less than 25¢; 1% costs more; 94% is yours for the asking. Use this material privately, or in schools from elementary to college, for discussion, vocational guidance, projects. 59 categories include health, trucking, textiles, language, weather, the blood, office practice, wild life, atomic energy, other important topics. Each item described according to contents, number of pages or running time, level. All material is educationally sound, and without political or company bias. 1st publication. Extensive index. xii + 289pp. 5⅜ x 8.

> T663 Paperbound **$1.35**

THE WORLD'S GREAT SPEECHES, edited by Lewis Copeland and Lawrence Lamm. 255 speeches ranging over scores of topic and moods (including a special section of "Informal Speeches" and a fine collection of historically important speeches of the U.S.A. and other western hemisphere countries), present the greatest speakers of all time from Pericles of Athens to Churchill, Roosevelt, and Dylan Thomas. Invaluable as a guide to speakers, fascinating as history both past and contemporary, much material here is available elsewhere only with great difficulty. 3 indices: Topic, Author, Nation. xx + 745pp. 5⅜ x 8. T376 Paperbound **$2.49**

CATALOG OF DOVER BOOKS

THE ROMANCE OF WORDS, E. Weekley. An entertaining collection of unusual word-histories that tracks down for the general reader the origins of more than 2000 common words and phrases in English (including British and American slang): discoveries often surprising, often humorous, that help trace vast chains of commerce in products and ideas. There are Arabic trade words, cowboy words, origins of family names, phonetic accidents, curious wanderings, folk-etymologies, etc. Index. xiii + 210pp. 5⅜ x 8.　　　　　T710 Paperbound **$1.25**

PHRASE AND WORD ORIGINS: A STUDY OF FAMILIAR EXPRESSIONS, A. H. Holt. One of the most entertaining books on the unexpected origins and colorful histories of words and phrases, based on sound scholarship, but written primarily for the layman. Over 1200 phrases and 1000 separate words are covered, with many quotations, and the results of the most modern linguistic and historical researches. "A right jolly book Mr. Holt has made," N. Y. Times. v + 254pp. 5⅜ x 8.　　　　　T758 Paperbound **$1.35**

AMATEUR WINE MAKING, S. M. Tritton. Now, with only modest equipment and no prior knowledge, you can make your own fine table wines. A practical handbook, this covers every type of grape wine, as well as fruit, flower, herb, vegetable, and cereal wines, and many kinds of mead, cider, and beer. Every question you might have is answered, and there is a valuable discussion of what can go wrong at various stages along the way. Special supplement of yeasts and American sources of supply. 13 tables. 32 illustrations. Glossary. Index. 239pp. 5½ x 8½.　　　　　T514 Clothbound **$4.00**

SAILING ALONE AROUND THE WORLD. Captain Joshua Slocum. A great modern classic in a convenient inexpensive edition. Captain Slocum's account of his single-handed voyage around the world in a 34 foot boat which he rebuilt himself. A nearly unparalleled feat of seamanship told with vigor, wit, imagination, and great descriptive power. "A nautical equivalent of Thoreau's account," Van Wyck Brooks. 67 illustrations. 308pp. 5⅜ x 8.
T326 Paperbound **$1.00**

TREASURY OF THE WORLD'S COINS, Fred Reinfeld. The finest general introduction to numismatics, non-technical, thorough, always fascinating. Coins of Greece, Rome, modern countries of every continent, primitive societies, such oddities as the 50 lb. stone money of Yap, the nail coinage of New England; all mirror man's economy, customs, religion, politics, philosophy, and art. An entertaining, absorbing study, and a novel view of history. Over 750 illustrations. Table of value of coins illustrated. List of U.S. coin clubs. Bibliographic material. Index. 224pp. 6½ x 9¼　　　　　T457 Paperbound **$1.75**

HOAXES, C. D. MacDougall. Shows how art, science, history, journalism can be perverted for private purposes. Hours of delightful entertainment and a work of scholarly value, this often shocking book tells of the deliberate creation of nonsense news, the Cardiff giant, Shakespeare forgeries, the Loch Ness monster, Biblical frauds, political schemes, literary hoaxers like Chatterton, Ossian, the disumbrationist school of painting, the lady in black at Valentino's tomb, and over 250 others. It will probably reveal the truth about a few things you've believed, and help you spot more readily the editorial "gander" and planted publicity release. "A stupendous collection . . . and shrewd analysis." New Yorker. New revised edition. 54 photographs. Index. 320pp. 5⅜ x 8.　　　　　T465 Paperbound **$1.75**

A HISTORY OF THE WARFARE OF SCIENCE WITH THEOLOGY IN CHRISTENDOM, A. D. White. Most thorough account ever written of the great religious-scientific battles shows gradual victory of science over ignorant, harmful beliefs. Attacks on theory of evolution; attacks on Galileo; great medieval plagues caused by belief in devil-origin of disease; attacks on Franklin's experiments with electricity; the witches of Salem; scores more that will amaze you. Author, co-founder and first president of Cornell U., writes with vast scholarly background, but in clear, readable prose. Acclaimed as classic effort in America to do away with superstition. Index. Total of 928pp. 5⅜ x 8.　　　T608 Vol I Paperbound **$1.85**
T609 Vol II Paperbound **$1.85**

Dover publishes books on art, music, philosophy, literature, languages, history, social sciences, psychology, handcrafts, orientalia, puzzles and entertainments, chess, pets and gardens, books explaining science, intermediate and higher mathematics mathematical physics, engineering, biological sciences, earth sciences, classics of science, etc. Write to:

　　　　　Dept. catrr.
　　　　　Dover Publications, Inc.
　　　　　180 Varick Street, N. Y. 14, N. Y.